Created and Directed by Hans Höfer

INSIGHT GUIDES

DRESDEN

Edited by Wieland Giebel
Translated by David Ingram and Susan Bollans
Managing Editor: Andrew Eames

HOUGHTON MIFFLIN COMPANY

APA PUBLICATIONS

DRESDEN

First Edition (Reprint)
© **1993 APA PUBLICATIONS (HK) LTD**
All Rights Reserved
Printed in Singapore by Höfer Press Pte. Ltd

Distributed in the United States by:	Distributed in Canada by:	Distributed in the UK & Ireland by:	Worldwide distribution enquiries:
Houghton Mifflin Company	**Thomas Allen & Son**	**GeoCenter International UK Ltd**	**Höfer Communications Pte Ltd**
2 Park Street	390 Steelcase Road East	The Viables Center, Harrow Way	38 Joo Koon Road
Boston, Massachusetts 02108	Markham, Ontario L3R 1G2	Basingstoke, Hampshire RG22 4BJ	Singapore 2262
ISSN: 1064-7864	ISSN: 1064-7864		
ISBN: 0-395-65769-5	ISBN: 0-395-65769-5	ISBN: 9-62421-166-3	ISBN: 9-62421-166-3

ABOUT THIS BOOK

according to the English author Jerome K. Jerome, writing in 1900 in *Three Men on the Bummel*: "Dresden, perhaps, is the most attractive town in Germany; but it is a place to be lived in for a while rather than visited. Its museums and galleries, palaces and gardens, its beautiful and historically rich environment, provide pleasure for a winter but bewilder for a week. It has not the gaiety of Paris or Vienna, which quickly palls; its charms are more solidly German and more lasting. It is the Mecca of the musician."

It had long been thus. Even 250 years ago, the Baroque splendours created by Augustus the Strong drew artists, writers, composers, royalty and common tourists from all over Europe to the capital of Saxony. Now, after the collapse of the Berlin Wall and the reunification of Germany, visitors flock to Dresden, drawn by its magnificent buildings, works of art and wonderful situation in the rolling hills of the Elbe Valley. Its proximity to the beautiful crags and forests of "Saxon Switzerland" make it a prime destination for visitors to eastern Germany.

But in admiring the historical part of Dresden, the tourist is confronted with the dark shadow cast on 13 February 1945, when the work of centuries was destroyed in a single night by British bombers. The firestorm in the old city was so devastating that memories of that "living hell" are bound to linger even after reconstruction is finally completed in the second decade of the 21st century. So, while describing all the buildings, the works of art, and those who created them, *Cityguide: Dresden* also puts special emphasis on the people of the city – on how they view their past and, since the momentous political and social changes of 1989, how they are coming to terms with their present and their future.

The book's project editor, **Wieland Giebel**, was born in Thuringia, one of the new federal states. He grew up in Kassel, in the state of Hesse, and, through his work as a journalist and his involvement with the European Parliament, he always managed to keep in touch with developments on the other side of the Iron Curtain. He has also produced new editions of Insight Guides to Germany and Berlin and has edited *Cityguide: Frankfurt*.

The Writers

Giebel set about recruiting an expert team of writers and photographers who could share their expertise on the city and its surroundings. He turned first to **Werner Kohlert**, who spent 36 years as a cameraman, scriptwriter and director in the documentary department of the DEFA film studios. He now makes films about the Saxon Switzerland, Meissen wine and other Dresden topics. In this book, he writes about famous people who have lived in Dresden, and examines the city's historical role as the capital of Saxony.

Until recently, **Dr Hans Joachim Neidhardt** lived at Pillnitz, Augustus the Strong's pleasure palace on the River Elbe. Neidhardt is a Saxon through and through. He was born in Leipzig, where he went on to study art history. Since 1959 he has been curator at the Dresden Picture Gallery, responsible for modern art. In these pages, he writes about the delights of Pillnitz, and also details the city's artistic treasures.

A born Dresdener, **Reinhardt Eigenwill** traces the city's development in the Middle Ages. He has worked since 1977 in the Saxon

Giebel

Neidhardt

Eigenwill

Klieme

National Library, an institution founded in 1556 and more recently regarded by the Communist SED rulers as a "dangerous breeding-ground of the intellect".

Dr Günter Klieme studied cultural history, German and English language and lectured at the Dresden Technical University. He was also one of the founders of the Dresden Museum for Early-Romanticism. In this book, he writes on the theatre.

The cultural historian **Dr Walter May** also lectured at the Technical University and has published material about the Baroque in Saxony. He takes us on a tour of Dresden's main Baroque sights, from to the Royal Palace to the famous Zwinger.

Historian **Dr Gerhard Schmidt** has written about countless topics in and around Dresden (anything from the Reform Movement in Saxony to churches in Saxon Switzerland) and has provided this book with an article on Dresden's historically rich villa-suburb of Loschwitz.

Dr Christian Mühne, who writes about Wagner and Weber in Dresden, has been director of the Richard Wagner Museum in Graupa since 1987. Before then, he worked at the Saxon National Library, of which **Hans-Jürgen Sarfert**, who describes the garden city of Hellerau, is another veteran.

Darmstadt-based **Dr Jutta Schütz**, editor of Insight Guides to Mexico City and Corsica, is a frequent visitor to Dresden. Here she takes us to some of the towns round about and reveals the beautiful scenery of "Saxon Switzerland". The area is a paradise for climbers; Germany's best-known climber **Bernd Arnold** traces the development of the sport.

Michael Bienert, a regular Insight contributor, took on a number of features, including a tour to the famous porcelain centre of Meissen, a discussion of environmental issues and an essay on Dresden's famous musical tradition. He also looks at the events of 1989 and how life has changed since.

Heike Leisch examines the idiosyncrasies of the Saxon dialect and reveals one of the darker aspects of the city's history by describing the fate of the Jewish cemetery. **Matthias Stresow** introduces Dresden's "in scene", particularly in the "Multicoloured Republic of Neustadt". Finally, **Armin Conrad** stops at that lasting symbol of the horrors of war, the ruins of the Frauenkirche.

The Photographers

Cityguide: Dresden maintains the high standard of photography for which the series is renowned. **Werner Neumeister**, who lives and works in Munich, grew up in Dresden. **Erhard Pansegrau**, a regular Insight contributor, is also well represented. **Sabine and Karl-Heinz Kraemer** have also worked for the series before, as has **Hector Barrientos**, a Chilean living in Berlin. **Wolfgang Fritz** from Cologne and **Rainer Kiedrowski** from Düsseldorf provided their usual high-quality contributions. Further material came from **Jens Rötsch** from East Berlin and **Jens Koshofer**, a photo-journalist from Ratingen. Assistance with archive material was given by the **German Photo Archive** in the Saxon National Library.

The main text for this English edition was translated by **Susan Bollans** and **David Ingram** and the Travel Tips section by **Susan Sting**, all under the supervision of **Tony Halliday**. Proofreading and indexing was completed by **Carole Mansur**, under the direction of managing editor **Andrew Eames**.

May　　*Schmidt*　　*Schütz*　　*Bienert*

History

Features

Places

Maps

TRAVEL TIPS

Compiled by Wieland Giebel

For detailed information
see page 241

YESTERDAY AND TOMORROW

Under the Saxon elector Augustus the Strong (1670–1733), Dresden became one of the most prosperous cities in Europe. When he first came to power the city's population numbered 20,000; by the end of his era, three and a half decades later, it had increased to 45,000.

"Princes become immortal through their creations," was Augustus's motto. His vision and architectural extravagance resulted in the creation of a series of buildings for which Dresden is still famed to this day: the Zwinger, the cathedral, the Royal Palace, the Taschenbergpalais, the Great Garden, Moritzburg and Pillnitz.

To do honour to this architectural golden age, this book opens with a series of views, or *vedutas*, of the city by the Venetian painter Bellotto (1721–80), better known as Canaletto. On pages 12–17 he provides us with a highly accurate document of Dresden's panorama at the height of its baroque glory.

In the first *veduta*, dating from 1748, Canaletto portrays the construction of the Catholic Hofkirche, which was built between 1738 and 1755 by Frederick Augustus II, Augustus the Strong's son and successor. The church was to stand at the head of the Augustus Bridge and grandly point the way to Warsaw, the Saxon electors' second residence. The monumental cupola of the Frauenkirche in the next *veduta* was a Dresden landmark at that time. The Altmarkt in the final scene was crowded with houses, and is now to be recreated once more into a harmonious whole.

Life today for Dresden's 500,000 or more inhabitants of these baroque surroundings is a tense mix of the city's recent history and optimistic plans for the future. Saxony is well-placed from the economic point of view. Saxon inventiveness goes hand-in-hand with the Protestant work ethic and a real zest for life.

After years of having to toe the official line, the people of Dresden have finally regained their Saxon self-confidence and love of life. There is a definite atmosphere of cheerful, almost Mediterranean serenity about the place. This new charisma has also brought the old rhyme, *"Sachsen, wo die schönen Mädchen wachsen"* ("Saxony, where the pretty girls come from") back into circulation, and visual evidence in the rest of this book proves the saying. In the old days, the local womenfolk had quite a reputation. In the *Ladies' Conversation Manual* of 1834 one reads: "Saxon women combine French attractiveness with the German temperament, physical charms with an intellectual education, and hard work in family life with an aesthetic sense for all that is noble and beautiful in nature and in the arts." And long may they continue to do so!

Preceding pages: the height of Dresden baroque as observed by Canaletto: Dresden as seen from the left bank of the Elbe (1748); Dresden from the right bank of the Elbe (1747); view of the Altmarkt from the Royal Palace (1749–53). **Left,** the *Weisse Flotte* moored on the banks of the Elbe.

FESTSCHRIFT
ZUR
800 JAEHR. JUBELFEIER
DES HAUSES WETTIN

Verfasst von Prof. OTTO KAEMMEL.
Künstlerisch ausgestattet von Historienm. Prof. E. A. DONADINI.

Brene

Groißh

Burggſ zu storbeg

Burgg zu Aldemburg

Kefferubergg

Burgaw

M. DCCC. LXXXIX.

Gagan

Pfalz

The inhabitants of Dresden have always been exceedingly proud of their world-famous buildings and art treasures, and also of the long history of their city. They can therefore be forgiven for having wrongly believed, even up to the 18th century, that Dresden was founded back in the time of Charlemagne, in 800. Dresden was actually founded some 350 years later. Today's visitor will nevertheless look in vain for the remains of old city gates or even a Gothic church: the heritage of later epochs has removed most of the traces of medieval Dresden.

The name of the city is itself a reference to its origins: "Drezdany", the place of the wooded river valley dwellers, was what the Sorbian inhabitants called their village on the River Elbe. It was located in the vicinity of the present-day Frauenkirche (Church of Our Lady), which in the Middle Ages was the parish church of Dresden, even though it lay outside the town walls. The church originated in the mid-11th century as a centre of Christian missionary work amongst the Sorbs, who were gradually Germanised over the centuries. The first actual mention of Dresden is in a document issued by a member of the Wettiner family, Dietrich der Bedrängte, dated 31 March 1206, but no further details are given. Here, at a natural crossing point, the trade routes from Meissen and the silver-mining town of Freiberg traversed the Elbe in a north-easterly direction. Even before the town's foundation by Margrave (a German nobleman) Dietrich there was thus in all probability a trade settlement on this spot.

Dresden becomes a town: Dresden was first mentioned as a *civitas*, a town, in 1216. At the end of the 13th century the castle on the Elbe was the favourite residence of the ageing Margrave Heinrich der Erlauchte, a prince famous throughout the realm for the splendours of his court. He not only promoted the

culture of the knights, but was also himself a composer of *minnelieder*, the lyrical poetry that became so popular in medieval Germany. For a long time after the town's foundation its affairs were dictated from the castle by a resident margrave, and it was not until a much later date that the citizens became masters of their own affairs.

In the Middle Ages the oldest bridge across the Elbe – built at the point where the Augustusbrücke now spans the river – was

already one of the town's main attractions. The astonishing thing about it was that even in those early days it was built of stone; there were few other bridges in the empire of such construction and size.

The bridge linked Dresden with the small settlement of Altendresden on the opposite bank. The latter received its city charter only in 1403 and was subsequently merged with Dresden in the 16th century. Apart from the castle there were a few large secular and sacred buildings which stood out amongst the densely-packed little houses of the two towns, with their thatched or shingle roofs.

Preceding pages: Pillnitz Palace; the sundial of the Stallhof. Left, the coat-of-arms of the Wettin family which guided the fortunes of the city for 800 years. Above, the residence of the Wettins.

As in all medieval towns, much of public life was enacted on the marketplace, on what today is known as the Altmarkt.

Markets and crosses: In the town hall, which was originally also used for trading purposes, tailors and cloth merchants laid out their materials. They occupied a position of great prominence in the town and the town council was recruited almost entirely from their ranks. It was not until the end of the Middle Ages that they were forced to vacate some of their seats in the council to representatives of the rich craftsmen's guilds, which had long been envious of their power. The small dealers and shopkeepers offered

its new name in the mid-13th century when Konstanze von Babenberg, the first wife of Margrave Heinrich der Erlauchte, brought a fragment of the Holy Cross to Dresden as part of her dowry. The chapel built for the precious relic became a popular place of pilgrimage. Even more people, however, were probably attracted by the "black crucifix", a mysterious crucifix that was allegedly covered with human skin.

First tourists: In 1319 the Dresden clergy obtained a 40-day absolution from the Curia in Rome for all believers who came in penitence to the Kreuzkirche on St John the Baptist's Day or who made donations to the

their wares from booths and stalls outside the town hall. On such days the town centre was peopled by buyers, onlookers, pickpockets and other dubious sectors of the population and was a rough and lively place.

Medieval man was, however, also very unsure of himself and particularly in need of religious support. Mysterious symbols or signs of the Christian faith thus had a special attraction. High above the houses on the market towered the spire of the ancient Kreuzkirche (Church of the Holy Cross). Originally dedicated to St Nicholas, the patron saint of merchants and travellers, it acquired

Elbe bridge (part of the church's estate). And so it was that in the late Middle Ages more than 10,000 visitors would pour into the city on this day – quite remarkable when one considers that the population totalled scarcely 4,000 souls.

Starting from the Kreuzkirche, the priests and members of the guilds went through the streets of Dresden enacting biblical scenes, in particular the passion of Christ. The highlight, after the procession was over, was the performance of the "Beheading of John the Baptist" on a stage erected in front of the Kreuzkirche. From 1489 the council also held races for runners and carts on the market square: first prize was a live ox. However, reformist zeal and puritanism put an end to the annual festival in 1539.

Work and festivities, fires, epidemics, war and death – these were the dominant features of the age. In the 15th century, which marked the end of the Middle Ages, they were compounded in Dresden by political and religious unrest, which also led to war.

Heretical doctrine: At the beginning of the century the town was visited by a virulent "bacillus" in the eyes of the church, that of the Hussite doctrine. The teachers, who had been "infected" in Prague, preached their

of the Wettiner family's sphere of influence began to change. Duke Albrecht der Beherzte (Albert the Bold) had ruled the lands of Saxony with his brother Ernst from 1464. But in 1485 they agreed, in the treaty of Leipzig, to divide their inheritance between them. As the holder of the electoral entitlement, Ernst acquired the duchy of Saxe-Wittenberg-Thuringia; his brother was left with the Meissen Marches, including Dresden and the Erzgebirge.

The two branches of the Wettiner family henceforth became known as the Albertine and Ernestine lines. The capital of Albertine Saxony was now Dresden and this fact was

"heresies" at the Kreuzschule, Dresden's esteemed Latin school founded about the year 1300. These teachers had left Prague University with other German students and professors in 1409 and in 1412 were forced to leave Dresden again at the instigation of the Bishop of Meissen.

The modern age: As it emerged from the Middle Ages, Dresden's insignificant status as a small country town on the eastern edge

Left, the Wettin Duke Dietrich in battle dress. **Above**, Margrave Conrad lays down his arms in Meissen cathedral.

to have a decisive influence on the fortunes of the city until well into the 19th century: the requirements of court and the society it attracted had an ever-increasing effect on the prosperity and economic development of the city. Without the rulers' preoccupation with the maintenance of a particular image and the patronage of the aristocracy, the cultural achievements of subsequent centuries in Dresden would have been unthinkable. The way in which the court was gradually also beginning to influence the mentality of the Dresdeners was later viewed with mixed feelings: the widespread uncritical acceptance of the aristocratic life style as the focal point of society at the time actually was detrimental to the development of the bourgeoisie as an independent social class, particularly in the 18th century.

In the 16th and 17th centuries, however, there was an ideal symbiosis between the bourgeois instinct for achievement, the rulers' love of power and prestige, and the major forces of the Renaissance and the Reformation. After a massive fire reduced 230 houses and the Kreuzkirche to ashes on 15 June 1491, Duke Albert, who was usually away fighting in the service of the emperor and spent very little time in the city, was

commenting that the houses being built there would be regarded as palaces if they'd been anywhere else.

The Reformation: Hieronymous Emser was an opponent of the Reformation, as indeed was the Duke himself. George the Bearded could not accept the teachings of Martin Luther, although he did acknowledge that certain pressing reforms were necessary within the Church. The shameless sale of indulgences by the Pope's emissaries, aimed at raising church funds, was a matter that had to be resolved.

The famous Dominican monk and seller of indulgences, Johann Tetzel, appeared in Dres-

Alten-Dresden wie es am 6. Aug: Anno 1685. im Feuer gestanden.

quick to act: in order to encourage rapid reconstruction, he exempted the effected citizens from paying their taxes for some years. And the new houses were to be built of stone.

Under Albert's successor, Duke Georg der Bärtige (George the Bearded), the new creative forces began to take effect, even though initially they were eclipsed by the unrest and confusion connected with the Reformation. In 1505 the court chaplain, Hieronymous Emser, was disappointed by the "wretched little town" he found. Only three decades later, his successor, Johannes Cochlaus, enthused about the "fine city of Dresden",

den in 1508 and 1509; here too the licentiousness of the clergy had reached scandalous proportions. Tetzel's indulgences were intended to finance the building of St Peter's in Rome and ended up provoking Luther's 95 Wittenberg Theses.

Prior to the outbreak of these fundamental conflicts Luther himself had been in Dresden twice, in 1516 as a local vicar of the Augustine order based in the monastery of Altendresden and responsible for Meissen and Thuringia, and in 1518 – when he was still on friendly terms with Emser – to preach a sermon in the palace chapel. Thus it was that the spirit of the Reformation had penetrated the residence city of the Albertines. In 1521, when the news came out of Pope Leo X's bull of excommunication against Luther, an angry crowd smashed the windows of Emser's house. After George the Bearded's death his brother, Heinrich der Fromme (Henry the Pious), who had long become a follower of Luther, took over the reins of government.

Renaissance heritage: In 1547, Henry's son Moritz acquired the electorship for the Albertines. He and his successor Augustus transformed Dresden into a magnificent Renaissance city, metropolis of the most power-

long arcade was completed, in which splendid tournaments were held; there was also an execution in front of the building, when the Calvinist chancellor Nikolaus Krell was beheaded in 1601. In 1560 Augustus founded the Dresden collections, at a time which coincided with an economic upswing. It was no longer the cloth merchants but the craftsmen who were catering for the needs of the court who reached unknown heights of prosperity. Now Dresden rose in status above towns such as Pirna and Freiberg and the number of inhabitants trebled between 1500 and 1600 to around 15,000.

The Thirty Years' War put an end to this

ful territory of the empire after the dominion of the Habsburgs. In 1546 the medieval town wall was replaced by modern fortifications along Dutch lines. The final section, completed in 1591, has been preserved as the Brühlsche Terrasse.

In 1563 Elector Augustus completed the Zeughaus (arsenal) – today the Albertinum – one of the largest of its day in Europe. Under Elector Christian I the Stable Court with the

Left, in 1685 Altendresden was destroyed by fire (artist unknown). Above, Johann A. Thiele painted Castle Moritzburg in 1736.

first golden age. Life in Dresden was marked by hunger, inflation, war, taxes and plagues, and the crafts and trade in general were on the verge of ruin. Fortunately for the city, however, the massive fortifications spared the inhabitants the immediate terrors of wars. So many people wanted to take refuge within the walls "that all the gates and bridges seemed too narrow". In 1645, the Thirty Years' War, the worst ever in the history of Central Europe, was over for Dresden. A completely changed world emerged from amongst the horrors of superstition, plagues and religious conflicts.

AUGUSTUS THE STRONG AND THE BAROQUE AGE

Dresden is the most beautiful city in Germany – or at least that's what the locals say. Millions of annual visitors come to marvel at its magnificent buildings and gardens, the splendid voluptuous baroque creations which provided such a sumptuous stronghold for Augustus the Strong (1670–1733). The highlights of Dresden today are mostly down to the fantasies of that one man, the Hun with the boyish soul, who not only enjoyed life to the full but as a man of great vision also set about the planning of this, *his* city.

The baroque age can only be understood against the background of the Reformation and the Thirty Years' War, with its heritage of "ghastly emptiness, broken people, ravaged earth, lifeless homesteads and a godless world". The true meaning of the word "baroque" has nothing to do with the history of art. It was a world in itself, an overflowing of life in the wake of a world crisis. That it was also the outcome of its own particular constellation of circumstances, however, becomes immediately evident when compared with the more recent past: the period following the end of World War II was by no means as fruitful as that which followed the end of the Thirty Years' War in 1648. In those days, too, there were ruins to be cleared away, just as there were in 1945, but it was done with a totally different aim in mind: while we remove the traces of war by restoring old facades, our predecessors built a whole new world. They created, we recreate.

Survivors: It is difficult to form a picture of baroque Dresden. Only a few isolated features have survived the intervening waves of history. The Zwinger, the cathedral, the Grosser Garten (Great Garden), Moritzburg, Pillnitz, the art collections including the Grünes Gewölbe (Green Vault), the orchestra and the opera (the institution not the house, which was built later). And when the

palace is eventually rebuilt, the audience room and the bedchamber of Augustus the Strong will also once again be on display. All these things are, however, merely set pieces, and while we can appreciate their beauty as individual items, we can no longer see them in their full context.

This should not come as a surprise, since even Frederick the Great was no longer able to understand the baroque world: when Prussia invaded and occupied Saxony in the

Seven Years' War (1756–1763), destroyed Dresden and subjected Augustus III's prime minister, Count Brühl, to such humiliation that he died as a result, the Prussian king was horrified at the unbelievable luxury of the count's lifestyle. Every suit had to be worn with a particular watch, snuffbox, stick and dagger, and each outfit was depicted in a book from which Brühl made his selection every morning. Two hundred pairs of shoes, 800 dressing-gowns and 1,500 wigs completed his wardrobe. Frederick the Great commented that it was "a lot of wigs for a person with nothing in his head!"

Left, Augustus the Strong, elector of Saxony, portrayed here as Augustus II, king of Poland, by Louis de Silvestre, 1718. Above, his wife Christiane Eberhardine was devoutly pious.

The great baroque age of Dresden covers the reigns of Augustus the Strong and his son Augustus III (1694–1763). As early as 1719 a contemporary writer described it as a city that had attained "the height of perfection, rapture and magnificence". A good impression of what the city was like can be gained from the famous *vedutas* of Bernardo Bellotto (1721–80), otherwise known as Canaletto, some of which are reproduced in the early pages of this book.

Augustus: As the second-born son of Elector Johann Georg III, Augustus the Strong was not the crown prince. His obligatory educational journey did not therefore take him,

to the Catholic faith. As a result, Saxony was immediately exposed to the overwhelmingly baroque influence of the Catholic states of France and Italy, which was soon reflected in its architecture, painting, music and poetry.

Dazzling festivals: The baroque love of life and art, the importance of the here and now, was particularly evident in the splendid Dresden festivals which became the talk of Europe. Staged by Augustus the Strong himself, their underlying purpose was of course to demonstrate the elector's power in the absolutist sense. The magnificent buildings which remind us of these events today were basically only a backdrop. Zwinger,

like his brother, to Holland, which at the time enjoyed supremacy, but to France, Spain, Portugal and Italy. After three years on the throne his elder brother Johann Georg IV died suddenly and Augustus took over the electorship – a happy conjunction of circumstances. Had Augustus been the first-born, he would have taken his lead from Holland, and if he had not become elector he would not have been able to give expression to the ideas inspired by his educational journeys.

An equally fortunate circumstance was the acquisition of the crown of Poland, which demanded a changeover from the Protestant

Grosser Garten, Pillnitz, Moritzburg and Japanisches Palais (Japanese Palace) all provided a setting for the great festivals. The Elbe became Augustus the Strong's "Grand Canal" and the Zwinger his open-air banqueting hall. By 1719 the construction of the latter had progressed to the point that it was possible to use it for the wedding ceremony of the crown prince Augustus III with the empress's daughter Maria Josepha, a celebration completed in imitation of a festival of Jupiter.

Contemporary descriptions help us to picture what it must have been like: "The king himself took part in the carousel of the four elements, the high point of the festivities, also his son the electoral prince and the dukes of Saxony-Weissenfels and Württemberg. Each prince was followed by 16 riders and horses all in the same colours. Most splendid of all was Augustus himself, dressed as fire in bright red satin studded with diamonds and decorated with salamanders and flickering golden flames."

The legends surrounding Augustus: The Brühlsche Terrasse does not only attract those who are interested in the beautiful view. Those visitors who can sometimes be seen painstakingly searching the railings are credible is his reputation for being able to break silver cups, plates and hard coins as if they were paper – he was also called the Saxon Hercules. "He broke the hearts of the ladies," says the historian Vehse, "as easily as he broke horseshoes," and with this remark introduces a second phenomenon: Augustus was the royal version of Don Juan. In her memoirs the Marchioness of Bayreuth wrote that he had 354 natural children and a French professor credited him with 700 women (300 fewer than Solomon).

To do Augustus justice it should be remembered that the age in which he lived had become incredibly corrupt. To keep a mis-

looking for the thumb-prints of Augustus the Strong on the handrail, on which he is said to have demonstrated his strength. They have, however, failed to notice that these railings are at the very earliest a 19th-century construction and therefore far too recent for Augustus's grip. The legend is nevertheless an attractive one because it fits his image and was responsible for the epithet "the Strong".

His enormous strength was supposedly derived from drinking lion's milk, but more

Augustus built the Zwinger, left, as a stage for his extravagant parties, above (J.A. Thiele).

tress was good form and his most famous mistress was Countess Constantia Cosel whom he subsequently imprisoned in Burg Stolpen for 17 years, and thereafter she remained there voluntarily to the end of her life. His wife, on the other hand, the electress Christiane Eberhardine of Bayreuth, was pious and serious, and popularly known as the "shrine of Saxony".

A king's career: Augustus was born in 1670. From 1687 to 1689, he travelled Europe, visiting France, where he met Louis XIV in Versailles, Spain, Portugal and Italy. He became elector in 1694, and two years later his son and heir Augustus II was born. With the help of his friend, the emperor Joseph of Austria, he became King Augustus II of Poland. First, however, he had to join the Catholic Church, an unusual step to take in the country that had given birth to the Reformation. The cost of acquiring the throne ran to some 11 million talers.

Augustus the Strong soon became involved in the Great Northern War in which Sweden – or, to be more exact, Augustus's young cousin King Karl XII – fought against Russia, Denmark and Saxony-Poland. In 1702 Augustus was driven out of Poland and in 1704 deposed as Polish king in favour of

personal tax, the excise tax, which caused food prices to rise by a third. From 1713 onwards he maintained a standing army of 16,000 men. His sources of wealth in the country were the rich mines, high agricultural yields and an industrious people with a reputation for good work. The enormous power of the aristocracy had been bolstered by the long absence of the elector king, and his ministers were more the masters of the land than he was. Augustus employed a chancellor who was responsible for raising funds, a head chamberlain who was in charge of festivities and entertainment, and a field marshal who regulated diplomatic affairs.

Stanislaus Leszczynski. In the Peace of Altrandstadt Augustus was forced to renounce his claim to the Polish throne. After the battle of Poltava/Ukraine, in which Sweden was defeated, Augustus regained the throne in 1709 – by which time he had been ruling the country for almost a quarter of a century. His son, King Augustus III of Poland, managed to keep the crown and the personal union of Saxony and Poland thus continued until 1763.

After a seven-year absence, Augustus returned to Dresden in 1704 to find that the state coffers were empty. He borrowed money from Holland, sold land and introduced a

He finally died in Warsaw in 1733. His coffin is in Cracow, but his heart was brought to Dresden and kept in a silver urn in the crypt of the Hofkirche (cathedral), where it can still be seen today.

Festive centre: It was not the state but the court which experienced a golden age under Augustus the Strong, during an era of unprecedented splendour in the German-speaking world. Augustus planned the court festivities himself. There were Mars, Venus, Diana, Neptune and Saturn festivals. The peasant festivals were extremely popular with the people of Saxony because they brought visitors to the country, stimulated the arts and sciences and promoted the circulation of goods and money.

Everything that makes Dresden what it is today was the creation of Augustus the Strong. In his day, the city's houses were still made of wood; in 1708 he ordered that stone was to be used instead. The most important buildings created during his reign were the Zwinger, the Frauenkirche, the Japanisches Palais (Japanese Palace), Moritzburg and Pillnitz. The art treasures he accumulated are still the best exhibits in the Grünes Gewölbe (Green Vault) and the art gallery. He promoted French comedy, the ballet, the Dresdner

tried to present Saxon history in a bad light in order to improve its own image. Heinrich von Treitschke, a Prussian historian, wrote: "When the Albertines' craving for splendour was combined with the licentiousness of the Polish aristocracy, German absolutism reached the height of depravity."

End of a dream: It is hard for today's visitor to picture the Zwinger as the centre of festivities. The sandstone has been eaten away by pollution and is very black. Those who find it difficult to imagine Dresden in the baroque age should visit the Grünes Gewölbe, where the painting by Johann Melchior Dinglinger (1664–1731), *Household of the*

Kapelle and the Italian opera. A production cost 40–50,000 talers, but all "respectably dressed persons" were admitted free.

Augustus the Strong transformed Saxony from a quiet backwater to a country occupying a central position in European politics. His defeats were therefore of great advantage to Brandenburg/Prussia. Prussian propaganda, especially under Bismarck, always

Great Moghul in Delhi, is a representation of Augustus the Strong's dream of a great Wettin kingdom.

The Seven Years' War and the bankruptcy of the state put an end to the great baroque age. In the words of Helene von Nostitz: "A new style, emerging from the more objective outlook of the bourgeoisie, was on its way, and everyday life asserted its rights at the cost of creative zest. Even the princes became more conscientious, bourgeois and cautious. These virtues, however, did not produce such an enduring heritage of great works as the excesses of Augustus the Strong."

Left, the Neumarkt with the Frauenkirche in the background, Canaletto, 1749. **Above**, the pomp for which Augustus strived: *The Moghul court in Delhi* by Johann Dinglinger (early 18th-century).

CONSTANTIA VON COSEL

They were passionately in love, Augustus the Strong and his mistress Constantia. She hosted festivities with him, led the court and skilfully represented Saxony to foreign diplomats, engaged the best artists, was charming, beautiful and desirable, and took great pleasure in the presents he gave her. Constantia also ran her own town residence, the manor of Pillnitz, and was involved as an independent businesswoman in money-lending activities, in particular at the Leipzig fair. Augustus wanted her with him all the time – not just in bed, but also on his trips of inspection round the country, when he made use of her analytical abilities. In shooting competitions, often as the only woman competitor, she far outstripped the cavaliers of the court. There was not a man at court who was not attracted by her sensuality and not a man who was spared her ready wit.

Augustus had never given a mistress so much. She had two guards in front of her house, while his ministers had only one, and it was for her that he built the grandiose Taschenbergpalais, which was linked to the palace by a covered passage. He bought her Pillnitz Palace and obtained for her the title of countess from the emperor. Her love for him was so great that she still believed in and supported him even when he dropped her as a consequence of political intrigues.

Constantia was not only his mistress: in secret, but with the backing of a marriage contract, she was his other wife. She was born on 17 October 1680 on the estate of Depenau, near Plön. On her mother's side she was descended from a family of rich Hamburg merchants, and on her father's side the impoverished family of the Holstein knight Brockdorff, which was closely connected with the Danish royal family. Her father taught her to ride and shoot and organised her education, while from her mother she learned the attributes required of the lady of the house. As the maid of honour of a Danish princess, she became familiar with the etiquette of the aristocracy.

In 1703 she married Adolf Magnus of Hoym, 12 years her senior and hated by aristocracy and peasants alike as Augustus's tax collector, and went with him to Dresden. The marriage did not go well: Hoym isolated her, in retaliation for which she refused him his conjugal rights, and finally asked for a separation. At a ball she went up to Augustus, introduced herself and talked to him for a long time. Scandal followed. Shortly afterwards there was a fire at Constantia's house. The king himself had driven to the site because of the danger for the city and saw Constantia giving decisive instructions for extinguishing the fire.

She resisted his courtship for a long time and it was not until he offered her a house near the palace that she agreed to become his mistress. In return, however, she insisted on the secret marriage contract, which stipulated that Augustus must separate from his previous mistress, pay Constantia 100,000 talers a year (almost as much as the queen), but above all officially acknowledge their children. Augustus accepted. In the ensuing years Constantia was present at all Augustus's meetings, excluding his ministers and favourites and provoking jealousy amongst her female competitors. Constantia reacted naively to the intrigues at court, trusting completely the two rival groups involved and relying on her great love for Augustus.

Augustus's prime minister and closest adviser was Lieutenant General Jakob Heinrich von Flemming. His relationship with Constantia was a mixture of attraction and controlled distance; they were rivals for the king's favour. It was Flemming who advised Augustus to take a Polish mistress on account of his involvement in Poland. Constantia was outraged. She was pushed aside, and both the marriage contract and presents she had been given were demanded back. Finally, she was imprisoned in Burg Stolpen, where she lived under surveillance for 49 years, outliving Augustus by 30 years.

Right, Anna Constantia Countess Cosel was the most famous of Augustus's mistresses.

When Francis II resigned as emperor in August 1806, the "Holy Roman Empire of the German nation" officially ended, after 1,000 unbroken years of existence. Its dissolution had, however, already been signed and sealed on 12 July 1806, when 16 German estates of the empire put their names to the document of the Confederation of the Rhine, which was under the protectorate of Napoleon. On 11 December 1806 peace was concluded in Poznan between France and Saxony, as a result of which Elector Frederick Augustus III joined the Confederation of the Rhine and took the title of king of Saxony. From then on, he called himself Frederick Augustus I.

Seven kings: The electoral residence became the royal capital and residency of Dresden. For the next 112 years between 1806 and 1918 seven kings of the Wettin line resided in Dresden. They are depicted in 19th-century style in the *Procession of Princes* (10,300 sq. ft or 957 sq. metres) on the exterior of the *Langer Gang* (long arcade) of the Stallhof in Augustusstrasse; originally executed in sgraffito technique (1876), the mural was later transferred to 24,000 tiles made of Meissen porcelain. The city lost its status as a seat of government on 13 November 1918 when Frederick Augustus III was forced to abdicate and Saxony ceased to exist as a kingdom.

Originally, the new importance of Saxony made little initial difference to Dresden's appearance, but an order by Napoleon paved the way for future change: between 1809 and 1829 the old fortifications were knocked down. The town, so long confined by its medieval bonds, was now free to expand, and the driving force behind this expansion was the bourgeoisie, because the aristocracy was gradually waning in importance.

The visible symbol of this is the Brühlsche Terrasse. It was connected with the city by means of a wide staircase and taken posses-

sion of by the self-confident bourgeoisie. Houses were built and avenues laid out on the site of the former fortifications, particularly in the Neustadt. Building standards were improved by new regulations; the last wooden houses had already disappeared long ago in 1710. Since then most of the buildings had been made of plastered brickwork, and from 1830 on solid sandstone was also used. With the appointment in 1834 of Gottfried Semper, whose monument stands on the

Brühlsche Terrasse, the appearance of the city was increasingly enriched by the neo-Renaissance style. New landmarks in the city centre were first the opera house (1838–41) and later the art gallery (1847–54).

Industrialisation: After 1870 both public and private buildings became increasingly cluttered in their architectural style. Industrialisation, which had begun to make massive inroads in Dresden, and the constant increase in the city's population, led to the appearance of tenement blocks in the suburbs. Hans Erlwein, head of the city planning department and building control from 1905

Left, King Johann, who ruled from 1854 to 1873. **Above**, the town hall in the Altstadt.

Napoleon In Dresden

The poet and composer Ernst Theodor Amadeus Hoffmann came to Dresden for the first time on 25 April 1813 as the musical director of Joseph Seconda's opera company. On 10 May he wrote to his publisher describing how Napoleon had once again taken the city; part of his letter is reprinted below.

Napoleon had smashed the French Revolution but nevertheless shaped the whole of Europe according to its ideals. In 1812 he invaded Russia with 600,000 soldiers, only to retreat in October when he was defeated. His former ally Prussia deserted him and concluded a neutrality treaty with Russia. For the first time, the Prussian king called on the people to resist: "It is the final battle on which our existence, our independence and our prosperity depend!"

Napoleon moved with lightning speed, and in Bautzen was initially victorious, but was then defeated in the Battle of the Nations at Leipzig in October 1813. Germany was liberated as far as the Rhine, Paris was occupied and Napoleon was exiled to Elba. For the time being, however, Dresden is under siege:

"We are living through a time when there is such a rapid succession of events that only the most recent seems important; do not therefore expect a full account of what has been happening to me. What I would like to say, however, is that this splendid city, even in these critical times and even in my highly precarious situation, is a source of great encouragement to me. On 3 May large numbers of Russians began crossing the Elbe, and continued to do so all day and all night. On 7 May the Chancellor of State, von Hardenberg, left Dresden with the city councillors. The next day the King of Prussia rode through the city. The thunder of the cannons was shaking the windows of the houses on the Elbe. At 11 o'clock a French trumpeter rode through the streets followed by cavalry and infantry, and at five, with all the bells of the city ringing, Emperor Napoleon entered the city and was received by various deputations.

"The Russians stayed in the Neustadt and now there was a great deal of rifle fire. How the Russian officer rushed about trying to find where his enemies were and how frantically he gestured at the population who had gathered out of curiosity to go away! The bullets bounced off the palace gate, a woman was badly wounded and a boy shot. On 9 May French riflemen were posted on the gallery and the tower of the Catholic church and fired across the river. Now bullets of a different kind even reached the Neumarkt – the Russians had emplaced guns – and at 1.30 a grenade exploded in the middle of the Altmarkt.

"Unaware of this danger I went to the Brühlsche Palais at 10 in the morning and found a number of people by the palace gate, but at that very moment was hit in the shin by a bullet rebounding from the wall, so slightly however that only the turnover of my boot was damaged and all I got was a bruise. I picked up the bullet, which had been pressed as flat as a coin, to take home as a souvenir, and very satisfied with this, unselfishly requiring nothing more, I removed myself rather quickly and also abandoned the idea of visiting the ramparts where French guns were being positioned at the remaining embrasures.

"One could not think of attending a service or vespers as the bullets were shattering the windows of the churches and hitting the doors; even early in the morning an old man had been shot on the church steps and bullets were raining against the palace gate. In short, it was possible to die of curiosity anywhere in the city. Whether I now remain in Dresden and how and when I will get to Leipzig is in the lap of the gods. I have therefore left my expensive hotel and am lodging on the fourth floor of Altmarkt No. 33, at Madame Vetter's, in a romantic little room near the Uranus where I am sitting now, and full of my own heroic courage am writing of the fear and danger I have survived.

"You cannot imagine, my dear friend, the extent of the troubles and awful tumult we have been going through in the last few days. For this reason, therefore, the promised essay is not yet ready, but I am enclosing a copy of 'Ritter Gluck'. My literary tools are of no use at all – how can anyone write decently with pale ink and a blunt pen? But it should and will get better."

on, brightened up the city by reintroducing baroque elements; one example of which is the Italian village restaurant (built between 1911 and 1913).

After the Reichstagsgebäude (parliament building) had been constructed in Berlin, Dresden, not to be outdone, commissioned the same architect, Paul Wallot (1841–1912), to build the Landtagsgebäude (state parliament building) which was finished by 1907; the central location chosen on Schlossplatz meant that substantial old buildings had to be pulled down to make way for it (Palais Brühl, Palais Fürstenberg).

Building boom: The combination of the would be today. Moreover, the solid construction of those 19th-century edifices meant that many of them withstood the bombing better than the historic buildings of old Dresden, with the result that the former now really do dominate the city. They have recently gone up in public estimation, so sharply do they contrast with the unimaginative new postwar buildings.

The city redesigned: The right bank of the Elbe with the Neustadt, as seen from the Brühlsche Terrasse, is dominated by two massive buildings. On the left is the former finance ministry (1892–94), on the right the former general ministry (1900–04). These

growing administrative burden and a state that was becoming increasingly prestige-conscious resulted in the construction of further official buildings in the centre of Dresden rather than on the new land available on the edge of the city. Numerous private buildings were also put up during this period, naturally in the same style as the official ones, so that in the late 19th century the appearance of Dresden underwent considerable alteration. Of course, in those days such radical change was more acceptable than it

Above, the Japanese Palace in Neustadt, 1835.

authorities were responsible for the administration of the kingdom of Saxony, and these buildings are today the seat of the Saxon state government. In the Schiessgasse next to the Museum für Stadtgeschichte (City Historical Museum) are the police headquarters, built from 1894 to 1898 and massively extended in the 1970s as far as the Frauenkirche without the department responsible for the preservation of historic monuments being able to do anything about it. The Rathaus (town hall) was also rebuilt from 1905 to 1910; its massive tower is higher than any other building in the city (308 ft or

98 metres), and provides a good view of the surroundings. The gilded figure on the top of the tower has become the symbol of the city, and after the war the people of Dresden joked that it showed how high the rubble was.

In 1839 the first German long-distance railway line began operating between Leipzig and Dresden, followed by six different lines of the Saxon State Railway. The main station (1892–95) and the III Neustadt station (1898–1901) are still impressive.

When the first steamships began plying the Elbe in 1837 the only bridge between the Altstadt and the Neustadt became a problem: its arches were too narrow and too low. The

it now functions as the central box-office for the state theatres. The Yenidze cigarette factory (1912), in the guise of a mosque, is by contrast something of a curiosity amongst the buildings of Dresden.

A city out of balance: At the beginning of the 19th century there was a harmonious relationship between houses, squares and streets and the people for whom they were designed. This was only maintained until just after the middle of the century. After 1870 things began to get out of balance and by the end of the century the principle had been abandoned altogether. This negative tendency was closely linked with social developments:

old bridge was replaced and five other bridges were constructed across the Elbe. It can be said with some justification that it was not until this time, when Dresden was also equipped with street lighting, sanitation, banks, warehouses and hotels, that it acquired the status of a major city.

There are two architectural outsiders in the heart of the city: on the central square between the palace, the opera house and the Zwinger (art gallery) stands the Altstädter Wache, built from 1830–1832 to a design by the Berlin architect Karl Friedrich Schinkel (1781–1841). Preserved in its original form,

the Prussian way was increasingly taking over even in the country that was Prussia's old rival, Saxony.

Vanished past: The visitor who comes to Dresden to see the famous baroque city will be disappointed. Only a few isolated buildings remain from its great past: what the age of capitalism before World War I did not destroy was finished off by the age of communism after World War II.

Above, Saxon and Prussian troops attacking the barricades in 1849. **Right**, a battle in the revolution year of 1848.

RICHARD WAGNER AND THE DRESDEN UPRISING

Composer Richard Wagner was in Dresden when the city's democratically-inclined burghers rose up against the Saxon government in 1849. Although a large majority of the townspeople had close links with the court, the Saxon democrats succeeded in consolidating their position during the 1849 state parliament elections. The monarchy promptly dissolved the parliament. It was this move, combined with a rejection of the imperial constitution drafted by the Frankfurt parliament, which sparked off an open confrontation.

It was only when shots were fired on the population that the "Fatherland Association" called for armed resistance. Though successful at first, the inexperienced rebel troops were defeated by the Prussian army which had been hurriedly called in to assist the Saxon court. The rebellion was quashed and the prisons were filled to overflowing. Wagner and Semper, the architect, fled abroad. Nevertheless, democratic reforms did develop all over Germany with the advent of industrialisation. But for the time being, Wagner is witnessing the Dresden uprising:

"Sunday 7 May 1849 was one of the best days this year; I was awoken by the sound of a nightingale singing. Fog descended, however, towards sunrise: suddenly we could hear the sound of the *Marseillaise* coming through it loud and clear, getting closer and closer, then the fog dispersed and the rays of the bright red rising sun glinted on the rifles of a long column of soldiers marching into town.

"It was impossible not to succumb to the impressions this lasting vision created; that particular element, whose presence I have missed for so long in the German people, and whose absence has contributed in no small measure to my moods until now, was suddenly presenting itself to me in its freshest possible aspect: there they were, at least several thousand well-armed and well-organised *Erzgebirgler* [mountain people], most of them miners, and they had all arrived to protect Dresden. Soon we saw them marching up to the Altmarkt, opposite the town hall, and pitch camp there in order to rest from their march, to a jubilant welcome.

"What I witnessed at around eleven o'clock, however, was altogether less impressive: the sight of the old opera house, in which I had conducted the last performance of the Ninth Symphony only weeks previously, suddenly going up in flames. People had always been worried that this building, only a temporary construction in its time, and filled as it was with wood and canvas, would one day fall victim to fire damage. I was informed that it had been set alight on purpose, for strategic reasons, in order to fend off an attack by the troops on this vulnerable side of the city, and to protect the famous Semper barricade from surprise attack; from which I inferred that strategic reasons are far more powerful than any aesthetic motives, which had already – and in vain – been calling for the demolition of this ugly edifice, which so disturbed the elegance of the Zwinger.

"Filled as it was with such incredibly inflammable material, this building, which was actually of quite respectable dimensions, burst into an enormous sea of flame within a very short time. Zeal for the arts ensured that the fire was stopped from spreading to the Zwinger and its galleries.

"Our observation point, which until then had been relatively peaceful, began to fill with ever greater numbers of armed men who had been sent to the church in order to defend the entrance to the Altmarkt, which it was feared would be attacked from the direction of the only thinly-defended Kreuzgasse. There was no place for unarmed men here now; moreover I had received a message from my wife, filled with fear and concern, bidding me to return home. It was only with the greatest difficulty that I managed to do so, having taken all manner of circuitous routes in my secluded suburb, which sheltered me from the parts of the city where the battle was raging, as well as from a volley fired from the direction of the Zwinger. My apartment was filled with frantic females. My young nieces, in daredevil mood and thoroughly enjoying the shooting, restored my good humour."

MARTIN LUTHER

DRESDEN IN THE TWENTIETH CENTURY

A 20th-century history of Dresden is still waiting to be written, for the tendentious depictions of the GDR era are massively flawed. In the Stadtmuseum (Municipal Museum), Dresden's historians cleared away the relevant exhibits at the beginning of 1990 without replacing them. Since then the history of the city in the 20th century has remained a complete blank for its visitors.

The official historical version furnished by the state was supposed to represent the victory of the working class under the leadership of the Communist party. Local history has also been falsified in much the same way. Not a word is mentioned about such reformist projects as Hellerau, the garden city to the north of Dresden, which a humanistically-minded factory owner had built for his workers before World War I. Politics in the democratic free state of Saxony after World War I have remained unresearched, as have municipal policies of that time, which were to a large extent influenced by the Social Democrats. The state regime was just as happy not to be reminded of them as of the division of East Germany into its component federal states, which were dissolved in 1952 before finally being reinstated in 1990. Jewish history has also been cloaked in silence.

Since the 1970s, special workshops had been formed in West German cities with the aim of researching local history. Virtually nothing of the kind happened in the East, however – and when it did, it was in secret and very much against the will of the state. Anti-Fascism became the official doctrine of the GDR, and there was never a proper evaluation of National Socialism. The state's representations of history during the postwar period were nothing more than touched-up lists of achievements of the party in power.

Normally, in a historical survey like this, one is able to draw on the work of professional historians. However, against such a

Left, Luther by the ruined Frauenkirche. **Above**, Ernst Grämer presents his bust of Lenin on the occasion of the 1st Pioneer meeting in 1952.

rough background, the pages that follow can constitute only an attempt to assemble the pieces of the jigsaw.

Between the wars: In 1930, in his novel *Fabian*, the author Erich Kästner described his native city thus: "Towards evening, Fabian crossed over to the Altstadt. From the bridge he saw the old buildings once again, the buildings he had known all his life: the royal palace, the imperial opera house, the Hofkirche, everything here was wonderful,

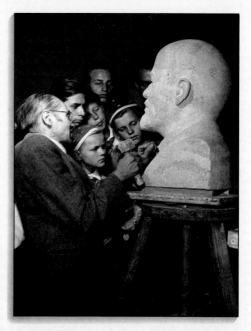

unique. The moon slowly rolled across from the top of the palace to the top of the church tower as if sliding along a high-wire. The terrace extending along the river embankment was overgrown with ancient trees and dignified museums. This city, its life and its culture – all had gone into retirement. The panorama resembled nothing more than an expensive funeral."

Like many young artists and intellectuals of that time, Kästner was strongly drawn to Berlin, which had long since outstripped Dresden as cultural metropolis of the empire. From the mid-1920s onwards, Dresden began more and more to assume the character of a quiet provincial town, until it was shaken to its foundations by the economic crisis of the early 1930s.

But the period before the crisis was, politically at least, very exciting. On 9 November 1918, the revolution spread to Dresden. A revolutionary soldiers' and workers' council announced the removal of the government of Saxony, and proclaimed a "socialist republic". The king of Saxony was forced to abdicate, and the red flag was hoisted above the palace. The state art collections still bear visible traces of those days: on most picture-frames the wooden crown

travelled on to Stuttgart. On 15 March there was a general strike in Dresden in protest at those who had started the *putsch*. The 59 demonstrators were shot on the Postplatz.

At the very first elections for the Saxon state parliament and for the Dresden city council, the moderate left (SPD and USPD parties) were able to achieve an absolute majority. In November 1920 Saxony was given a new constitution, under which it now re-defined itself as a "free state". The state parliament and state government were now both based here. Just how little room for manoeuvre the government of this new "free state" actually had, became very clear in

above the picture – the symbol of its ownership – is missing, having been broken off during that period.

During the so-called "Spartacus Rebellion" of January 1919, counter-revolutionary troops shot 14 Communist workers. In April, the Saxon Minister of War, a Social Democrat, was thrown into the Elbe by demonstrators, whereupon the imperial government immediately announced a state of emergency.

During the right-wing "Kapp Putsch" in Berlin, in March 1920, the imperial government fled to Dresden, but, refused permission to stay by the commander there,

October 1923: when Social Democrat Erich Zeigner reshuffled his cabinet and allowed the Communists to take part in the state government, the entire administration was removed from office by the army and an imperial government decree. The elected state government wound up in prison, and an army officer took over instead.

City of hygiene: During the first three decades of the 20th century, Dresden was nearly as well-known for its leading role in health education as it was for its opera and its art treasures. In 1911 Dresden industrialist Karl August Lingner co-operated with the city of

Dresden to stage the first ever International Hygiene Exhibition. Its huge popularity led to the foundation of the Deutsches Hygienemuseum (German Hygiene Museum). This building on the Lignerplatz, designed by architect Wilhelm Kreis, which the museum moved into in 1929, is the only significant building achievement of the period (apart from Hellerau) in all Dresden. In the following year, a second International Hygiene Exhibition was held in a vast exhibition park surrounding the new building. The park railway in the Great Garden is all that remains of it. Despite the increasing severity of the world economic crisis, an

in 1946. Klemperer had been teaching French literature at Dresden's Technical University since 1920. A Jew, he lost his professorship there in 1933 before being gradually deprived of all his civil rights. He survived the Nazi era because his "Aryan" wife was able to protect him.

Viktor Klemperer kept a secret record of those years. He is unable to tell us of any opposition on behalf of the people of Dresden to National Socialism. His book describes the insidious way in which people's minds were infected by the ubiquitous Nazi terminology, which gradually poisoned their attitudes and ways of thinking – even those

even more enlarged version of the exhibition was held yet again in 1931. However, under the National Socialists the progressive efforts made by the Hygiene Museum were reversed: in 1933, courses in "racial studies and racial cultivation" were embarked upon.

The path to destruction: Only one published source survives that gives us an idea of what everyday life in Dresden between 1933 and 1945 must have been like: Viktor Klemperer's book *LTI*, a study of Fascist language, printed

Left, the last royal parade in Dresden took place in 1914. **Above**, the Altmarkt in 1937.

who were not committed Nazis at all.

Others exiled from Dresden in 1933 included painter Otto Dix, who taught at the Academy of Fine Arts, and conductor Fritz Busch. The latter was taken away by the Nazis on 7 March 1933 while conducting a performance of Verdi's *Rigoletto* in the opera house. The state art collections were purged of several works, notably those of Dix, Kokoschka, Schmidt-Rottluff and Barlach. The synagogue designed by Gottfried Semper was burnt down in the 1938 pogrom, and nearly all the Jews of Dresden were either exiled or murdered.

THE BOMBING

After the destruction of Dresden, Erich Kästner wrote: "What was formerly known as Dresden is no more. Fifteen square kilometres of city have been destroyed for ever. Solid rock usually takes whole geological ages to metamorphose – here it took only a single night to do so."

The city centre, filled with refugees, was totally destroyed during the British bombing raid that took place on the night of 13–14 February 1945, less than three months before the end of the war in Europe. The target sector markings on RAF photographs leave no doubt that this attack went exactly as planned, into the heart of the city. Military areas to the north of Dresden, factories, and freight stations were scarcely damaged at all.

The bombardment created a firestorm in the city centre – a firestorm that was impossible to extinguish. Even the Great Garden and the Elbe Meadows, where many sought refuge on that night, were bombarded. 35,000 or 135,000 – nobody knows for certain how many – died. So many people were killed, however, that it was impossible to bury the corpses quickly enough, even in mass graves. In the Altmarkt, tram rails were used to create makeshift grids upon which the bodies could be cremated.

Speculation continues to this day as to what motive Air Vice Marshal Sir Arthur Harris might have had when he gave the order for this raid – an order that was approved by Churchill. One theory is that it was an act of revenge for the destruction of Coventry in 1941. Whatever the reason, the justification has never been clarified. "Bomber Harris" organised what was by far the most murderous carpet-bombing operation of the entire war. Over half a million German civilians and over 55,000 RAF airmen fell victim to his "firestorm strategy".

The victims were either killed instantly under the hail of bombs, or died horribly from suffocation. Even British military historians consider these attacks to have been "a waste of men and materials which was far from delivering heavy, let alone decisive, losses on the enemy."

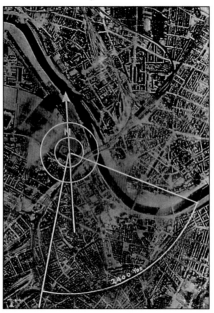

Before Dresden was bombed, the cities of Lübeck, Rostock, Pforzheim, Hamburg, Hildesheim, Cologne, Magdeburg, Mainz and Würzburg had all been subjected to tactical bombardments, where the maximum possible number of bombs were dropped within as large a target area as possible. The German magazine *Der Spiegel* sums this up as "the first pre-nuclear mass murder from the air in military history", and the *Presse* in Vienna considered Sir Arthur Harris's attack to be "the forerunner of Hiroshima".

The controversy continues: several of Harris's wartime comrades recently collected over £10,000 in order to be able to dedicate a monumental bronze statue to the memory of the Air Vice Marshal, who died in 1984, and have it erected in front of the RAF church of St Clement Danes in The Strand in central London. The plan was approved by Westminster City Council and the Air Force, and went ahead despite the fact that mayors from the German cities that had suffered bombardment had implored the British government to abandon it.

Public criticism of the "architect of destruction" would have had worldwide implications – and would also have led to a discussion of Winston Churchill's role. The reason the latter agreed to the bombardment, in the opinion of military historians, lay in the RAF's fatal lack of accuracy during operations.

According to British military historian Ralph Baker, as quoted in Germany's *Der Spiegel* magazine, one reason Churchill approved Harris's annihilation strategy was because "it was better to bomb what we could hit than to carry on bombing what we couldn't."

In his childhood reminiscences entitled *When I Was a Little Boy*, the writer Erich Kästner warns: "To this day the governments of the great powers are still arguing about who was responsible for the murder of Dresden, and nobody wants to be accused of it. Everyone says that everyone else was to blame. Well, I don't know what they're on about. They won't bring Dresden back to life like that. In future, make the government suffer, not the people! And not just after the event either, but straightaway. Does that sound simplistic? Well, it's actually simpler than it sounds."

Between 1933 and 1939, the city's population dwindled from 642,143 to 625,117.

The catastrophe: Dresden's belief in Hitler and in "final victory" lasted longer than that of many other German cities. While the other cities had been subjected to bombing raids, Dresden remained unscathed until almost the end of the war. This is how the legend developed that Dresden was taboo as far as the Allied bomber squadrons were concerned. The city was considered so safe, in fact, that its anti-aircraft installations were shifted to another location in 1945.

The bombardment that took place on the night of 13–14 February 1945 was an act of May 1945 Dresden already had a new municipal administration, with Rudolf Friedrichs, a Social Democrat, at its head as acting mayor. The first daily newspapers appeared that summer, and the State Theatre and Philharmonic Orchestra began performances once more. A monument in front of the town hall stands as a reminder that it was mostly the women of the city who cleared away the 17 million cubic metres of rubble.

Reconstructing the Dresden of old was unthinkable in the face of so much destruction, and the urgent need to house the homeless. Apart from the desperate situation there were also quite sensible reasons in favour of

terrorism against the civilian population. There was no need to attack this city, which was filled to overflowing with evacuees, refugees and war wounded. Within the space of a single night, the centre of Dresden was totally destroyed, and tens (possibly hundreds) of thousands of people were killed. Militarily important targets, such as the barracks, remained unscathed.

Reconstruction: At the beginning of May 1945, the Soviet army entered the city. By 10 a more spaciously-planned modern construction programme: however beautiful the former city may have been, hygiene standards and sanitation conditions in many of its old buildings were quite unacceptable by modern standards.

Another noticeable feature, though, is that the areas that were in really desperate need of new housing are not all that ugly – not, at least, the parts of the city that were rebuilt before 1958, when the faceless concrete-slab style of building was introduced. Far worse are the remains of attempts during the 1960s to turn Dresden into a representative-look-

Left, a bomber's view of Dresden. **Above**, Pioneers march past Stalin's portrait.

ing "socialist metropolis". The huge wedge of that oversized parade ground, the Thälmannstrasse, was driven into the city centre, and the Altmarkt (Old Market) was turned into a large and deserted open space to accommodate state-run mass rallies. The Palace of Culture, completed in 1969, made as much of a mockery of the city's rich building heritage as did the redevelopment of the Prager Strasse.

Since the mid-1970s there has been a gradual shift towards taking more care of the various historic municipal buildings Dresden still possesses. In 1979 the Strasse der Befreiung (Liberation Street) was officially

had suffered less damage and were situated away from the centre could not be properly maintained. A lot of streets and houses have thus become dilapidated through neglect only during the past 40 years.

Small businesses and the self-employed were at a huge disadvantage under the socialist system, and this in turn meant that whole shopping streets which had contained rows of craft businesses, small shops and pubs right up until the 1960s became completely desolate. The people of Dresden, who have always kept a distance between themselves and the official view of the rest of the world as prescribed by the Party of Unity,

opened. The way it integrated the historic buildings and scaled everything down to human dimensions earned it much praise, even from the West. In the 1980s, the focus shifted to historicisation as far as construction was concerned, in the area near the fashionable Dresdner Hof hotel.

With the reconstruction of the Zwinger, the Frauenkirche and the Semper Opera House, and with various exhibitions and congresses, Dresden tried to re-establish its former reputation as a city of culture. However, the ambitious reconstruction projects meant that the sections of old Dresden which

gradually realised that the last two decades of the GDR had been a period of progressive paralysis. The gulf between what the papers said and reality became ever deeper. The standard of living worsened, pollution increased and the supply of consumer goods never matched demand. But hospitality and helpfulness continued to survive, somehow, within the huge authoritarian state structure.

Above, the pride of the proletariat – the mobile concrete mixer. **Right**, Hans Modrow, the SED district secretary from Dresden, the GDR's last leader before reunification.

THE WALL COLLAPSES

The East German (GDR) economy was on the brink of collapse – yet no-one believed it. Tired of drab everyday life, of the all-powerful state and of the way they were continually being forced to adjust to it, most people scarcely dared even dream of change. The dissatisfaction did not lead to mass protests but instead to one enormous mass desertion.

The Dresden region was nicknamed the "Valley of the Clueless" because it could not receive Western TV and therefore couldn't see what it was missing. However, the number of exit visa applications in the Dresden area was above-average – 22,000 people apparently fled during the summer of 1989, when the border was suddenly opened. Trains full of GDR "refugees" travelled through the main station. On Wednesday 4 October a large crowd gathered there: "We're staying put, we demand reform," they shouted.

Others whose escape plans had been thwarted by the closing of the Czech border tried to jump on to the trains. The station was stormed, and the police and the army took drastic measures. Worries about a possible "Chinese solution" were rife: many feared that the government would send in tanks, just as the Chinese Communist party had done in Peking earlier in the year.

On 8 October Communist party leader Erich Honecker told the regional secretaries to use every means at their disposal to suppress the demonstrations in the province. In Dresden, thousands took to the streets, and, although he brought in massive "reinforcements", the police chief did not attack the peaceful crowd.

There was no organised opposition in Dresden; no-one had prepared what were quite spontaneous demonstrations. One of the first groups to join the courageous Protestant church in speaking out in public was the State Theatre Ensemble: after each of their performances, the actors read out protest announcements, informing the audiences of events in Berlin and Leipzig and inviting public discussion. That evening the local party leaders bowed to the crowd's demands. The next morning Wolfgang Berghofer, the mayor, received a deputation of 20 demonstrators. The "twenty" wanted dialogue, free from violence, and sweeping changes from the bottom up. They demanded that he grant the people press freedom, the freedom to travel and the right to demonstrate, and also release political prisoners. The group then delivered its report to the population that evening, in churches packed to overflowing.

The climate for discussion was more favourable in Dresden than elsewhere because the hated state party was represented locally by two politicians who had been shifted from the party's central Berlin headquarters to the province, and had since won great respect there.

Mayor Wolfgang Berghofer and local party chief Hans Modrow were considered would-be reformers and secret supporters of Gorbachev. Modrow in particular was held in exceptionally high esteem because he had not moved into the usual private villa but had instead opted for a three-room apartment, and queued up like everyone else in the local supermarket (rechristened the "Modrow-market"). His strained relationship with Berlin was also a well-known fact. His suggested reforms received no reply.

With his *realpolitik*, Berghofer was the first SED functionary in the entire country to engage in dialogue with the population. On 6 November both men took up positions at the head of the Monday demonstration, in which 70,000 took part. After the collapse of the old leadership, the party then placed its hopes in these two: on 13 November 1989 Modrow was elected president. He went on to rule the GDR until the first free elections in March 1990, and, unlike Berghofer, did not resign from the party.

With demands for unification of East and West Germany becoming ever more vocal at the Monday demonstrations, Chancellor Kohl visited Dresden on 19 December. In front of the ruins of the Frauenkirche, the people of Dresden greeted him with a huge sea of black, red and gold flags. It was this more than anything else that made Kohl realise that German reunification should take place as swiftly as possible.

EIN HERZ FÜR KINDER

9 - 91

Ich hab'
den West-Test
gemacht!

LIFE SINCE THE WALL CAME DOWN

Dresden has become more colourful since the reunification of Germany. The black-and-grey tones of the old city are steadily receding, and the loud colours of free enterprise are upstaging that uniform greyish-brown which was once so typical of cities in the GDR. There are advertising posters up everywhere, even plastered across the Czech trams, still very much the backbone of the public transport system. There are street stalls, sausage vendors on every street-corner, and cigarettes being sold on the black market. But construction machinery and scaffolding from the West is speeding up reconstruction work on the old Residenz (Royal Palace), and, although the sales halls are still furnished in the old style, the goods they display are predominantly Western.

Many people in Dresden are not at all happy about how their city is changing. They are unused to the permanent firework display of neon signs and flashy lettering. The days when one could proudly display Western packaging in the living-room cupboard are long gone.

A change in opinion: In local votes as well as in the Bundestag elections in 1990, the people of Saxony supported speedy union with West Germany by a large majority. Black, red and gold flags fluttered throughout Dresden's streets during the months before final reunification.

A small minority of those who have profited from the change are now proudly displaying how readily they have learned to fit in with the advanced Western lifestyle. But others – especially people aged 50 and over – feel they have reached a dead end. To a large extent, they defined themselves by their jobs, which they have since lost; many now have little chance of finding new ones, despite the economic upswing.

Take Barbara, for example: Barbara is a dyed-in-the-wool Dresdener, a woman of

Preceding pages: a sticker after the collapse of the Wall. **Left,** "We Are One People." **Above,** Trabi, digital watch and boundless optimism.

around 50, with a Canaletto hanging in her living-room and neo-baroque fitted shelves along one wall, which she decided she could afford after monetary union. "I'm not myself these days," she says. She hasn't had a good night's sleep since the summer of 1990. She is a member of the works council at what used to be a state-owned planning concern which was sold to a West German firm.

Actually, a West German electronics concern had wanted to take it over, but that

firm had made the dismissal of the entire management a precondition of the takeover, and the "reds" among the management knew how to hinder this. They got the *Treuhandanstalt* (the trust responsible for the privatisation of the formerly state-run enterprises) to listen to them, and it sold the concern to a new owner, who came to an agreement with its former management.

Barbara had to stand there and watch as two-thirds of the staff were sacked, but not even a single former Communist was among them. Barbara was one of those people who had high hopes after the Wall came down, and who now feel powerless and betrayed. Moreover, Barbara has been living alone since the summer of 1990. Both her daughters are in West Germany – a reflection of the mass migration of young and qualified people from East to West that is still going on despite reunification and monetary union.

Local economics: The economic situation is still hard to define because privatisation has only just got properly into gear. The city's two most famous concerns – the Robotron combine, and Pentacon, the camera manufacturers – have been broken up, with some parts of the companies shut down and other parts already sold off.

partners have simply become too expensive.

The consumer goods industry – the more profitable parts of it at any rate – is in West German hands. The firm of Philip Morris has taken over the cigarette factories formerly owned by the Dresden tobacco combine. The famous non-filter Karo cigarette has survived the onslaught of Western brands. A hamburger firm has bought up the Mitropa catering combine. The largest department store in the city, Centrum, in Prager Strasse, has now been taken over by Karstadt AG, a major West German retailer. It took the municipal commission for de-unionisation of trade nine months to persuade the Spar chain

Dresden is suffering more than most from the economic collapse that has been taking place ever since monetary union. Up to 60 percent of its industrial products – whether children's clothing, railway trucks, packaging, machinery, gas pipelines or microchips – used to go straight to the Soviet Union. A certain amount of business is guaranteed even today – replacement parts for computer systems, for example, manufactured by Robotron. But new contracts are thin on the ground, despite this continuing demand. Since the changeover to the D-mark, most products manufactured for former Comecon

of stores to withdraw from 57 of a total of 138 sales outlets in Dresden, thus making genuine competition possible.

Most of the investment has been in subsidiaries owned by Western firms, and in sales outlets for Western goods, although the Aufschwung Ost Community Initiative has won extra contracts to the tune of DM 110 million for Dresden businesses. The main obstacles in the way of the economic upswing are the worn-out infrastructure, the unsettled question of what property belongs to whom, and unfamiliarity among administrators with the new legal system.

New government: There have been several complaints from people out of work, students applying for grants, small businessmen and entrepreneurs willing to invest and those taking early voluntary retirement, that they have often had to wait for months at a time for their various applications to be processed. The situation in the Municipal Property Office is particularly critical: here, in mid-1991, a mere 13 employees were faced with 40,000 applications from people who claimed ownership of property. It is this lack of certainty about the legal situation that is having such a crippling effect on people's readiness to invest.

lems. Another fly in the ointment is the *Stasi* (secret police) past, which has yet to be properly confronted: because no thorough investigation into the representatives of the people has ever taken place, renewed suspicion about key individuals keeps springing up all the time, and the parliament keeps getting caught up in unproductive debates which only serve to postpone the solution of urgent problems.

Apartments and rents are a highly controversial issue in the city, and are causing a lot of worry and misery for the population. Because of numerous price-rises, the ratio between income and the cost of living is al-

The worn-out infrastructure is also creating unnecessary difficulties. The telephone system is so bad that local politicians cannot even be assured of a smooth information flow within the city itself. One year after the new municipal government was formed, the city's deputy mayor still had no private line. The MPs in the Saxon Diet as well as members of the state government, which is based in Dresden, are struggling with similar prob-

ready so out of joint in East Germany that rent increases since October 1991 have taken on existential and threatening dimensions in many people's eyes.

The rents do have to go up, though, finally to cover costs and successfully to hinder any further structural collapse of rental accommodation. Dresden needs another 30,000 apartments – a deficit that is not at all easy to make up. The lack of accommodation is not only affecting young people who want to start families, but also the various investors, qualified personnel and officials the city is trying to attract from the West.

Left, "Reunification – only this way," claims the graffito. **Above,** where East meets West – street markets have a universal appeal.

Town planning is in top gear. New office blocks and hotels are soon to be constructed in the suburbs. In the historic centre, where new buildings have to take the remains of the old city into account, the planners are still rather hesitant. They are unanimous, however, that at least half of the Altmarkt in its present condition will need to be rebuilt. Many of Dresden's inhabitants would love to see the ugly square red building near the Zwinger, which the Sophienkirche had to make way for during the 1960s, vanish as soon as possible. Not far away, in a magnificent location on the Elbe embankment, a new building for the Diet is being planned.

Partners: Dresden will be able to adapt fully to the new era only with outside help. Assistance on the municipal and state level has earned much praise, and this applies in particular to the swift and unbureaucratic support the city has received from its partner city in the West, Hamburg.

Dresden is profiting considerably from its role as capital of Saxony in its relations with its partner state of Baden-Württemberg. The Swabians have assigned hundreds of civil servants to Dresden, and are making up the difference in their wages. The sheer scale of this assistance has already resulted in objections on the grounds that it constitutes a threat to Saxon identity. Furthermore, the city has also recently signed another partnership contract with Salzburg, a city to which Dresden feels particularly close because of its baroque and musical heritage.

Neo-Nazis: Unfortunately, Dresden has earned itself a reputation for right-wing activities. Attacks by bands of neo-Nazi thugs seem to have become the order of the day; they take place on occupied houses in the Neustadt section of the city, on foreign students and on Vietnamese "guest-workers" who, dismissed from their jobs, have to save themselves from starvation via illicit street-trading. The first fatality was 28-year-old Jorge Gondomai from Mozambique; he was beaten up by a group of skinheads on a tram on Easter Sunday 1991 and then thrown head-first out into the street. The radical right was provided with its first martyr: Rainer Sonntag, a known right-wing organiser, who was shot in broad daylight at the beginning of June 1991, probably by some members of the city's pimp fraternity. His funeral attracted 2,000 demonstrators, the largest neo-Nazi procession in postwar history.

The right-wing scene is not homogeneous, and is hard to define. For many youths – particularly those from authoritarian families with an SED or Stasi background – membership of a gang is often the only way of gaining any social recognition. The people in control of the gangs are older, and some have moved across from the West. Using Dresden as a base, they are attempting to transform the latent radical right-wing potential in the new federal states into an

organised force and an increasingly powerful political weapon.

In the meantime, a new interior minister for Saxony has been appointed, and programmes have now been started with the aim of reaching young people, above all in schools and youth centres. In the long term, the government is setting its hopes on a revitalised economy – the firmest basis for uprooting right-wing radicalism once and for all.

<u>Above</u>, after 1989 the population turned to the West. <u>Right</u>, Dresden's partner city Hamburg and private sponsors support the reconstruction.

THE TWINS ON THE ELBE

In the 1980s, local government officials, who are often surprisingly susceptible to current fashions, promoted the idea of "twinning" towns in Europe. Mayors and council dignitaries embraced with enthusiasm the notion that international understanding would be inestimably enhanced if they were to pay official visits to each other's countries – all expenses paid, of course.

Dresden and Hamburg did not need any spurious excuses to justify establishing close links. These two cities on the River Elbe had been isolated from each another for 40 years and old historic ties could be quickly re-established. Just after the Wall came down, the mayor of Hamburg, Henning Voscherau, jumped at the opportunity to give Dresden a helping hand and offer his city's services as a logistical centre for Dresden's modernisation programme. In January 1990 he flew into the city with 75 top managers from Hamburg in order to put economic contacts on a firm footing. It was the first Lufthansa flight to Dresden since the end of World War II.

Before then, the GDR had already become Hamburg harbour's largest transit customer (2.6 million tons a year), almost half of Hamburg's transport network had been geared towards the East.

After Voscherau's visit, events moved at great speed: Dresden city officials went to Hamburg for informational talks, school exchanges between the two cities were organised, local medical societies organised exchanges of medicine, and female members of the alternative Green Party took part in the opening of a new women's centre in Dresden. The two cities have finally become partners once again. Plenty of other partners are also involved in the city.

Reconstruction of the Royal Palace, due to be completed in the year 2006, will cost something like DM 500 million alone, and DM 130 million is the figure estimated for the Frauenkirche – one which will be impossible to realise solely with municipal funds. Private sponsors have come together to form the "Dresden Foundation".

On the initiative of the Dräger Foundation, such leading names as Daimler Benz, Axel Springer, the *Frankfurter Allgemeine*, the Dresdner Bank and the Norddeutsche Landesbank have joined forces in order to signal their "optimism and readiness to help".

The money is channelled through people like Erich Jeschke. His job-title is a prime example of the socialist predilection for linguistic precision: "construction management leader (Dresden district) for the reconstruction of cultural and historical buildings".

The title almost belongs in the archives too – as a "listed" expression. Erich Jeschke stands in the art gallery, surrounded by the decayed walls and ripped-up parquet flooring, telling stories which often fill his listeners with disbelief. Such as the time, for example, when all the masons and stone-

cutters had already climbed the ladders leading up to Augustus the Strong's throne-room when they received a message that the elevated tank at the waterworks in the Neustadt was in urgent need of repair. The workmen duly descended their wobbly ladders, climbed into their Trabants and drove off to the waterworks.

Erich Jeschke would often not see them for weeks at a time, but now he is quietly confident. "We've finished work on the opera house too." The international praise the city received for the successful restoration work is still ringing in his ears. He mentions the Charter of Venice, under the conditions of which teams working on the preservation of public monuments are requested to leave as much of a building's historical substance in as original a condition as possible.

"Tearing them down and rebuilding them is a lot cheaper, of course," he points out. For the past few years, Jeschke has been particularly busy with the Royal Palace in Dresden, which has received several additions over 700 years from the Saxons.

Public and private assistance is closely connected in these projects. The sponsors from the Dresden Foundation are responsible for the restoration of individual sections of buildings: the Jürgen Ponto Room, for example, in the famous Grünes Gewölbe (now containing a museum containing the finest Saxon treasures) was paid for by the Dresdner Bank.

THE SAXON DIALECT

A typical Saxon remark, overheard in a café, might run something like this: *Ei forbibbsch, nu is mir doch schon wieder so viel Bähbe beim Didschen in Gaffe gebroggd* (rough translation: "Oh dear, I've gone and got too many crumbs in my coffee again from dunking cake"). The tone is tired and conveys annoyance. Nothing beats *Gemiedlichkeid* – the Saxon equivalent of *Gemütlichkeit* or sense of personal comfort – nor the Saxon's favourite drink, his *Gaffe*, or coffee – which he wouldn't mind drinking in peace, thank you very much, and the more sugar the better. Coffee drinking is a real Saxon cult.

The Saxon dialect is a reflection of an easy-going, peace-loving attitude to life: it is soft, quiet and comfortable-sounding. Critics say Saxons only slightly open their mouths to let the words spill out because they are lazy. Saxons disagree vehemently. Their dialect has been too often ridiculed over the past century, and in films they have been cast as the fat, stupid characters, the south-east German twits, and more recently, the incompetent ex-citizens of the GDR.

Loyalty to the King: Beware! The calm exterior hides a very deep sense of pride. Pride in a beautiful homeland with its wild mountains and rolling hills, pride in great thinkers, a rich cultural heritage and beautiful towns and villages. Not to mention that incompatible mixture of *Nischel* (brains, intelligence) and loyalty to the king. Both these characteristics, which have already left their mark on Saxon history, were reflected once more in the events of 1989 and 1990: in the rebellious anger towards the GDR state on the one hand, and in the subsequent government elections on the other.

The "true Saxon" doesn't really exist, though. Ask someone from Leipzig or Dresden where genuine Saxons are to be found and they won't surrender their rights to one another. But ask that same person from Leipzig who speaks the worse-sounding dialect and he'll always tell you it's people from Dresden – and, of course, vice versa.

A noble language: The Saxon can always tell quite distinctly which part of Saxony his conversation partner comes from, for there are actually several different variants of *sächsisch*. These subtleties are usually lost on film-makers, who swiftly shift the finest Chemnitzer to Dresden. These subtle differences in the dialect have individual names too: in Chemnitz they speak *vorerzgebirgisch*, in Leipzig *südwestosterländisch*, in Bautzen *neulausitzisch*, in Riesa *nordmeissnisch* and in Dresden *ostmeissnisch*. All these dialects also have Slavonic features as especially clear from place-names (Dresden = *Drezdany* = "the place of the wooded river valley dwellers"). To this day the colloquial language still contains expressions such as *Hitsche* (footstool) and *Bähbe* (traditional cake baked in a mould). The German word for "border" is *Grenze*, and comes from the Slavonic word *granitsa*.

It used to be fashionable to use Saxon expressions in the north of Germany. Goethe considered the Saxon dialect to be the best and clearest in all Germany, and Saxons still get very annoyed by observations such as those made by Karl Barth ("a horrible, dreadful German dialect") and Franz Grillparzer ("a formal, sheep-like baa-baa sound", "a bleating E-language").

The hated Prussians: This defamation of the dialect was accompanied by a sense of shame forced on Saxons – so they themselves say – by the Prussians, who never really managed to establish total dominion over Saxony. And the Prussians have often denied Saxon accusations that they spread the legend about Augustus the Strong having more than 250 children. We thus have yet another Saxon characteristic: an intransigent hatred of Prussians, who in their eyes are overbearing, loudmouthed, hectic, aggressive and arrogant, and of Berliners in particular, because on top of everything else the latter took away Dresden's role as capital city.

Preceding pages: on the streets for the Dixieland Festival; the young people of Dresden. **Left**, a typical Saxon.

It was one the first warm days of the year, and the cracked walls of the city were bathed in magnificent sunlight. The old man was sitting by the side of the road, next to the busy traffic, with a newspaper on his lap, sunning himself. He was sitting in such a way that it was still possible to make out the graffiti on the back of his bench. "KOHL NEIN DANKE", it said, with the "NEIN" obliterated by black paint. A perfect subject for a photograph.

The man asked what the photograph was

He'd no idea what we were all in for. A right mess it turned out to be."

The old man asked about the philosopher Nietzsche, the atheist. Friedrich Nietzsche was a Saxon, you see, born and bred. Then he got on to "that Goethe fellow", but said that he had lived in Weimar and only came to Dresden on visits. Finally there was "that Kästner bloke", and the nice monument to him on the other side of the street.

And the old man, whose name was Herr

going to be used for. "For a book? I don't believe it. Well, well, you don't say! But of course I want to be in the book, of course I do!" Then he opened the newspaper and pointed to a photograph. "See that there? See that? That's the Palais de Saxe. That was the finest building in all Dresden, that was. And up there – see the window? – that's where I was born. On 2 September 1914. Know what happened on that day? Bet you don't. That was Sedan Day, the anniversary of the Prussian victory over the French in 1871. And my dad used to say: he's a lucky lad, never has to go to school on his birthday.

Trautner, said that he'd also been "on Bautzner Strasse" – meaning he'd visited the Stasi headquarters there – because he'd sent anonymous letters to Eduard von Schnitzler, the chief demagogue of East German television.

Herr Trautner lives in Löbtau, a nice area for walks with plenty of parkland situated between high blocks of flats of red and yellow brick. Old photographs hang on the walls in his flat. "That's me on the balcony of the Palais de Saxe when I was a young boy, and that's my younger brother. I'll be visiting him in Munich this summer. We haven't seen each other for 40 years. He wants to come to Dresden after that. God knows what he'll say when he sees my flat. And this is my other brother. He was killed in Russia on 24 December 1942, you know, when all that was going on. That destroyed Christmas for us for good. My parents never bought another Christmas tree after that."

He went on to say that he had had a job in the catering trade and had also spent three years as a prisoner-of-war in Russia. He was married twice; his second wife left him 15 years ago. When asked about the city he goes and fetches a plan on which every house is depicted individually, and the huge military

of 1989, Herr Trautner answers that he's much better off and can afford more these days. He goes on to say that he drives off every lunchtime to eat in the "Pikant" restaurant, where you can get still get a good barley stew for DM 2.80. He considers everything else a luxury. Sometimes he goes to "that Russian place" (a restaurant) in the Hospitalstrasse, too.

He still remembers a bit of Russian from the old days. "Most people are frightened of the Russians. Not me. Russians aren't bad. It's us who've made them bad." Herr Trautner gets a hot meal in their canteen for as little as DM 1.50. German-Soviet friendship.

areas to the north are individually coded according to their functions. His most exciting moment was the discovery of several pontoons opposite the Brühlsche Terrasse on the Elbe – floating swimming-pools. One pool, known as the "Antonbad", was where Herr Trautner had first learnt how to swim, and he used to get dressed in the changing-rooms facing the famous skyline of the city.

Asked about the situation since the events

After this chance meeting, Herr Trautner sent the editor a travel guide dating from 1912 – a marvellous little collector's item, pocket-sized and well-written:

You pearl of the Elbe,
You hospitable city,
With your beauty, joy and peace
For all people!

God save your King,
God bless your treasures,
Whatever you do,
May heaven protect you.

Above, the story of Dresden in the past few decades is mirrored in what Herr Trautner tells about his life.

Dresden is one of the most magnificent treasure-houses of art in the world. The Saxon elector Augustus founded the "electoral chamber of art and wonders", a royal hall of fame with all kinds of curios and rarities, in 1560. From that time onwards Dresden became the venue for international art, reaching its peak in the 18th century when Augustus the Strong and his son, both of them avid collectors, purchased art treasures from all over the world and brought them back to Dresden.

In the 19th century these collections were reorganised and put on public display. In February 1945, during World War II, over 200 paintings were destroyed, while a further 500 were stolen from storage depots. After the war the Dresden collections were transferred to the Soviet Union, where they were carefully preserved in museums in Moscow, St Petersburg and Kiev. Ten years later they were returned to Dresden.

Art in Dresden today is on display in the 11 museums belonging to the Staatliche Kunst-sammlungen (State Art Collections), but it is very cramped. The space situation will only improve once the Residenzschloss (Royal Palace) has been rebuilt.

Reconstruction work on the Gemälde-galerie (Art Gallery) in the Zwinger, built around 1860 by Gottfried Semper, has been under way since 1988. Until its completion, some of the most important collections have been temporarily crammed into the Albert-inum on the Brühlsche Terrasse. This is advantageous for visitors, because here they can find all in one small space the very best works from the Alte und Neue Meister (Old and New Masters) gallery, the Grünes Gewölbe (Green Vault), the Skulpturen-sammlung (Sculpture Collection) and the Münzkabinett (Coin Collection).

Preceding pages: angels from the *Sistine Madonna* in the Dresden Art Gallery. **Left**, the baroque was a synthesis of everything beautiful: Egyptian motifs with the portrait of Augustus the Strong. **Above**, the *Sistine Madonna* on display.

The *Sistine Madonna*: The Semper Picture Gallery (Gemäldegalerie Alter Meister) is today still considered to be the most magnificent of the collections in Dresden, and Raphael's *Sistine Madonna* is its most famous picture. It was purchased in 1754 from a monastery in Piacenza for the sum of 20,000 ducats. King Augustus III is said to have exclaimed excitedly, "Make way for the great Raphael!" and vacated his throne for it on the day when the huge painting was

delivered to the palace in Dresden.

The purchase of the *Sistine Madonna* was the high point of a magnificent era of acquisition; in and around the year 1740 alone the city acquired a full 268 paintings from the Wallenstein Collection in Dux, 100 of the best pictures from the collection belonging to the Duke of Modena, and 69 more from the Imperial Gallery in Prague. In his private chambers, on his travels and military campaigns, Augustus III quite happily surrounded himself with gems from his picture gallery, and further purchasing was only stopped by the advent of the Seven Years' War.

The imposing Royal Gallery chiefly contains works from the Italian Renaissance and of the Italian and French baroque, as well as 17th-century Dutch and Flemish art.

As well as the *Sistine Madonna*, there are also several other works by leading masters of that period for the visitor to admire. Indeed, some connoisseurs even rank other works above Raphael's *Madonna*, such as Giorgione's *Sleeping Venus*, Titian's *Tribute Money*, Vermeer's *Girl Reading a Letter by the Window*, or Rembrandt's *Self-Portrait with Saskia*.

More recent masters: Many visitors who dislike modern art tend to steer clear of the Impressionists and Post-Impressionists, ranging from Manet to van Gogh and Gauguin. Magnificent examples of 20th-century art were on view here until the Nazi destruction of "degenerate art" in 1937.

The gallery owes its existence not to eager royal collectors this time, but to Saxon minister Bernhard von Lindenau and his democratic attitude to art. When he left his official duties in 1843 he made his retirement allowance available for the promotion of art and culture, and especially for the purchase of contemporary paintings. One of the first paintings to be thus acquired was Ludwig Richter's *Bridal Procession in Springtime*.

word "new" and avoid visiting the New Masters gallery. In doing so they miss out on some of Dresden's finest and most well-known paintings. Here one can find one of the richest collections of German Romantics and German Impressionists, with major works by Caspar David Friedrich, Ludwig Richter, Max Liebermann, Lovis Corinth and Max Slevogt, as well as *War*, the moving triptych by Otto Dix. The New Masters gallery contains all the paintings in Dresden dating from around 1800 onwards. The majority of them are by German artists, with the exception of a group of pictures by French

Today, only about a fifth of the 2,000 paintings can be exhibited at any one time.

Glittering emeralds, shining gold: The Grünes Gewölbe or "Green Vault", the legendary treasure vault of the princes of the House of Wettin, is the largest and most magnificent of its kind in all Europe. The treasure collection gets its name from its former location in the Royal Palace, to which it is soon to be returned when reconstruction work there has been completed. This vaulted group of rooms, with outer walls over 6.5 ft (2 metres) thick, and heavily barred windows, was considered to be the part of the palace that was safest against fire and theft. It was here in 1723–24 that Augustus the Strong had the first treasure museum in the world put on view. And here it remained, until its immeasurably precious contents had to be moved out, because of the war, to the strong rooms of the fortress of Königstein in 1942.

Amazingly, the collection, with its 3,000 or more artefacts made from gold, silver, precious stones, ivory, emeralds and bronze, survived the war totally unscathed. Roughly half of it is on display today in the Albertinum. Among the most fabulous works in this glittering array are the figurines from "the Imperial Household in Delhi on the Great Moghul's

Madonna statues and Renaissance bronzes, but also sculptures by Rodin, Maillol, Barlach and Kollwitz. At the heart of it all is the Antique Collection it was originally based on. This is one of the oldest in Europe, and after it was started by Augustus the Strong in 1723 for many years it was the only major collection of its type in all Germany. It owes its existence to the stinginess and lack of culture displayed by Frederick William I, the Prussian "soldier king", when he sold his fine collection of antique sculpture to Saxony in 1726. A short while later, in 1728, Augustus the Strong's agents in Rome acquired the wonderful Chigi Collection with such mas-

birthday", the Königsberg Emerald Cabinet, and also a cherry-stone made of gold with 183 heads carved into it, which can be observed through a magnifying glass.

The Sculpture Collection: The work here ranges from the 3rd century BC to the present day, with examples of sculpture from nearly all the cultures of Europe and the Near East: Assyrian reliefs and Egyptian mummies, Greek vases and Roman busts, medieval

Left, the *Sleeping Venus* by Giorgione (1478–1510). <u>Above</u>, *Leda and the Swan* by Peter Paul Rubens (1577–1640).

terpieces as the *Athena Lemnia*, the *Victorious Boy* by Polyclitus and the *Satyr Pouring a Glass of Wine* by Praxiteles.

Antiques and white gold: The Dresden Antiques – which were first displayed at great expense in the Great Garden – were internationally famous as long ago as the 18th century. They were later moved inside the Japanese Palace, where, lit by torchlight, they could be inspected of an evening by prominent visitors to Dresden. No less famous, though, was the Mengs'sche Collection of the original casts of antique statues, which was situated in the so-called "Stallhof".

"I now know the Greeks and I will never forget them as long as I live," wrote Jean Paul after his visit there.

One of the pavilions in the Zwinger houses the Porcelain Collection. The works of art here are made of the same "white gold" that was successfully invented for a second time by the alchemist Böttger in 1709, who was trying to make real gold, only a few hundred metres away in the catacombs of the old fortifications under the Brühlsche Terrasse. In the end porcelain proved equally valuable. The famous Meissen products, with their blue crossed swords symbol, became famous throughout the world, earning the

drawings, watercolours and pastels. The oldest of the exhibits, including 181 engravings by Albrecht Dürer, were formerly part of the Electoral Art Chamber. In 1720, Augustus the Strong had the 150,000 engravings brought together to form this collection, which flourished for a second time in 1882 when art experts from the city extended it. Showing courage and connoisseurship, they lent their support to artists who at that time were often very unpopular and misunderstood, such as Max Liebermann, Käthe Kollwitz and Toulouse-Lautrec. Alongside omnibus works by Old German and Dutch masters, and Rembrandt in particular, high-

Saxon rulers huge sums of money. This collection is the result of Augustus the Strong's obsession; in 1723 he had the so-called Dutch (later Japanese) Palace furnished as a porcelain palace, and thus had his agents, diplomats and merchants all over the world buy up Japanese and Chinese porcelain in huge quantities.

Copper Engravings: The former Arts and Crafts Academy on the Sachsenplatz also houses the Kupferstichkabinett (Copper Engravings Collection), one of the oldest of its kind in the world. The works on display here feature all the graphic techniques as well as

lights here include a magnificent collection of German Romantics, as well as works by Otto Dix. The Coin Collection is by far the oldest collection in Dresden; it was founded as far back as Luther's time, by Duke George.

The Folklore Museum (a collection of electoral weaponry and armour which became the History Museum) and the Copper Engravings and Coin Collections will in future be on display in the Royal Palace.

Above, *Nymphs and Children under Fruit Trees* **by Hendrik van Balen (1575–1632). Right, a somewhat more modern work.**

MODERN ART

Dresden is a city with a thriving art scene. At the beginning of the 1980s a new and expressive language of form developed here, a language very much frowned on by the GDR until then, because it was a reaction to social grievances as well as to the armament policy of that time. The young artists received support from the Dresden Academy of Fine Arts which, via the exhibitions it held, provided its students' work with an audience early on in their careers.

At the time, artists in Dresden tended to be far more daring than those in, say, Berlin or Halle. In January 1989, for example, the following provocative exhibit could be admired in the "Galerie Nord": in a huge room, the visitor had to make his way past a row of 14 red light-bulbs screwed into the wall at shoulder-height – a reference to the infamous indoctrination events, known familiarly as "the red-light treatment", that took place in schools and factories. A little further on the visitor will reach an aquarium filled with water containing a brigade of tiny model figures, all holding pick-axes and spades, digging into the sand at the bottom.

In those days, large-scale exhibitions made it possible to get a good overview of GDR art in general. The last GDR Art Exhibition in Dresden, held between 1987 and 1988, attracted over half a million visitors in six months. Entering the exhibition, one felt far removed from reality – a feeling which was hardly surprising, in amongst that mammoth collection of modern painting, graphics, sculpture, architecture, scenography, industrial graphics, commercial art and caricatures.

But political change has also brought changes to the art world, de-institutionalising it. The market has altered: local demand has dropped, and new clients from West Germany and abroad have now entered the stage.

The art scene is in a dangerous state of crisis. On the one hand the artists are suffering from the job insecurity that is so prevalent in eastern Germany; the local art market has collapsed to the extent that it is no longer possible, as it once used to be, to live for a few months off the proceeds from a drawing sold at black market rates to buyers in West Berlin. Furthermore, many popular galleries that used to receive great acclaim for their changing exhibitions have turned into shops and commercial agencies. The "Galerie Nord" on Leipziger Strasse is actually the last communal gallery to keep its doors open particularly for the work of local Dresden artists.

The art-scene cafés in the Neustadt, which often double as galleries, have created a whole new milieu, fashioned by artists for artists.

These are good venues for the casual visitor. A well-known address on the free art scene is the "Stadt Riesa" in the Adlergasse, a pub much frequented by artists, with a gallery on the first floor. Another exhibition room very close to the old-established Galerie Kühl on Zittauer Strasse, and contrasting nicely with it, is the Autogen gallery in the Pulsnitzer Strasse. After her spectacular years in the Villa Marie, Wanda, the owner, has now found a new home here.

And another newly-founded gallery, also a product of determination and idealism, is the Fotogalerie belonging to the Zadniceks at 20, Niederwaldstrasse, the first place of its kind in Dresden.

Among Dresden artists still living today, Max Uhlig, born in 1937, certainly deserves special mention. After five years' training at the Dresden Academy of Fine Arts he spent three years studying as a master craftsman at the Academy of Arts in Berlin, and has achieved international fame with his landscape and portrait paintings.

A younger artist on the scene is Lutz Fleischer, born in 1956, who attended evening classes at the Dresden Academy of Fine Arts and then went on to teach himself. He has been working freelance since 1981 and in 1983 he was a co-founder of the "Leitwolf" publishing house. His drawings, collages and sculptures employ the simplest of means to expose subjects taken from everyday life, and excite all manner of emotional responses in the onlooker, ranging from humour to horror.

There are, of course, many more than these two: the scene keeps changing all the time.

DRESDEN THROUGH ARTISTS' EYES

"He who has not experienced the beauty of Dresden has not experienced beauty at all." These words were written in 1749 by Johann Joachim Winckelmann, rediscoverer of antiquity and one of the most prominent visitors to the Saxon Royal Palace.

But Dresden's reputation as one of the finest cities in Europe has not only found its reflection in words but also in pictures. From the 16th century onwards the city's appearance provided creative inspiration for a host of draughtsmen, engravers and painters. Indeed there were very few capital cities surrounded by such magnificent natural scenery as the Saxon metropolis. Dresden lies in a basin-like extension of the Elbe valley, with gently-sloping hills to the south and north. The Elbe itself, with its green banks, winding its way through Dresden and reflecting the palaces, towers and bridges in its waters, provides ever-changing, picturesque views of the city.

The earliest views we have of the city date from the 16th century and show a Dresden quite unlike the one we know today: the Dresden of the late Middle Ages and the Renaissance. Engraved *vedutas* of the city at this time are highly detailed and accurate, and present a scene of harmonious unity. The magnificent buildings of the Saxon electors of the Renaissance, especially the Palace and the Arsenal, are situated above the city's extensive fortified walls, and alongside them stand the high roofs and towers of the old churches, which look so different today.

Indeed, hardly anything at all remains of that old and magnificent Dresden of the 16th century apart from the Residenzschloss (Royal Palace), at present being rebuilt, and the remains of the Jägerhof (hunting lodge) in the Neustadt, where the electors used to keep animals for the hunt.

Canaletto's vistas: It was the king's son and heir Augustus III who invited Bernardo

Dresden was an inspiration to Romantics. Left, *View of Dresden at Full Moon* by Johan Christian Dahl (1788–1857).

Bellotto, better known as Canaletto, to come to Dresden from Venice and chronicle the city's magnificence in paint. Canaletto painted 14 large-format *vedutas* in six years, and to this day they have remained the most famous pictures of the city. The fact that the Italian used a *camera obscura* to assist him means that they are also highly accurate and realistic documents. What is more, they give us interesting insights into everyday life in Dresden's streets and squares in the mid-18th century.

Bellotto was ordered to provide the all-powerful minister von Brühl with smaller reproductions of each of the paintings for the

in the late 18th and 19th centuries for cheaper artistic reproductions. Etchings by Professor Adrian Zingg (1734–1816), printed in large numbers and often coloured and sold as souvenirs, became the forerunners of the picture postcard. They show Dresden from a distance, as seen from prominent observation points in the area surrounding the city.

After Zingg, a few dozen minor masters engraved, etched and lithographed the outline of Dresden for the growing stream of tourists. Thus it was that by the first half of the century, Dresden became the most-portrayed city in all Germany. Even today, with a bit of luck, one can still find fine prints

price of 200 thalers each, a sum that von Brühl naturally forgot to pay him. His pictures are the first to show the complete silhouette of Dresden, with the cupola of the Frauen-kirche and the tower of the Catholic Hof-kirche. As two of his later works (painted between 1760 and 1763) make clear, he did not flinch from portraying the destruction wrought by Prussian brutality during the Seven Years' War.

Forerunners of the picture postcard: Although Bellotto created his extravagant Dresden scenes for the representative needs of the royal court, there was great popular demand

dating from that period in art galleries.

Romantics: Far superior to these "everyday" products are the Dresden pictures by Romantics such as Carus and Dahl, who painted famous nocturnal views of the Elbe Embankment in the Altstadt by moonlight. Gotthard Kuehl, on the other hand, the energetic reformer of the city's art scene, saw the city in quite a different light around the year 1900: like a drop of ink on blotting-paper, quickly spreading in all directions.

While industrial areas and workers' tenements were springing up in its suburbs, Dresden's city centre retained the flair of the

well-preserved Residenz, and in his paintings, Kuehl discovered new beauty in the
appearance of the old city. Even where he
portrayed the seemingly chaotic side of the
city as it went through the process of change,
with its construction sites and its demolished
buildings, he endowed the whole with a new
sense of unity. The old Augustusbrücke
provided him with a particular artistic chal-
lenge. Just like Monet, with his series of
paintings of the facade of Rouen Cathedral,
Kuehl portrayed the bridge again and again
under differing light and weather conditions.

Expressionists: In 1905, *Die Brücke* ("The
Bridge") became the name, symbol and trade-
mark of the young Expressionists who spread
the new message of their painting throughout the world.

Several of them, Kirchner and Heckel in
particular, concentrated on painting views of
the city. They were not so much concerned
with the beautiful side of Dresden, however;
they tended instead to draw and paint street-
corners and iron bridges in the industrial
suburbs of Löbtau and Friedrichstadt. In

their work the city is no longer portrayed, but
rather subjectively transformed. They chose
ugly motifs, and made fine and colourful
pictures from them.

Another great Expressionist painter also
ended up in Dresden during World War I:
Oskar Kokoschka was a professor at the
Academy of Art from 1919 to 1924. His six
lively views of the Neustadt and the Elbe
bridges were painted from his studio on the
Brühlsche Terrasse. The glowing, almost
tapestry-like magnificence of their colours
makes one forget the topography of the
subject completely.

Otto Dix, the gruff *enfant terrible* of the
1920s, often used his adopted home of Dresden as a subject for his paintings. Propheti-
cally, in 1939, he painted the city in flames in
the background of his great picture *Lot and
his Daughters*. Six years later, in February
1945, his vision of disaster was to become
horrifying reality.

The finest tribute to *Immortal Dresden*
(the title of his painting) was paid by Ernst
Hassebrauck. He has been justly referred to
as the "legitimate heir to the Dresden of
Augustus", having pursued a creative dialogue with Dresdener baroque like no other
before or since.

Left, Caspar David Friedrich (1774–1840) painted
The Great Enclosure Near Dresden. Above, *Elbe
Landscape in Dresden* by Oskar Kokoschka.

The Saxon Royal Palace was one of the centres of the Romantic movement in Germany – its picture gallery played an important role in its development. Raphael's *Sistine Madonna* became an object of passionate adoration for young Romantic poets such as Wackenroder, Tieck, Novalis and the Schlegel brothers; it became the "altar" before which they knelt. Raphael was the idol and patron saint of the alternative crowd, who met in Dresden in the summer of 1798 and rebelled as much against the outmoded traditions of the 18th century as they did against Classicism. The religious concerts in the Catholic Hofkirche also attracted a lot of these young intellectuals, all of them in the grip of a new religious fervour.

After literature had thus paved the way, young painters began arriving in Dresden: in 1798, Caspar David Friedrich, in 1801 Philipp Otto Runge and in 1804 the Riepenhauer and Olivier brothers. All of them were determined to give new impetus to German art.

Runge's period in Dresden (1801–04) was a source of lasting inspiration to him. Even he, intellectual iconoclast and profound theoretician of German art as he was, was so moved at the sight of the *Madonna* in the gallery that "he did not know where he was." But in the summer of 1801 another "Madonna" had appeared in front of the 24-year-old: he had fallen in love with the dark-haired Pauline Bassenge, 15 years old, the daughter of a glove manufacturer. He portrayed Pauline in numerous paintings as well as in his thematic work, such as the Romantic allegory entitled *The Nightingale's Lesson* (1804). It was during the years he spent in Dresden that Runge developed his artistic concept. It first took shape in his graphic cycle *Zeiten* ("Times"), which he intended for later exhibition using large-format wall paintings in a neo-Gothic room, with musical accompaniment. Runge thus anticipated

the idea of the Romantic *Gesamtkunstwerk* (synthesis of the arts), a concept which Richard Wagner later realised in his operas.

The advent of war: Between 1806 and 1815, Germany was marked by the occupation and suppression of Napoleon's armies and power structures as well as by the wars of liberation. In Saxony, growing intellectual resistance took the shape of patriotic Romanticism (or Romantic patriotism). The most well-known figure in this movement, and also its sym-

bolic leader, was the young freedom-fighter and poet Theodor Körner, actually an affable good-for-nothing who was forced to spend some time in prison during his student days in Leipzig because of fighting and not paying his debts, and was eventually expelled from the university there. A lieutenant in the Lützow Rifles, he died in 1813 aged 22, during a battle against the French. His collection of wartime songs, *The Lyre and the Sword*, is filled with heroic pathos.

The circle of opponents of Napoleon in Dresden contained large numbers of artists and intellectuals. It was here that Heinrich

Left, *The Lady on the Balcony* by Carl Gustav Carus (1789–1869). **Above**, *The Cross in the Mountains* by Caspar David Friedrich.

von Kleist wrote his nationalist drama *The Battle of the Teutoburg Forest* as well as his novel *Michael Kohlhaas*; Gerhard von Kügelgen painted political allegories and Caspar David Friedrich his "patriotic" works.

One of Friedrich's fellow artists, Georg Friedrich Kersting, fought in the Lützow volunteer corps. Kersting has gone down in art history as the creator of a special kind of portrait. He had the idea of portraying various Dresden artists and scholars in the environments in which they lived and worked, and did this in an admirably sensitive and subtle manner while retaining a sharp documentary realism and precision. Thanks to

composers, poets and artists. As soon as "the king called" in 1813, they mounted their battle horses and joined the wars of liberation.

Inner visions: The work of Caspar David Friedrich was not highly regarded by the public at large during his lifetime. The naive inhabitants of Dresden had no idea that in the bare studio in the house known as An der Elbe 33 the greatest ever German landscape painter was working away at his easel. Friedrich, a north German from the harbour town of Greifswald, had come to Dresden while still a young man, and he remained there until his death. He caused something of a stir during Christmas 1808 when he exhib-

him, we know exactly what Caspar David Friedrich's studio looked like. His depiction of the artist Kügelgen in his studio enabled a room in the Gottessegen house on the Strasse der Befreiung to be reconstructed, and it is still in existence today.

Strange habits: On a steep mountain on the Elbe, between Dresden and Meissen, lies the half-ruined castle of Scharfenberg; it was partly restored in 1812 by Carl von Miltitz, and he invited his fellow nationalist friends there. Here, they used to tell each other terrifying stories for the thrill of terror, play medieval games and support one another as

ited his huge devotional picture, the famous *Tetschen Altar*, in his darkened studio, lit only by candlelight, to the general public. People at the time were shocked that it was a landscape. Fierce controversy in the press both for and against the painting soon ensured that the courageous iconoclast's name was on everyone's lips – so much so that in the years that followed the King of Prussia, the Grand Duke of Weimar and the Tsar of Russia all purchased paintings from him, including some of his large-format main works such as *Monk by the Sea*, and *The Abbey in the Oak Forest*.

Friedrich's range of subjects was unusual: snow-covered cemeteries, bare oak trees, ruined churches, megalithic graves, beaches by night under a sickle moon, and, again and again, solitary people standing on riverbanks, on high mountain peaks or high up above the white chalk cliffs of Rügen, gazing into the distance, rapt in contemplation. He loved the atmosphere of autumn and winter, of twilight and fog; his work was, in short, "pretty strange stuff", to quote Wilhelm von Kügelgen. "Why don't you give us something cheerful, a genre piece that can be hung above a sofa or an aquarium?" was the advice once given to him by an art dealer.

What is clear to us now, so many years later, was impossible for his contemporaries to grasp: Friedrich was Germany's first Modern, he was actually an Expressionist, for – as he himself said – the painter should, first and foremost, paint what he sees within himself and not what lies before his nose. His landscapes are portrayals of these inner visions, and are often allegories of religious or political hope.

Other Romantics: One of the most interesting figures in the Romantic movement in Dresden was Carl Gustav Carus, a highly gifted and versatile native of Leipzig, who earned himself two doctorates at the age of 22, was named professor and director of the Dresden maternity clinic at 25, and was active thereafter in the city not only as a doctor and natural scientist but also as a philosopher, writer and painter.

Both Friedrich and Johan Christian Dahl were among his friends, and although painting was for him a spare-time pursuit, something he did for his own enjoyment and edification, he had very high standards. He defended Romantic propositions in his many scientific works, but also remained loyal to the views of Goethe, a person he respected highly and modelled himself after. Today, his paintings hang next to those of Friedrich in the Gemäldegalerie (Art Gallery). He expounded his artistic theories in his *Nine Letters on the Subject of Landscape Painting*, which was later to provide Friedrich with his basic theories.

The Romantic movement was equally alive in the world of music. In the dazzling figure of Ernst Theodor Amadeus Hoffmann lies the embodiment of the Romantic interplay of the arts. Hoffmann, who began by studying law, was a poet, a composer, a dramatic adviser and a painter. Between 1813 and 1816 he was theatrical musical director of the famed "Secondasche Theatertruppe", which used to perform in the summertime. It was in Dresden, too, that he composed his Romantic opera *Undine* and also wrote the fairy-tale novella *The Golden Pot*.

Music has always been the most effective way of conveying Romantic emotion, and was highly popular in the Dresden of that time. Carl Maria von Weber, with his *Freischütz*, *Euryanthe* and *Oberon* created a German national opera to compete with that of Italy. Richard Wagner worked as conductor at the court opera in Dresden, where his *Rienzi* was performed in 1842. He also wrote *Tannhäuser* and *Lohengrin* here, until the threat of arrest because of his pro-revolutionary activities and the active part he played in the failed Dresden uprising of 1849 forced him to flee abroad. Robert Schumann, too,

Left, *The Crossing of the Elbe at Schreckenstein* by Adrian Ludwig Richter (1803–84). **Above**, *Spring Landscape II* by Caspar David Friedrich.

claimed to have spent his happiest and most creative years in Dresden.

The Late Romantic: Ludwig Richter is one of the few Dresden Romantics who did not move to the city from elsewhere; he was a native Dresdener through and through, and was at his happiest at home. The intellectual appeal and calibre of his work are rather modest when compared with that of Friedrich or Runge.

Richter came from the comfortable middle-class milieu of the Dresden Friedrichstadt, and his bourgeois origins were to characterise his entire life. He set his sights on greatness, however, visiting Rome at the age of 20 to

was not his paintings, however, that earned Richter his huge popularity, but his extensive graphics. With over 3,000 woodcut illustrations for calendars, fairy-tales, songbooks and other literary works, he became the most famous illustrator in Germany. Though his pictures are childlike, cosy, prettified and very middle-class, they also give us a very good idea of the taste of the time.

Where to find them: Anyone keen on tracking down where Dresden's various Romantics lived will have a hard time, for today nearly all their former haunts have disappeared. One house, though, which almost all of them visited at some time or other, still

study landscape painting with Koch. Two of the finest of his paintings dating from this early period can be seen in the Leipzig Museum: *Rocca di Mezzo* and *Valley near Amalfi*. His transition from Italian to German landscapes was almost like a religious conversion. It was an experience he had on the Elbe near Aussig, beneath the ruins of Schloss Schreckenstein, which opened his eyes to the natural beauty of his home country, resulting in his famous painting *Überfahrt am Schreckenstein* (Crossing at Schreckenstein) which often used to hang in Saxon classrooms as a coloured lithograph in former days. It

stands: Gerhard von Kügelgen's former home in the the Neustadt, which now houses the Museum of Early Romanticism in Dresden (No. 13, Strasse der Befreiung).

A memorial to Caspar David Friedrich has stood at the Albertinum on the Brühlsche Terrasse since 1990. His grave can be found in the Trinitatis Cemetery in Johannstadt (Fiedlerstrasse). Ludwig Richter lies in the New Catholic Cemetery on Bremer Strasse.

Above, Adrian Ludwig Richter's *July Landscape with Rainbow* (1859). **Right**, photographer Hermann Krone in a self-portrait taken in 1850.

HERMANN KRONE

"I tell you, a man can lose his reason when faced with such an image, one that appears to have been fashioned by Nature herself." These words were written in 1839 by Berlin art and photography dealer Louis Sachse when he saw his first daguerreotype – the first ever photographic technique, named after its inventor, Daguerre. Never had an invention been so eagerly awaited or more enthusiastically greeted than this one.

Not long afterwards Hermann Krone (1827–1916) built a camera and succeeded in taking his first photograph. He opened his first photography studio in Dresden in 1852.

Krone provided the impetus for the "Dresden Photographic Society" (1869), and as early as 1853 he was probably the first ever person to request that a professorship be made available in photography. In 1870 he received a university lectureship and in 1895 he became a professor at the technical university.

Krone's activities in Dresden were highly versatile, to say the least. He successfully combined art and commerce. The fruits of his labours, as well as providing us with so much pleasure today, are also of great scientific value, particularly as far as the preservation of public monuments is concerned.

Krone's pictures turned him into a unique chronicler of the city and its inhabitants during the second half of the 19th century. He took several portraits of famous personalities from the world of science, art and politics. In 1853 he photographed the Sächsische Schweiz ("Saxon Switzerland") under conditions that to us today seem almost unimaginable, using a plate-back camera with a 30 cm by 40 cm format. Up amongst these inhospitable peaks he pulled his darkroom tent and the chemicals he needed along behind him, in a small handcart.

In memory of this pioneering achievement in landscape photography, some friends of his had the following words chiselled into the Bastei rock peaks: *Hermann Krone Hic Primus Luce Pinxit 1853* ("Hermann Krone was the first person to paint with light here"). Even today, if you take care not to allow your gaze to wander off into the distance when crossing the Basteibrücke, it is still possible to read this inscription.

Krone published his set of photographs, which became famous under the name of *Königsalbum* ("King's Album"), around the year 1872. In 142 photographs he had recorded all the towns in Saxony. A second album then appeared containing 60 photographs of towns in Saxony-Altenburg. Krone's photography not only took him all over Germany, but also to Bohemia and Switzerland.

In 1874 he took part in an expedition to observe the passage of Venus across the sun's disc on the Auckland Islands to the south of New Zealand. It turned out that his photographs could be used for purposes of astronomical measurement, and the explorer Alexander von Humboldt subsequently invited him to Berlin. The Dresden Technical University still possesses a unique treasure: in 1907, when he went into retirement, Krone donated his "Historical Educational Museum for Photography" to the institute.

The collection comprises not only cameras, lenses, equipment and negatives, but also 141 large-format educational charts, complete with more than 1,000 photographs and around 100 daguerreotypes which Krone made himself and which bear his signature. The charts provide an excellent overview of the development of early photography from 1843 onwards and, considering when they were made, they provide what is probably the most thorough documentation of the subject anywhere in the world.

Krone used these charts when giving lectures, and they also reflect his vocation as a teacher of photographic technique. He wanted "the progress required by the modern age to grow repeatedly from the renewal of past experience", as he put it in the introduction to his text-book entitled *Basic Photographic Methods*.

The Photographic Society of Saxony commissioned a medal in honour of Krone's 100th birthday, bearing his personal motto: *Im Licht – durchs Licht – zum Licht!* (In the light – by the light – to the light!).

Bach-Händel-Schütz
Ehrung der Deutschen
Demokratischen
Republik

Heinrich-Schütz-
Festtage der DDR
Dresden
Oktober 1985

The people of Dresden are proud of their city's long-standing tradition as a metropolis of music, and are convinced that their Staatskapelle, Kreuzchor and opera house still occupy leading positions in the music world. Ask any professor of music in the city to write a brief survey of musical life in Dresden and he will provide a long list of achievements, as much as to say: the target quota has been achieved, we were not just one of the world's foremost musical cities once, we still are.

The myth about Dresden being a metropolis of music is true insofar as the city's inhabitants tend to identify themselves more with local musical life than elsewhere. But despite much effort, Dresden has not succeeded in regaining the rank it once possessed as a music city – its isolation from many areas of international musical life has hindered this.

The city is rich in choirs, orchestras and chamber music ensembles, in which new generations of musical talent can learn from an early age what it means to study thoroughly musical works at a high level. The most famous source of talent is the Dresden Kreuzchor, which has produced many soloists: the singer Peter Schreier is just one example.

The choir of the Kreuzschule, which was founded in the 13th century, is the oldest musical institution in the city. It has worked with great orchestras, toured internationally and made several recordings.

The city's most famous orchestra is the Staatskapelle Dresden, the Semper Opera Orchestra, which has also found fame as a concert orchestra far beyond Dresden. The Staatskapelle was founded on 22 September 1548, the day that Elector Moritz of Saxony signed the foundation charter for a court choir consisting of just 20 singers and an

organist. Heinrich Schütz conducted the orchestra for 55 years, from 1617 until his death in 1672.

In those days of the Thirty Years' War, musical life often came to a complete standstill. The court musicians were not paid at all by the state; they had to flee from the atrocities of war, and some of them died of the plague. Schütz switched to the Copenhagen court on several occasions to make money, but despite enormous difficulties he always kept coming back to Dresden. He was the first person ever to compose an opera with a German libretto, by the poet Martin Opitz.

Italian domination: In the following century it was Italian opera that dominated the musical life of the city. Pompous works that synthesised many of the arts simultaneously were in great demand, thus ensuring that the Saxon court could continue to compete with the other absolutist ruling houses of the day. This was also the reason why it took just 11 months in the year 1719 to build an enormous opera house at the Zwinger, with a stage 105 feet (32 metres) deep and room to

Left, believe it or not, the lettering on this poster in honour of Heinrich Schütz by Hans Wiesenhütter was done by hand. **Above**, a performer at the International Dixieland Festival.

seat over 1,500 people – in a city whose population then numbered only 30,000 or so.

In fact, in those days music played only a subsidiary role in the opera performances, during which highly sophisticated stage devices were used, including fountains and waterfalls, along with up to 400 people and 100 horses. Mozart, who spent a few days in Dresden in 1789, called the opera there "truly miserable".

Composers: One harbinger of cultural improvement in the 19th century was lawyer, poet, painter and musician Ernst Theodor Amadeus Hoffmann. He spent some time in Dresden in 1813 and finished his Romantic opera *Undine* there.

In 1816 Carl Maria von Weber was appointed musical director of the newly-founded German Opera. Weber wanted to end the predominance of Italian opera and build up a national musical theatre in Dresden that was closer to the people. He was a major reformer, not just in his role as composer of *Freischütz* but also as a conductor, for he introduced several important innovations in performance practice and strove for realism in opera performances. After some initial resistance, the admiration which the orchestra and public felt for this unorthodox musician knew no bounds.

Nine-year-old Richard Wagner, who was attending the Kreuzschule in those days, had first-hand experience of Weber's performances with the Staatskapelle and is said to have made his fortunate decision to become a conductor, rather than "Kaiser or King", at that time.

In 1843, after the successful first performances of his operas *Rienzi* and *The Flying Dutchman*, Wagner was given a lifetime post as musical director of the court orchestra. He had Weber's remains brought back from London to Dresden and reburied. Wagner also met Robert Schumann on several occasions; the latter lived in Dresden from 1845 to 1850. It was in Dresden, too, that Schumann composed his famous A-minor piano concerto – Clara Schumann was the soloist at its first performance.

After the 1849 May uprising, Richard Wagner was forced to abandon his beloved orchestra, which he often referred to as his *Wunderharfe*, or "magic harp". Because of the active part he had taken in the uprising, a warrant had been issued for his arrest, and not a single Wagner opera was heard in Dresden for the next 10 years. It was only after an amnesty in 1862 that he was finally allowed to attend performances of his work in Dresden once more.

The Staatskapelle achieved its greatest fame because of its links with the conductor Ernst von Schuch and the composer Richard Strauss, whose operas were given first performances in Dresden (including *Der Rosenkavalier* in 1913) from 1901 onwards. Music-lovers from Berlin used to travel by special train to Dresden to go to the opera there. The orchestra's conductor during the Weimar Republic, Fritz Busch, lent his support to new composers such as Busoni, Weill and Hindemith, but rampaging Nazis forced Busch to leave the podium in the Semper Opera House in 1933.

An independent civic music culture had been developing alongside the court opera since the 19th century. In 1854 the Tonkünstlervereinigung, or Musicians' Association, was formed with the aim of fostering contemporary music. The Conservatory then opened in 1856, and in 1870 the Staatskapelle was faced with its first serious competitor: the Dresdner Philharmonie. The orchestra has since been conducted by many famous composers, including Brahms, Tchaikovsky, Dvorak and Strauss.

The Carl Maria von Weber Academy of Music developed from the Staatskapelle's conservatory and orchestra school; musicians from both orchestras train the younger generation here.

Another important Dresden institution is the Contemporary Music Centre, which promotes living composers and holds a festival of new music at the beginning of October each year. This complements the Dresden Music Festival (May/June) with its essentially conservative programming.

Dance: Mary Wigman, choreographer, dance-teacher and founder of modern interpretative dance opened her first school in Dresden in 1920; it was later closed down by the Nazis. The school founded by her most famous pupil, Gret Palucca, is still in existence today, and its students undergo an eight-year-long period of training and study for their school examinations at the same time. The youngest are still taught by the school's founder in what has become known as the Palucca-Stunde, or "Palucca Lesson".

At the start of German reunification, all of the city's artistic institutions suffered from low attendances and financial difficulties. The uncertain situation has now begun to stabilise somewhat. After the success of the 1991 event and Bonn's agreement to provide timely financial assistance, even the continuation of the International Dixieland Festival became assured – happily, since this

ised benefit concerts in churches on his own initiative, and founded a chamber music ensemble independent of state subsidy. Güttler and his ensemble then played old music of the Saxon court that he had found in the Saxon State Library while studying Dresden's musical history. During the Dresden Revolution, he was one of the spokesmen at the people's mass demonstrations.

Imports from the West are also giving music in Dresden a new lease of life. The Semper Opera House has a new director, Christoph Albrecht from Hamburg, and top Italian conductor Giuseppe Sinopoli has been appointed head of the Staatskapelle.

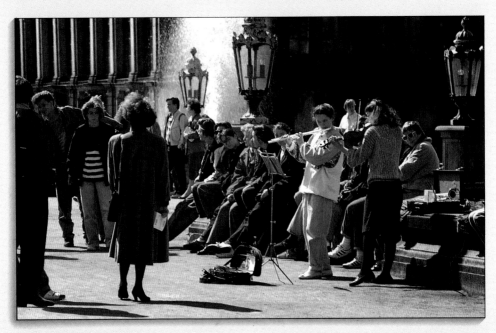

celebration used to attract thousands of jazz fans from all over the GDR to Dresden in the early summer of each year.

Today's stars: The two most famous names on the Dresden music scene at present are probably singer and conductor Peter Schreier and internationally renowned trumpeter Ludwig Güttler. Even before the GDR revolution, Güttler was a nuisance to the authorities because of his criticism of state cultural and educational policies. He organ-

Above, street musicians in the Zwinger continue Dresden's centuries-old music tradition.

Before the music metropolis of Dresden is fully restored to its former glory, however, many other obstacles will have to be overcome. Most Strauss operas, for example, still cannot be staged in the building where they were originally performed – the Semper Opera – because of sloppy restoration work. The movable wood section between the orchestra pit and the auditorium was replaced by a concrete wall, since when there has no longer been enough room in the pit to accommodate the number of musicians required for works such as *Rosenkavalier* or Wagner's *Ring*.

Actors first came to Dresden in the shape of wandering "bands" of dancers, acrobats, comedians and clowns who, accompanied by instrumentalists, would provide entertainment of varying quality in pubs, marketplaces and squares. "Itinerants" such as these, though enjoying full artistic freedom, were more often than not exposed to the dangers of starvation if their public lost interest.

An actor's chances of survival were slightly improved if the elector granted him a patent – a kind of performance permit, letter of safe-conduct and passport rolled into one – which ranked him very slightly above the itinerant mob. It was very rare that renowned acting troupes succeeded in organising regular work on a temporary basis.

The Royal Dresden Actors' Society, the first official company, managed to last only 10 years at the Dresden court. There again, the actors had the same status as lowly servants, and their combined annual income amounted to that earned by a single soloist at the Italian court opera.

A permanent ensemble: It was only during the reign of Augustus the Strong that the city built its own small theatre in 1696–97 for actors from France, who in keeping with the fashion performed the great dramas of Corneille, Molière and Racine at the electoral court – in French, of course, a language incomprehensible to the average citizen.

For a long time, German drama led a troubled and shadowy existence. Performances took place in the suburbs, and were given their first real boost only when the actress Friederike Carolin Neuber reformed theatrical life in Dresden. The attractive young actress's art of presentation received great public acclaim in many German cities at that time. From 1724 onwards, she appeared on stage several times in the old Merchants' Hall in Dresden, where she had been granted a patent by the Electorate of

Saxony to perform with her fellow-actor and husband of several years.

In Leipzig, "Die Neuberin", as she was affectionately known, finally succeeded in properly reforming German drama by banning the bawdy, farcical Harlequin from serious theatre. Encouraged by the young playwright Gottholt Ephraim Lessing, she made sure that far more demanding works were selected, and that high-quality performances could be introduced, given by

permanent ensembles. She insisted that their members learn their parts carefully, rehearse thoroughly and lead a moral lifestyle.

Realism in acting: In 1789 the successful Italian impresario Franz Seconda took over control of the Royal Dresden Patented Actors' Society. Its leading light during the previous decade had been his compatriot Pasquale Bondini, who had given Lessing's *Nathan der Weise* its first performance in Dresden in 1779. Franz Seconda soon left matters of artistic management to a member of the ensemble known as Friedrich Reinecke, who as performer/director set high standards

Left, the Semper Opera. **Above**, the actress Friederike Carolin Neuber radically reformed theatrical life in Dresden.

for the ensemble and aimed at realism in performance, particularly in Shakespearian drama. He also introduced several other works to Dresden, including Lessing's *Emilia Galotti* and *Minna von Barnhelm*, Goethe's *Clavigo* and Schiller's *Die Räuber, Cabal and Love*, and *Fiesco*.

Other performers were also at work. "King of Romanticism" was the name given to Ludwig Tieck during the many years he spent in Dresden (1819–42). At his famous evening readings in his one-man wooden theatre he would recite the great dramas of world literature to a select audience, while tea and biscuits were handed round. An ex-

rical reform during the 1848 revolution: he had wanted the court theatre, which belonged to the monarchy, to be changed into a democratically controlled national theatre. However, Gutzkow's tragedy *Uriel Acosta* was, despite royal objections, given a successful first performance in Dresden, as was the fateful drama (recommended by Gutzkow) *Der Erbförster* by Otto Ludwig, who lived in Dresden from 1849 to 1865.

Gottfried Semper's first theatre celebrated its opening in 1841 with a performance of Goethe's *Tasso*. The building was unfortunately destroyed by a fire in 1869, to be replaced by a second building which opened

cellent and astute drama critic, he also reviewed the many performances given in Dresden, and encouraged the performance of Heinrich von Kleist's *Prince of Homburg*, which resulted in theatre director von Luttichau appointing him adviser and critic at the court theatre, a post that was entirely new. Tieck also succeeded in organising a magnificent performance of *Faust* on the occasion of Goethe's 80th birthday.

After Tieck's departure, the new dramatic adviser Karl Gutzkow, a member of the Young Germany movement, was soon faced with failure because he had demanded theat-

in 1878 with Goethe's *Iphigenie*, and staged not only plays but operas. The monuments to Goethe and Schiller on both sides of the theatre today stand as a reminder of that time.

Popular theatre: From the turn of the 20th century onwards the royal theatre gradually adapted to the cultural needs of broad sections of the population of the ever-expanding industrialised city. From 1902, up to 15 annual "popular performances" were put on, most of them featuring established classics, and seats were priced at between 20 *pfennigs* and 1.25 *Reichsmarks*. But the artists of Dresden never got further than a few faint-hearted attempts to form a popular theatre movement on the Berlin model.

During the early years of World War I, theatre in Dresden paid tribute to the ruling establishment with jingoistic, patriotic plays aimed at distracting people from the misery and tragedy of their lives. Increasing weariness with the war made it possible in February 1918 for Reinhard Goering's anti-war drama *Seeschlacht* ("Sea Battle") to be given a successful, one-off private performance at the Dresden Literary Society. After sharp protests from high-ranking army officials, all further performances were forbidden.

The Golden Twenties: The upheaval of the

scandal at the first performance of Ernst Toller's *Hinkemann* in 1924, and the work was banned outright – a foretaste of the far more serious interference in the city's cultural life that was to take place after 1933.

After the war: In July 1945, after the war was over, the curtain rose in the smashed city of Dresden once more, on the temporary stage erected in the Tonhalle. A performance of Lessing's *Nathan der Weise,* a work that had been outlawed until then, once again announced its message of tolerance and international understanding. Hopes and expectations blossomed, none of which were to be fulfilled in the following four decades.

November Revolution of 1918 also resulted in sweeping changes to what was now the State Theatre in Dresden. During the 1920s, the State Theatre developed into a leading centre of German Expressionist drama. Works by Wedekind, Sternheim and Hasenclever, though readily accepted by young people, tended to shock the average bourgeois citizen. Nationalist hecklers, who would never listen to reason, caused a theatrical

Left, **Victor Klemperer (1881–1960), relieved of his post by the Nazis, at the Artists Congress in 1946.** Above, **the cabaret group** *Zwinger Two*.

It soon became clear that in the GDR too, all artistic life was being controlled and manipulated, and that actors, directors, dramatic advisers and playwrights alike were being forced to compromise between real art and deliberate propaganda, with the result that far too much tendentious and worthless drama was performed. In October 1989, however, at the end of each of their performances, the actors of the Dresden Ensemble began reading out many stirring pleas that were eventually to play their part in bringing about German reunification. The stage had once again proved its power.

PLACES

The first thing one notices about Dresden as one approaches its historical centre from the motorway, the airport or the station is that it looks very much like most other large cities. Since the days of Augustus the Strong, the city has grown more than tenfold, into an economic, industrial and administrative metropolis, and its outlying areas, with the exception of the banks of the Elbe, are similar to those of other German cities, with concrete housing estates and buildings blackened by what used to be until recently a high level of environmental pollution.

The Prager Strasse, the pedestrian precinct between the main station and the Altmarkt, was considered bigger, better and far more beautiful than anything the cities belonging to the subdued masses of West Germany could offer, a "model of Socialist magnificence" during the days of "goulash communism". But, to be fair to Dresden, what about all the architectural evils perpetrated on other cities in Europe at that time? Concepts such as individuality, humane living conditions, or even attractiveness weren't discussed there either.

It's easy to cover the historic centre of Dresden, including the Neustadt, on foot. The aerial photograph on page 126 of this book will certainly help you get your bearings. The Zwinger, the Royal Palace, the Semper Opera House are all right next to each other. One good way of getting into the proper mood would be to walk down the Procession of Princes, the frieze of 24,000 ceramic tiles depicting the 35 margraves of the House of Wettin, dukes, electors and kings; this should give you a feel of the spirit in which the nobility steered the fortunes of this city over the centuries. At the end of the frieze you will have reached the palace, where you can form your own opinion of Augustus the Strong's urban aesthetics.

This book doesn't detail any restaurants on the route through the centre – they are still changing hands far too rapidly. So are streetnames. The new names are mentioned on the map on the preceding page, but other streets are still having their names changed. It's not as confusing as you might think, though, because Dresdeners are familiar with both the old and new names; in fact, it provides a good chance to communicate. You'll soon notice that Dresdeners like to chat; they often have a detailed knowledge of the city's history and the individual buildings, and will happily share it with you.

Dresden is definitely "in". Hotel capacity is limited, so make sure you book your room in good time via the Dresden Information Service. They can also offer you cheaper private accommodation a little further outside the city.

Preceding pages: the Semper Opera House at night; the Hofkirche with the palace to its right, seen from above; Theaterplatz and the cathedral; a view of the Zwinger courtyard. Left, the palace in a puddle.

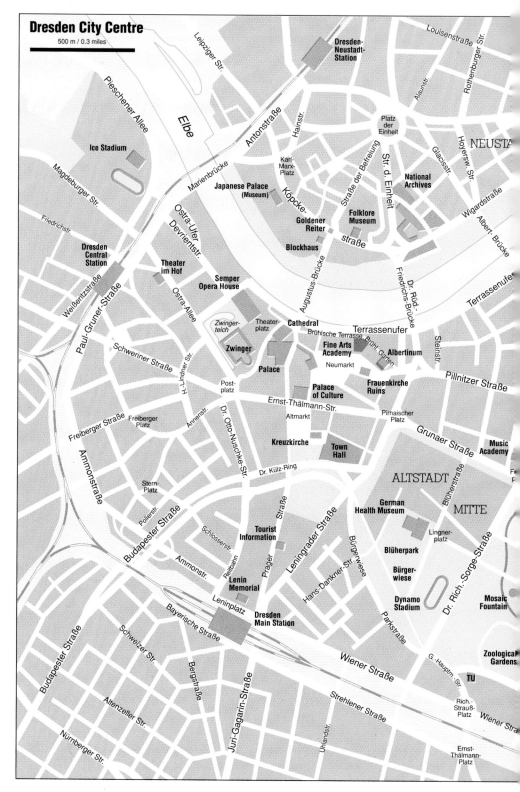

Dresden City Centre

500 m / 0.3 miles

Leipziger Str.

Elbe

Pieschener Allee

Ice Stadium

Magdeburger Str.

Friedrichstr.

Marienbrücke

Ostra-Ufer

Devrientstr.

Dresden Central Station

Weißeritzstraße

Paul-Gruner-Straße

Theater im Hof

Ostra-Allee

Schweriner Straße

Zwinger-teich

Theater-platz

Zwinger

Palace

Post-platz

Dr.-H.-Lindner Str.

Annenstr.

Freiberger Straße

Freiberger Platz

Ammonstraße

Stern-Platz

Polierstr.

Budapester Straße

Dr. Otto-Nuschke-Str.

Ammonstr.

Schlosserstr.

Reitbahn

Prager Straße

Straße

Tourist Information

Lenin Memorial

Leninplatz

Bayerische Straße

Budapester Straße

Schweizer Str.

Bergstraße

Altenzeller Str.

Nürnberger Str.

Juri-Gagarin-Straße

Dresden Main Station

Antonstraße

Hainstr.

Karl-Marx-Platz

Köpcke-straße

Japanese Palace (Museum)

Goldener Reiter

Blockhaus

Semper Opera House

Straße der Befreiung

Augustus-Brücke

Cathedral

Brühlsche Terrasse

Brühl Garten

Fine Arts Academy

Neumarkt

Palace of Culture

Ernst-Thälmann-Str.

Altmarkt

Kreuzkirche

Town Hall

Dr. Külz-Ring

German Health Museum

Blüherpark

Bürger-wiese

Hans-Dankner-Str.

Bürgerwiese

Wiener Straße

Strehlener Straße

Uhlandstr.

Dresden-Neustadt-Station

Louisenstraße

Rothenburger Str.

Alaunstr.

Platz der Einheit

Str. d. Einheit

NEUSTA

National Archives

Glacisstr.

Hoyersw.-Str.

Wigardstraße

Albert-Brücke

Folklore Museum

Dr. Rüd.-Friedrichs-Brücke

Terrassenufer

Terrassenufer

Steinstr.

Albertinum

Pillnitzer Straße

Frauenkirche Ruins

Pirnaischer Platz

Grunaer Straße

Blüherstraße

Music Academy

ALTSTADT

MITTE

Leningrader Straße

Lingner-platz

Dynamo Stadium

Parkstraße

Dr. Rich.-Sorge-Straße

Mosaic Fountain

Zoologica Gardens

TU

Rich.-Strauß-Platz

Wiener Stra

G.-Hauptm.-Str.

Ernst-Thälmann-Platz

106

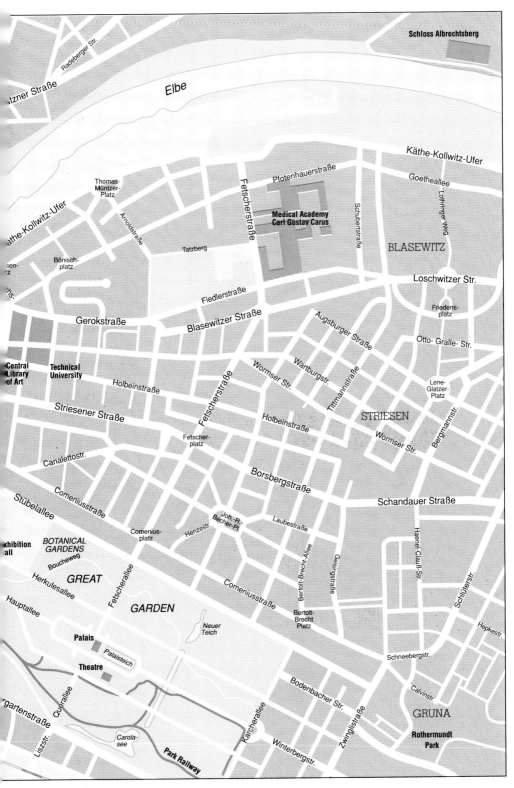

Schloss Albrechtsberg

Elbe

Käthe-Kollwitz-Ufer

Radeberger Str.

tzner Straße

Thomas-
Müntzer-
Platz

Pfotenhauerstraße

Goetheallee

Fetscherstraße

Medical Academy
Carl Gustav Carus

Schubertstraße

Lothinger Weg

BLASEWITZ

äthe-Kollwitz-Ufer

Arnoldstraße

Tatzberg

Bönisch-
platz

sen-
z

hu-

Fiedlerstraße

Loschwitzer Str.

Gerokstraße

Blasewitzer Straße

Augsburger Straße

Friedens-
platz

Otto- Gralle- Str.

Wartburgstr.

Central
Library
of Art

Technical
University

Holbeinstraße

Wormser Str.

Tittmannstraße

Lene-
Glatzer-
Platz

Striesener Straße

Fetscherstraße

Holbeinstraße

STRIESEN

Wormser Str.

Bergmannstr.

Fetscher-
platz

Canalettostr.

Borsbergstraße

Schandauer Straße

Comeniusstraße

Stübelallee

Joh.-R.-
Becher-Pl.

Laubestraße

Comenius-
platz

Henzestr.

xhibition
all

BOTANICAL
GARDENS

Boucheweg

Bertolt-Brecht-Allee

Geisingstraße

Haenel-Clauß-Str.

Schlüterstr.

GREAT

Herkulesallee

Fetscherallee

Comeniusstraße

Hauptallee

GARDEN

Neuer
Teich

Bertolt-
Brecht
Platz

Hepkestr.

Palais

Palaisteich

Theatre

Schneebergstr.

Bodenbacher Str.

Calvinstr.

GRUNA

gartenstraße

Querallee

Karcherallee

Zwinglistraße

Rothermundt
Park

Liszstr.

Carola-
see

Park Railway

Winterbergstr.

ALTMARKT AND NEUMARKT

The best view of the old part of Dresden can undoubtedly be claimed by the highest man in Dresden: supported on his horn of plenty the golden athlete on top of the 328 feet (100 metres) town hall tower stretches his right arm over the city. This figure, 18 feet (5.60 metres) high and made of gilded sheet copper, was completed in 1910 by Richard Guhr.

The first-time visitor to Dresden is recommended to take the lift to the viewing balconies two-thirds of the way up the **Rathausturm** (town hall tower), built in 1905 (entrance from the courtyard, Kreuzstrasse 6). A 1945 photograph of the fire-blackened sandstone statue on the south side of the upper balcony with the ruins of the bombed city in the background became world famous – a stark reminder of the consequences of war.

The former old town: Seen from above, the first thing to catch the eye is the outline of the old town centre, with the streets neatly laid out at right angles to one another. This clear, grid-like design is typical of the towns which were founded as the Germans pushed their borders east in the early Middle Ages.

Leading from the market square, once approximately 2.5 acres (1 hectare) in area, were streets named after the part they played in the lives of the city's inhabitants and visitors – some of which are still in existence today. On what was once Scheffelgasse (Bushel Street) was a standardised dry measure on a chain for checking purchases of cereals and pulses.

Although Webergasse (Weavers' Street), which is now redesigned as a modern shopping street, was named after the craftsmen who once lived here, it was popularly known as "Fressgasse" (Grub Street) even before 1945 on account of its numerous grocery stores and restaurants. The Schössergasse (Tax Collectors' Street) is a reference to the officials, especially the tax collectors, of the former Saxon Electoral Chancellery, while Schreibergasse (Scribe Street) denotes the handful of educated people who offered their services to a primarily illiterate population.

The hygiene requirements of the city's inhabitants were taken care of at the old "Rats-Baderei" (Municipal Bathhouse) in Badergasse (Bath Street), and Schulgasse (School Street) was once the location of the Kreuzschule, which became a grammar school in 1539, and has a famous boys' choir which was founded more than 775 years ago.

Christmas market: In the midst of the cramped and gloomy streets of the old part of Dresden, hemmed in by double ring walls and moats, the **Altmarkt** (Old Market) was a welcome space used for a variety of purposes; on market days, when traders from the country came in, it was a mass of stalls selling wares of every kind. At Christmas the Dresden Striezelmarkt is still very popular, a market named after the loaf-

Preceding pages: Lenin in front of the main station on Prager Strasse. **Left**, the Altmarkt and the Kreuzkirche. **Right**, sunbathing at the end of Prager Strasse.

shaped, yeasted fruit cake – also called "Stollen" – that is the speciality of the local bakers. The Altmarkt was also the Dresdeners' favourite place for festivities, carnival plays or masquerades; and sometimes it had a quite different role as the site of executions conducted publicly as a deterrent. The murderer of the popular Dresden painter Gerhard von Kügelgen was beheaded here in 1821, and the people who lived on the square rented out their roofs and market-facing windows.

The Altmarkt was also used by certain groups of citizens, the "Spiessbürger", who had defence obligations, and the second-class "Pfahlbürger" from the suburbs, who assembled here for consultations.

Town hall: The fortunes of the city were decided in the **Rathaus** or town hall, which was located on the market square for 300 years from 1380 until the reign of Augustus the Strong. The latter had the building with its Gothic features pulled down; not satisfied with the palace precincts alone, he also wanted the Altmarkt as an additional arena for his glittering celebrations and even for repulsive animal spectacles where wild beasts tore one another to pieces.

The **Tower** located on the west side of the Altmarkt is now all that remains of the baroque successor to the pre-Augustus Altstädter Rathaus. It was incorporated into the facade of the Altmarkt in 1741–44 and was destroyed 200 years later during the World War II air raids.

Uprisings and marches: During the bourgeois uprising of May 1849 the provisional government had its headquarters in the new baroque town hall, and many Dresdeners started out from here to join the unsuccessful barricade against the superior regiments of the Saxon-Prussian royalists.

Towards the end of their regime the Nazis had large, open water-containers placed on the Altmarkt for fire extinguishing purposes. They proved useless against the inferno of February 1945, **Travellers in town.**

and in them burning people fleeing from the streets of the old town met terrible deaths. For days after the bomb attack hundreds of mutilated bodies were cremated openly on the Altmarkt to prevent the outbreak of epidemics.

In the late autumn of 1989, the Altmarkt was again the scene of a peaceful uprising when the people successfully overturned the outmoded regime of an aging monopoly party. During the reconstruction of 1953–58 the same party had intervened in Dresden's plans from Berlin and had the Altmarkt expanded to about three times its original size as a gigantic arena for Stalinist mass parades.

After the war, the bombed inner city remained an almost impenetrable wilderness of rubble for practically a decade before reconstruction began. **Prager Strasse**, the 700-metre (766 yards) boulevard with numerous fountains, four hotels, pavilions and rows of shops that runs from the main station to the Altmarkt, was completed only in the early 1970s.

Despite the floating hotels on the Elbe, there aren't enough hotel beds for visitors.

Here the attempt to continue the famous Dresden baroque tradition has not generally been very successful, since the extend of baroque architecture detailing is very limited.

Towering above the Altmarkt is the **Kreuzkirche** (Church of the Holy Cross), a late Gothic church documented in the 13th century as the Nikolaikirche (Church of St Nicholas). Its present name refers to an alleged fragment of the cross of Christ once kept here. The church has a tragic history. It was rebuilt in 1760 after destruction by Prussian artillery, and was gutted by fire in 1897 and 1945. The interior has now been restored in simple rough plastering. The set of bells in the Kreuzkirche is the second largest of its kind in the whole of Germany: five bronze bells tuned to E, G, A, B, and D.

Reconstruction: The Neumarkt (New Market) has been the address of many internationally famous figures in the course of its history: at the beginning of the 18th century the Russian Tsar Peter

the Great stayed in the Hotel "Zum Goldenen Ring"; from 1766 to 1813 the portrait painter Anton Graff and from 1877 to 1822 the composer Carl Maria von Weber lived on the south side of the square; the attic floor above the apothecary, the Löwenapotheke, accommodated Heinrich von Kleist in 1809 and the writer, composer and artist E.T.A. Hoffmann in 1813, and Seestrasse was the address of Goethe in 1813 and Chopin in 1835.

The Neumarkt has not yet been reconstructed as a complete architectural unit with continuous facades. Over the last four decades this traditional old Dresden square has constantly been the Cinderella of the planning authorities, probably also because it is dominated by the ruin of the main Lutheran church of Dresden.

Since the bombing, various solutions have been mooted, ranging from reconstructing the square as it was to redesigning it on modern lines. After the rubble was cleared away, however, only a few buildings were put up, some of them reconstructions and others new, which appear to have no connection with each other or the square as a whole and contribute little to its overall effect.

Almost in the middle of the Neumarkt, the first thing that catches the eye is the ruin of the **Frauenkirche** (Church of Our Lady), a stark reminder of the destruction of Dresden at the end of World War II. Toppled during the bombing, the statue of Martin Luther now stands once more in front of the church, right hand laid imperiously on the Bible (completed in 1885 by Adolf Donndorf; Luther's head is by the Dresden sculptor Ernst Rietschel).

Once one of the symbols of the city on the Elbe and a dominant feature of its skyline, the dome of the Frauenkirche was an impressive 309 feet (95 metres) high and crowned with a rotunda. Constructed from 1726 to 1743 and primarily the work of the city's master carpenter George Bähr, it was one of the most magnificent baroque Protestant

Far left, the Altmarkt arcades, a continuation of Prager Strasse. **Left,** the Rathaus.

LUDWIG TIECK

The object of poet and theatre critic Ludwig Tieck's first visit to Dresden was a woman. Together with fellow poet Wilhelm Heinrich Wackenroder (1773–98) the famous German romantic writer visited the *Sistine Madonna* in the art gallery, to indulge in romantic fantasies about art. It was the year 1796.

After many subsequent journeys which took him all over Europe, visiting places of importance and achieving great success with his work, Tieck made a second attempt to settle in Dresden. This time he was to stay for 23 years. He was now accompanied by his mistress, Henriette Gräfin von Finckenstein, his "saving financial rock".

It was not until the summer of 1842 that Tieck left Dresden again in response to an invitation by King Frederick William IV to go to Berlin.

Tieck moved into a house on what is today the Altmarkt, a building no longer in existence. Here he held court as the "uncrowned king of German Romanticism", and his famous readings took place every Saturday evening: "Countess Finckenstein lived in great style. People went to her home to see and listen to Tieck. He read dramatic poetry" (Wilhelm von Chezy, 1863). Clemens von Brentano summed it up by saying that Tieck was the "greatest mimic who had ever *not* gone on stage".

Every contemporary guidebook of Dresden included descriptions of Tieck's readings, which were experiences no culturally-minded traveller missed and ranked with a visit to an art gallery. The location of these readings quickly became the centre of cultural life in the court capital, and Ludwig Tieck found himself an institution in Europe's intellectual circles.

Tieck also made a name for himself by publishing the works of his friends after their deaths. He edited the collected writings of Kleist and Lenz (1751–1792), published the posthumous works of Solger (1780–1819) and new editions of the writings of Novalis (1772–1801).

During his years in Dresden, he naturally also produced works of his own. Among them were *Geschichte des Herrn William Lovell*, *Volksmärchen*, *Franz Sternbalds Wanderungen*, *Kaiser Oktavianus*, *Phantasus*, *Gedichte* and *Dramaturgische Blätter*. His collected novellas alone fill 14 volumes. They are critical reflections on contemporary conditions, both those peculiar to Dresden and those prevailing in Germany as a whole.

This particular period was overshadowed by reactionary political tendencies while freedom of expression was restricted. Rigorous censorship suppressed all burgeoning national movements after the victory over Napoleon. A person of the intellectual calibre of Tieck was of course able to disguise his reactions by giving them artistic form.

In 1825 Tieck was elevated to the rank of Court Counsellor and dramaturge at the Royal Court Theatre. In this way his influence was expanded enormously, since he now had a say in what was put on the stage. At an earlier date, in 1821, he had already been the motivating force behind a pioneering production of Kleist's play *Prinz Friedrich von Homburg*, and in 1829, in honour of Goethe's 80th birthday, he arranged a staging of *Faust*, Part I.

Together with his daughter Dorothea (1799–1841) and Wolf Heinrich Graf Baudissin (1789–1878), Tieck embarked in 1825 on a new German version of Shakespeare's plays, using Schlegel's translation as the basis. In nine years they completed one of the greatest translations in German literature. The writer Thomas Mann (1875–1955) spoke of "a genuine incorporation of the great literary heritage of one people in the intellectual assets of another". On Tieck's 60th birthday Pierre-Jean d'Angers made a colossal bust of him, as he had done years before for Goethe. The event is immortalised in a painting by Tieck's friend Carl Vogel von Vogelstein (1788–1868).

Summing up, Tieck wrote: "Basically my life has been a happy one... It has been granted to me to see and recognise the beautiful and the great." However, he also concluded with resignation that "I have no exciting friends here – there are good men around me, but they receive more from me than I do from them."

churches in Germany, with its huge sandstone dome rising above an interior supported by pillars (it had an organ by Silbermann which was played by famous musicians, such as Johann Sebastian Bach in 1736, 1738 and 1741). While the dome had stood up to the cannon fire of Frederick II of Prussia, it was damaged by the fire storm of 13 February 1945 to such an extent that it collapsed the following day.

Baroque palaces: Next to the remains of the Frauenkirche's choir walls are the two reconstructed side wings of the palace built from 1762 to 1763 for Count Cosel (acknowledged son of Augustus the Strong and Countess Hoym-Cosel), and also destroyed by bombs.

Behind it are the ruins of another baroque building, the Kurländer Palais, which from 1815 to 1864 was the seat of the "Royal Saxon Surgical and Medical Academy". Its massive cellar vaults are still intact; once used for the study of pathology they now reverberate to the rhythms of the jazz club **Tonne**.

The new five-star hotel **Dresdner Hof** next to the Frauenkirche was completed in 1989, filling a space once occupied by a whole block of old houses. The back of the building, which faces north, is connected by a bridge across the Terrassengasse with the neo-baroque **Sekundogenitur** (built in 1907 as a library for the princes of the royal family) on the Brühlsche Terrasse.

The Sekundogenitur houses the hotel's quality eating establishments **Le Gourmet**, **Café vis-à-vis**, **Espresso Reale** and **Wettiner Keller**. The Münzgasse leads past the restaurants **Bistro de Saxe**, **Ristorante Rossini** and **Blaues Ei**, also belonging to the Dresdner Hof, down to the Elbe and under the bottom of the Brühlsche Terrasse (the former fortress wall) to the landing stages of the Weisse Flotte, the passenger boat service.

The Münzgasse, which also features the **Bierhaus zum Dampfschiff**, the **Kleppereck**, an old street clock and the double stairway to the Brühlsche Ter-

The Turken-brunnen (Turks' Fountain) in front of the Johanneum (Transport Museum).

rassc (1873), something of the original atmosphere of Dresden has been recreated. On its east side it is connected with the bridge, the Friedrichs-Brücke, by the Brühlsche Garten, which is not directly visible from the Neumarkt.

At the end of the Brühlsche Garten the former **court gardener's house**, now an old people's home and church hall belonging to the Reformed Church, was rebuilt in 1957–58 in its original 18th-century style. The steps which lead up to the former corner bastion, the fountain featuring a putto and a dolphin, and the sphinx groups on top of the bastion, are all original. In the casemates beneath the bastion (they were destroyed by a powder explosion in 1747) European porcelain was invented in 1709 by Johann Friedrich Böttger.

Fine Art: Also located between the Frauenkirche ruin and the Elbe is the **Academy of Fine Art**, with its facade picturesquely overgrown with wild vines. It was built between 1890 and 1894 in the style typical of this period of rapid industrial expansion in Germany; the glass dome crowned with a figure above what was once the life drawing hall (with the *Fama* by Robert Henze) is popularly known as the "lemon squeezer".

On the far side of Georg-Treu-Platz is the **Albertinum** (built from 1559 to 1562 as the arsenal, previously the citadel of Dresden; and after rebuilding in 1889 used for the State Art Collections), in front of it is the sculpture *Large grieving man* by Wieland Förster, which was unveiled on 13 February 1985. It was originally intended for the Sculpture Collection, which was started with the antiquities purchased by Augustus the Strong. The Albertinum today also houses the **Neue Meister** ("New Masters" Art Gallery, the **Münzkabinett** (Coin Cabinet) and the **Grünes Gewölbe** (Green Vault) with its priceless collection of jewels and gold. These museums are described in the *Art Treasures* chapter in this book.

Tournaments in the Stallhof: One ex-

ample of the Neumarkt's once predominantly baroque architecture which has been preserved is the elegant building now housing the **Verkehrsmuseum** (Transport Museum). Although its show side facing the square has remained almost unchanged for the last two-and-half centuries, it was originally built in 1588 in the Renaissance style as the electoral stables.

The back of the building forms one side of the "Stallhof" (Stable Court), the eastern courtyard of the former Residenzschloss (Royal Palace), which is entered through the rustic side portal next to the Dresdner Hof Hotel. The Stallhof was once used for magnificent show tournaments and horseback competitions. The pond in front of the tournament area, which is separated off by planking, was used as a watering-hole for the horses. Next to it is a slope up which the horses were ridden to the stables on the first floor, an interesting example of a space-saving "multi-storey garage" from the Renaissance epoch.

In 1729–30 the centre portal of the Transport Museum's main facade was embellished with a flight of outdoor steps in the French style. In 1875 the valuable collections of the Historisches Museum (Historical Museum) were transferred to the stable building, which was renamed the "Museum Johanneum" after the ruling Saxon monarch and Dante translator Johann (a statue of this king on horseback stands on Theaterplatz), where they remained until the destruction in 1945, and since 1956 it has been the home of the Dresden Transport Museum.

The **Schöne Pforte** (Beautiful Gateway), Dresden's only remaining treasure from the Renaissance epoch, has been temporarily erected to the left of this museum. This portal was once part of the Lutheran palace chapel in the north-west wing of the Royal Palace: it was removed when Augustus the Strong converted to Catholicism in 1697.

Turkish spring: The fountain in front of the Transport Museum is the **Türken-**

The steps up to the Brühlsche Terrasse, topped by the statue of Gottfried Semper.

brunnen (Turkish Fountain), erected in 1649 to commemorate the peace treaty signed after the Thirty Years' War. The statue of the goddess of peace was replaced in 1683 by a goddess of victory when Elector Johann Georg III returned triumphant after participating in the liberation of Vienna from the Turks (a Turkish head entwined with snakes spouts water).

A few paces from the fountain a stone set in the pavement bearing the initials *NK*, marks the spot where the Chancellor of the Electorate of Saxony Nikolaus Krell was publicly beheaded in 1601. As a result of a few moderate reformist ideas he was accused by his enemies of "crypto-Calvinism", in those days a charge punishable by death amongst orthodox Lutherans.

On the western side of the Neumarkt there was once a synagogue, which was destroyed in a pogrom as long ago as 1430; by the east stairway to the Brühlsche Terrasse there is now a six-armed memorial stone for the victims of the pogrom of November 1938 (completed in 1974–75 by Friedemann Döhner). From the completely open south side of the Neumarkt, which is bordered only by the backs of the houses along the main east-west thoroughfare, a number of narrow streets originally led to the Altmarkt (Frauenstrasse, Kirchgasse, etc.). On the corner of Frauenstrasse and Neumarkt there was originally a house with a Renaissance oriel, the home of the court Kapellmeister, composer and doyen of Protestant church music Heinrich Schütz from 1629 to 1657 (his memorial chapel is in the Kreuzkirche).

Monarchy embodied: It is in this corner of the Neumarkt that the **statue of King Frederick Augustus II** still stands, having survived the bombing more or less intact. In his hand the king holds the document which in 1831 changed Saxony into a constitutional monarchy. The monument (by Ernst Ludwig Hähnel in 1866) looks rather out of context without the De Saxe and Stadt Rom

Semper's opera house on the Elbe and the base for the Weisse Flotte.

hotels – the latter the scene of fierce fighting in the May uprising of 1849 – the two establishments of elegance and renown that originally stood at the top of the old Moritzstrasse (today the site is occupied by the Szeged restaurant).

In Moritzstrasse, Christian Gottfried Körner welcomed to his home all the important intellectuals of the classic-romantic epoch, whether citizens or guests of Dresden, to participate in lively discussions.

Among those who visited his house were Goethe, the brothers Wilhelm and Alexander von Humboldt, (the former an educational reformer, the latter a famous scientist); the Schlegel brothers (critics and scholars); August Wilhelm, translator of Shakespeare; writers Ludwig Tieck, Novalis and Heinrich von Kleist and the patriots of the Wars of Liberation (in which Körner's son Theodor fell), Ernst Mortiz Arndt and Baron von Stein.

The history of Dresden is documented in the **Stadtmuseum** (City Historical Museum) in the Landhaus, recognisable in Landhausstrasse by its balcony supported at the centre by six Doric columns. A special feature of the Landhaus interior (it was built from 1770 to 1776 as the meeting place and administrative building of the Saxon provincial legislature) is the spacious hall with its widely curving stairs; an architectural masterpiece illustrating the transition from baroque to classicism.

On the other side of the Landstrasse the crenellated old building with the two towers (1895–1900) is the **police headquarters**, the main facade of which fronts the appropriately named Schiessgasse (Shooting Street). While perfectly adequate for the police administration of the city and its surroundings in the first half of the 20th century, it was massively extended over the past four decades, and other large buildings in the city were also appropriated for use by the regular and secret police forces. On the ground floor of this building there are a number of service institutions.

Meeting in front of the Johanneum.

THE DRESDNER BANK

Eugen Gutmann, founder of the Dresdner Bank, could almost have been the key player in a promotional campaign dreamed up by an advertising agency: he was definitely the right person to look after your money. Forget the slogans of the bank's media campaigns these days: Eugen Gutmann radiated solid respectability, almost enough to make you want to commit your entire life savings to his care.

The Dresdner Bank started life on 1 December 1872 with 30 employees, when it took over the Bankhaus Michael Kaskel in Dresden, an establishment with a 100-year pedigree. Several other establishments were involved in its foundation, alongside the bank belonging to barons Carl and Felix von Kaskel: the Allgemeine Deutsche Credit-Anstalt in Leipzig, the Berliner Handelsgesellschaft, the Anglo-German Bank in Hamburg, and the Deutsche Verkehrsbank in Frankfurt am Main.

This all took place at the time when Thomas Alva Edison had just invented the light-bulb, Ernst Abbe had made scientific improvements to the microscope and Werner von Siemens had just developed the first-ever electric railway in Berlin. It was not to be long (1884, to be precise) before the bank took the crucial decision to move its head office to Berlin.

Just as important as the bank's quick founding of new branches in Hamburg, London, Bremen and Frankfurt am Main were its first investments in industry. Railways were being built, and the Dresdner Bank took its opportunity: in 1890 it invested in the Bank für Orientalische Eisenbahnen in Zurich and the Eisenbahnbaugesellschaft in Frankfurt, and in Constantinople it also took part in the financing of the Saloniki-Monastir railway, as well as of the Deutsche Speisewagen Gesellschaft a few years later.

Its first business contact with the firm of Krupp was established in 1893, and developed further in 1896 when Krupp took over the Germania ship and machinery construction company in Tegel and Kiel. The Mexican Electric Works, based in London, was co-founded with Siemens & Halske in 1897. For a period of years from 1900 onwards, the Dresdner Bank had more branches than any other bank in Germany. It now occupies second place in the table, behind the Deutsche Bank and ahead of the Commerzbank.

At the turn of the century a great new era of expansion was dawning. Germany's interests were no longer bounded by its national frontiers, its capital was now being invested worldwide. The Dresdner Bank took over syndicate management when the Russian Electricity Company was set up in St Petersburg and Riga (1898); it also invested in the Deutsch-Atlantische Telegraphen-Gesellschaft and the railway and mining concerns in Shangtung (1899).

A bank was founded in 1904 in the merchant city of Hamburg in cooperation with the Deutsch-Westafrikanische Handelsgesellschaft for the purposes of trade with Togo and Cameroon; large investments in the Deutsche Orientbank and the Bank of South America followed one year later.

The Dresdner Bank was now represented in many well-known cities throughout the world: Constantinople, Alexandria, Cairo, Casablanca, Buenos Aires, Mexico, Santiago de Chile and Rio de Janeiro. These branches were closed during World War II, but then were re-opened by the bank's principal office in Hamburg during the 1950s.

In Dresden, the bank managed to gain a foothold even before monetary union was established between East and West Germany. Its first office was set up in January 1990, in the Dresdner Hof hotel; a temporary building in Waisenhausstrasse followed, and soon its own imposing-looking office block will be helping to fill one of the gaps in the Altmarkt.

In 1992, around 40 branches are providing services to private customers and giving advice on the formation of new businesses. Two-thirds of the bank's workforce comes from the new federal states. Women bank managers – who are something quite new for the East – are now being trained in the bank's special centres there, and most employees get their training through hands-on practical experience.

FRAUENKIRCHE

At regular intervals a crane is manoeuvred up to the Frauenkirche (Church of Our Lady). On the small platform the specialists from the Department for the Preservation of Historical Monuments are lifted up to examine each of the two stumps which are all that remain of the church, and tap them carefully here and there, but only very carefully, since the fear that both stone pillars might collapse is ever-present. The people in the Interhotel Dresdner Hof, almost in the fall line, also look up anxiously at the remains of the choir and one of the four corner towers, which are still over 81 feet (25 metres) high.

Dresden's Frauenkirche represented one of the highpoints of church architecture in Protestant countries. It was designed by George Ludwig Bähr, the great Baroque architect, who built it in eight years, from 1726 to 1734. The massive dome, over 325 feet (100 metres) high, was such a dominant feature of the panorama of buildings spread out along the Elbe in Saxony's capital that, as Ludwig Güttler, the world-famous Dresden trumpeter, put it: "reconstruction of Dresden without the Frauenkirche is simply unthinkable".

The older residents of Dresden still remember it as the Protestant Cathedral of St Peter, which was its name until the inferno of 13 February 1945. At the time it was not even hit by the bombs: weakened by the shock waves and by the heat, which melted its steel constructions, it simply collapsed. For a long time it was thought that there were still bodies buried under the huge mountain of rubble, but today it is known that there were no people in the church when it fell in.

Antiwar symbol: Younger people can only compare the old ruin and the mountain of rubble with old photographs. There was very nearly nothing more to compare: in 1958 the ruling party, the

The Frauenkirche today...

SED, wanted to remove the remains of the Frauenkirche altogether as part of the general clearing-up process. This plan was abandoned due to the perseverance of the monument's curators.

There is probably no other ruin in Europe today that has as much symbolic value as the remains of the Frauenkirche in Dresden. What is it a symbol of? It is a grim reminder to all who see it – and with the large empty space between it and the Kulturpalast (Palace of Culture) on the Altmarkt it is impossible to miss – of the senselessness of war and destruction. It's an affecting sight, one which moves tourists to tears.

Meeting point of the peace movement: In the 1980s, however, the Frauenkirche was also the meeting point and symbol of the peace movement in the GDR. Without the "swords to ploughshares" demonstrations the events of autumn 1989 would have been inconceivable. And in autumn 1991 the two "forefingers of stone", as a newspaper called them, were also the starting point of another movement with the slogan "We are the people!"

In Dresden there were arguments after the changes of 1989 as to whether the Frauenkirche should be rebuilt in all its former glory. A vigorous campaign in support of this was conducted by an action committee composed of professors, doctors and architects, and the first plans have already been submitted. It is a project that would cost over 160 million German marks. The campaigners believed that if the Zwinger and the Opera House have been reconstructed, the Frauenkirche should be too.

One argument against reconstruction is that the Frauenkirche would have no parish community: the Christians around the bombed Neumarkt have long since found new churches to belong to. Many Dresdeners expressed the view that it was more important to build new hospitals and modernise the city's infrastructure than to worry about the Frauenkirche. The action committee at least wants to prevent a "peace museum"

...and before World War II.

from being temporarily erected on the site. It is argued that this would make reconstruction impossible and put an end once and for all to dreams of returning the church and its mighty dome to Dresden's skyline.

Even 250 years ago building problems did not hold up the construction of the Frauenkirche. After the death of the architect Bähr in 1737, his successor, the court architect Caetano Chiaveri, discovered that the giant dome was not properly positioned, and that cracks had developed in the overloaded pillars and arches. The dome was not however removed and in spite of all it held – right up until February 1945.

In March 1991, after much hesitation, the Bishop of Saxony and then the synod of the Lutheran church voted for rebuilding, in close cooperation with the Frauenkirche Foundation. There is no lack of donors. Federal Chancellor Helmut Kohl converted the presents he received on his 60th birthday into money for the rebuilding project.

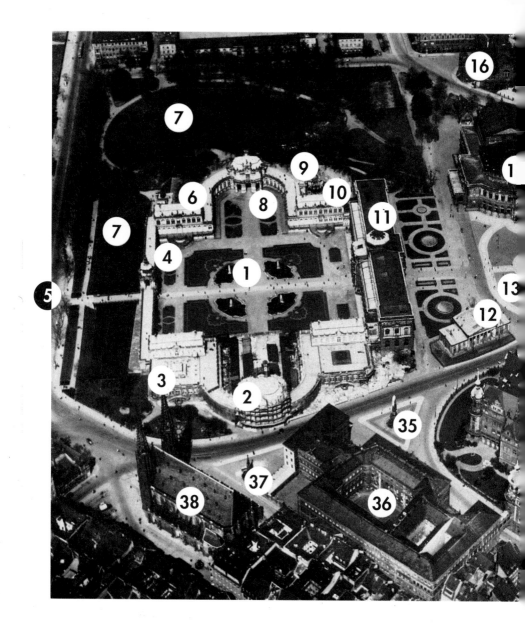

This aerial photograph, which was taken before the war, should help you find your way around the centre of Old Dresden, whose architectural ensemble made the city world-famous. The extent of the war-time damage is immediately clear; many of the ruined buildings were pulled down and simply vanished without trace. The picture does not take in the Altmarkt and the Neumarkt with its ruins of the Frauenkirche, whose reconstruction (at the time of going to press) is now on the agenda of the municipal and religious authorities.

The former beauty of the Altmarkt and Neumarkt can be seen from Canaletto's *vedutas* which are reproduced in this book on pages 12–17. The description of the photograph begins with the Zwinger in the top left-hand corner.

8 Wallpavillon (Rampart Pavilion)
9 Nymphenbad (Nymphs' Bath)
10 French Pavilion
11 "Old Masters" Gallery

City Centre
12 Altstädter Wache
13 Theaterplatz
14 Statue of King Johann on Horseback
15 Semper Opera House
16 Royal Heating and Electricity Works (pulled down after 1945)
17 Hotel Bellevue (pulled down after 1945)
18 River Elbe
19 "Italian Village"
20 Catholic Hofkirche (Cathedral)
21 Augustusbrücke
22 Brühlsche Terrasse (not in picture)
23 Schlossplatz
24 Georgentor
25 Stallhof (Stable Court)
26 Langer Gang (Long Arcade)
27 Procession of Princes (Augustusstrasse, not in picture)
28 Neumarkt
29 Schlossturm (Palace Tower, also known as the Hausmannsturm)
30 Grünes Gewölbe (Green Vault) in the Royal Palace
31 Gallery in the Grosser Schlosshof (Large Palace Courtyard)
32 Grosser Schlosshof
33 Kleiner (small) Schlosshof
34 Schlossstrasse
35 Wettin Column (destroyed 1945)
36 Taschenbergpalais (ruins, to to become a hotel)
37 Cholera and Gutschmid Fountains
38 Sophienkirche (pulled down after 1945)

OLD DRESDEN

Zwinger
1 Courtyard
2 City Pavilion
3 Porcelain Collection
4 Kronentor (Crown Gate)
5 Mathematics and Physics Salon
6 Schauspielhaus (not in picture)
7 Zwingerteich

FROM THE PALACE
TO THE ZWINGER

The area taken up by the Schloss or Royal Palace and the Zwinger, the architectural centre of Dresden, once lay at the edge of the city. When the first stone bridge was constructed across the Elbe in 1220, a fort was built to defend it on the left bank, a fort which gradually developed into a palace. From 1485 until the end of the monarchy in 1918 it was the permanent residence of the Albertines, with imposing state buildings concentrated around it on the periphery of the historic city centre. This area too was reduced to a field of smouldering ruins on 13 February 1945. Although reconstruction of the individual buildings, the Zwinger and the Hofkirche (Court Church), was begun immediately after the war, the complex has still not been completed.

The **Schlossplatz** (Palace Square), which forms the entrance to the Altstadt, (Old Town), dates back to the 16th and 18th centuries and was created by filling in several bridge arches and raising the land in front. The medieval bridge originally started at the Elbtor, (Elbe Gate), which was replaced in 1530–1535 under Duke George the Bearded by the **Georgenbau**, an extension to the late medieval palace and the first Renaissance building in Dresden. Most of its numerous ornamental sculptures were destroyed in the palace fire of 1701. The gateway on the Elbe side has been preserved, and was transferred to the west side of the Georgenbau when this was renovated in 1901.

The Royal Palace: The basic layout of the palace, which was destroyed in 1945, is much the same as it was after its reconstruction and extension under Elector Moritz in 1547 when the Albertines became electors. The resulting four-winged building with a large courtyard at the centre was one of the most magnificent palace complexes of the Renaissance era in Germany. The

addition to the medieval palace tower in 1674 raised it to a height of 315 feet (97 metres) and in 1693 a triumphal portal was built on to it for Elector Johann Georg III, the "Saxon Mars", who led the Saxon contingent against the Turks to end the siege of Vienna in 1683.

In the course of time the Royal Palace lost many of its Renaissance features, and from 1883–1901 it was comprehensively restored in neo-Renaissance style. Once the reconstruction begun in 1985 is completed, the buildings will be used to house the State Art Collections.

Princely frieze: On the east side of the palace complex is the **Stallhof** (Stable Court), which runs along the Augustusstrasse. The latter was laid out by Elector Moritz to replace the medieval city moat and is bounded by the Langer Gang (Long Arcade) connecting the Georgenbau with the former stable building (now the Transport Museum). The ground floor of this building is a colonnade open on the courtyard side and decorated with the coats of arms of the Wettin

dominions. The upper floor was originally covered on both sides with paintings, but only those on the inner side have been preserved.

To continue this ornamental style when the stable buildings were rebuilt as the Museum Johanneum, the whole exterior wall of the Long Arcade on the Augustusstrasse was decorated by Wilhelm Walter in 1872–76 with a frieze of figures, the **Procession of Princes**. Originally in sgraffito technique (a method of scratching plaster so that the underneath shows through), the mural was transferred in 1907 to more durable ceramic tiles fired in the Meissen porcelain factory. It represents the 800-year rule of the Wettin princes, depicted in a continuous horseback procession led by Margrave Konrad, the founder of the Wettin territorial state, and ending with King Albert, the ruling monarch when the picture was produced, and his brother and successor George, last but one of the Saxon kings. Representatives of the professions in Saxony, among them well-known artists and scholars of the time, bring up the rear.

On the opposite side of the street, with its main entrance on Schlossplatz, is the **Ständehaus** (Parliament House) designed by Paul Wallot, the architect of the Berlin Reichstag building, and built in 1901–06 for the Saxon Parliament. It replaced an old palace, the Brühlsche Palais.

A decorative flight of steps leads up from Schlossplatz to the **Brühlsche Terrasse**, which incorporates a section of the original ramparts surrounding the old town from the mid-16th to the beginning of the 19th century. From 1739 to 1750 the Brühlsche Palais gardens were laid out on top of the fortifications overlooking the River Elbe, thus opening the city to the water. The garden terrace with its attractive view of the Elbe and the hills sweeping down to it subsequently became known as the "balcony of Europe".

The **Hofkirche**, today the cathedral of the diocese of Dresden-Meissen, is **The Procession of Princes.**

located on the western side of Schlossplatz; built in 1739–55, it was designed by the Italian Caetano Chiaveri in the late baroque style of his home country. The building of a monumental Catholic church right in the middle of the capital of the region which had introduced Protestantism was at the time such an outrageous project that it was initially kept secret.

Behind the Hofkirche on Sophienstrasse opposite the palace is the **Altstädter Wache**, now the central box-office for the state theatres. This graceful building that looks rather like a temple was designed not by any of Dresden's architects but by the most important representative of Berlin neoclassicism, Karl Friedrich Schinkel, and dates from 1830–32.

Palace ruins: Also occupying a section of Sophienstrasse is the ruin of another palace, the **Taschenbergpalais**, which is connected by a bridge with the Royal Palace. In medieval times there was a rise in the ground in this part of the town, from which the palace takes its name ("berg" meaning "hill"). Built in 1705–09 by Augustus the Strong for his favourite mistress, Countess Cosel, the palace originally only consisted of what is now the central section, featuring a facade decorated with beautiful stucco work.

In the Zwinger: Opposite the Taschenbergpalais is an entrance leading into the **Zwinger** through the Stadtpavillon or Glockenspielpavillon (City or Carillon Pavilion). The area occupied by the Zwinger and the adjoining Theaterplatz was added to the city only in 1574 when new wider town walls were built. The land between the old and new fortifications remained empty for a long time, and was referred to as the Zwinger (Outer Bailey). In 1709 Augustus the Strong commissioned Pöppelmann to design an orangery here, which was followed by the Bogengalerien (Curved Galleries) and pavilions built against the ramparts opposite the Stadtpavillon. The royal project was

The Stallhof connects the Georgenbau with the Johanneum.

continued in 1714–15 with the building of the Langgalerie (Long Gallery) and the Kronentor (Crown Gate) on the ramparts above the moat.

In order to be able to use the unfinished garden courtyard in 1719 for the festivities at the wedding of the electoral prince with a daughter of Empress Maria Josepha the complex was provisionally completed, but it was never subsequently continued and has remained in its unfinished state; in 1728 Augustus the Strong decided to use the buildings to house art collections, a function they still fulfil today.

Nymphs and blossoms: The unusual appearance of the Dresden Zwinger, a product of the festive court culture which prevailed under Augustus the Strong and one of the highpoints of baroque architecture, is due to the extremely lavish decoration of the buildings, executed in stone to blend in with the architecture by Balthasar Permoser and his colleagues. The themes of the rich sculptural ornamentation are nature,

represented by elaborate fountains, blossoms and fruits, nymphs and satyrs; the rulers, represented by their insignias and coats of arms, and finally the world of the Olympic gods, in which nature is sublimated.

It was not until 1855 that the Zwinger courtyard was completed with the building of the **Gemäldegalerie** (Art Gallery), the work of Gottfried Semper. Although according to the architectural thinking of the 19th century the museum, built to house an extremely famous collection of paintings, should have been the dominant feature in the complex of baroque galleries and pavilions, Semper took the architecture of the Zwinger into account in his design, which owes much to the Italian Renaissance.

The ancient triumphal arch incorporated into the central part of the gallery is of symbolic significance as an arch dedicated to art as opposed to the Kronentor, which is the triumphal arch of absolutist royalty. The sculpture decorating the gallery, the work of Ernst

Left, the Nymphs' Bath in the Zwinger. Right, the Rampart Pavilion, part of the Zwinger.

Rietschel and Julius Hähnel, represents medieval and modern art on the Zwinger side, with Raphael and Michelangelo at the centre, and ancient art on the Elbe side. The return of the paintings from the Soviet Union in 1955, where they had been kept since the war, provided the impetus for rebuilding the gallery, which had been destroyed in 1945.

Opera house: The building of the Gemäldegalerie created a second open space next to the Zwingerhof, the Theaterplatz (Theatre Square). On the west side of this square is the **Semperoper** (Opera House), today the Saxon State Opera, which was also designed by Semper and built between 1871 and 1878. Its striking appearance with its facade of segmental arches is the combined result of years of preoccupation with theatre construction on the part of the architect and the adjustments required to blend the new building in with the art gallery. The rich structure of the exterior corresponds to that of the gallery building, and the portico over the central portal contains more than a suggestion of the colour and splendour of the interior, which has been reconstructed as Semper originally designed it. The Semperoper is as famous for its music as its architecture: most of the operas of Richard Strauss were premiered here with the Dresdner Staatskapelle (Dresden State Orchestra).

Schilling's **Statue of King Johann on Horseback**, the monument to the king who, under the pen name of "Philalethes", translated Dante's *Divine Comedy* into German, was erected in front of the theatre in 1889.

The restaurant with the name **Italienisches Dörfchen** (Italian Village) on the Elbe side of Theaterplatz was built from 1911 to 1913, but had a predecessor; it was all that remained of a small settlement that grew up on the site of the present square when Chiaveri built the Hofkirche. The name "Italian Village" thus serves as a memorial to the past of the square shaped by Semper with his famous buildings.

A lot to do in the Zwinger workshops.

CASEMATES

Dresden has a new tourist attraction. The special thing about it is that although it is right in the middle of the historic city centre, which was reduced to ashes by the Allied bombers in February 1945, it is nevertheless absolutely authentic. Moreover, it is not much smaller, and is certainly no less important or impressive than the landmarks of the old city that have already been rebuilt: the opera house, the cathedral, the Zwinger, or the half completed Royal Palace. And on top of this the new attraction is appreciably older than any of the above-named buildings.

Beneath the balcony of Europe: When what was known as "old Dresden" was destroyed in the bombing of 1945, the even older fortifications from the Renaissance epoch had already lain buried and forgotten for centuries. Buried underground, they survived. Some were filled in and built over, others used as a fuel depot by the ships of the "Weisse Flotte" or as general storerooms.

The **Casemates**, open to the public since autumn 1990, are located under, of all places, Dresden's treasured river promenade, the terrace built for Count Brühl which became famous as the "balcony of Europe". In the final phase of reconstruction work on the Brühlsche Terrasse, however, a large hole unexpectedly opened. Elegantly shaped in the form of a hexagon, it was identified as a former cannon yard.

At once there was a lively public debate as to whether the hole in the Terrasse should be left open. While some people were fascinated by this glimpse of history lying beneath the feet of generations of promenaders, for others the hole detracted from the charms of their favourite place, and they claimed that it spoiled the effect of the 1749 dolphin fountain right next to it. In the meantime the city came to a decision and the cannon yard was filled in again.

Once used by Böttger as a furnace for his porcelain...

The chairman of the society that has been excavating the site on a voluntary, non-profit making basis, Herr Apostel, does not even want to talk about the dispute any more. He has had enough problems with the authorities and is glad that he and the 40 members of his organisation have been allowed to continue excavating in peace.

Underground tours: The Society for the Preservation of the Fortifications, today a registered organisation, began its explorations in 1965. In 1968 the city administration forbade further excavation without giving any reasons. Since work started again in 1988 they have exposed a much larger complex of structures than they originally expected. On Saturday mornings, when the society's members use their free time to continue working on the excavations, there are guided tours for the public. Immediately behind the inconspicuous iron door at the back of the Brühlsche Terrasse (Georg-Treu-Platz) is the Ziegeltor, a gate built in the mid-16th century as part of the preparations for the imminent Turkish war. Herr Apostel and the members of his society explain to visitors where the drawbridge was, how the defence structures worked, and how the shafts for ventilation and communication were constructed. Curious about everything, at an earlier stage in the proceedings they even excavated the pit of the former latrine.

Some rooms are almost complete and will soon be used by the society for an exhibition documenting the pre-baroque history of Dresden, but most of the complex is still a building site. This makes a visit even more exciting.

The preservation society would have nothing against the conversion of some of the beautiful tunnel vaults into bars or music cellars. The society's members are enthusiasts like Herr Apostel, who would love most of all to unearth some fragments of wall from the Romanesque epoch: such fragments would then be the oldest remains of Dresden that have ever been found.

... the Casemates are now destined to house a restaurant, cinema and theatre.

THE GREAT GARDEN

All the gardens in the world are based on a single original model: paradise. Paradise, however, is as remote as heaven, an unattainable place no-one has ever seen or ever ventured into except perhaps in the imagination. A garden was once an enclosed space, a place of refuge from the noisy world outside and the ideal setting for meditation and philosophical discussion. It is a reflection of man's ideal society, embodying the social and cultural atmosphere of the time and changing not according to any particular fashion but according to the needs of its users.

In the year 1676 the Elector Johann Georg II bought the land between Dresden and the villages of Striesen, Gruna and Strehlen for use as a pheasant enclosure, 2,189 sq. yards (1,830 sq. metres) in area. It was divided into four parts by an east-west and a north-south axis, with an area at the intersection large enough for a palace. Two years later in 1678 the architect Johann Georg Starcke (1640–95) started work on this building, probably receiving help with the project from his teacher Wolf Caspar von Klengel (1630–91).

Augustan work of art: It was in 1698 that this garden came into its own, when it was transformed by order of Augustus the Strong into a complete work of art. Not intended for any practical purposes, its sole function was to be admired, and in keeping with the thinking of the baroque age it was no longer to be a private but a public garden. The designer of the new parkland, retitled the **Great Garden**, was Johann Friedrich Karcher (1650–1726).

The original square plot was enlarged to form a rectangle, and the Great Garden became the symbol of the power and wealth of the ruler. The underlying principle of its design is symmetry; the love of order and regularity in the baroque era, based on the principles of reason and geometry, meant that gardens increasingly became the responsibility of architects.

The Great Garden was inspired by Versailles and the Vaux le Vicomte garden designed by Le Nôtre, the famous gardener of the Sun King Louis XIV. Its similarities to Versailles are immediately evident.

Clear symmetry: The central point of the Great Garden is the *parterre*, a level area with a large pond; no baroque garden was complete without water, and it was for this reason the gardens were always laid out on level ground. In the middle stands the palace, the focal point of the main axis that runs through the park. The main part of the garden extends on either side of this central axis, which draws the eye to the edge of the park, thus having the effect of making the whole complex look even larger than it really is.

The Great Garden of Dresden has its centrally-positioned **palace**, which dominates the *parterre* and stands in the

Preceding pages: the Great Garden, laid out from 1676 in the French style. **Left**, Garden sculpture and (right) young visitor.

middle of an open space. The main axis points east to the distant mountains of Saxon Switzerland and west to the skyline of the city. It is intersected by an avenue running from north to south and two further avenues, the Herkulesallee and the Südallee, run parallel to the main avenue. The rectangular pond located on the side of the palace facing away from the city is used for water festivals and enhances the effects of firework displays.

The palace, a mixture of late Renaissance and baroque styles with of course a heavy French influence, was the first baroque building in Electoral Saxony. It is built in the shape of an H and has three floors; at the centre is the two-storeyed banqueting hall.

No longer used for residential purposes, the palace is today purely a setting for summer entertainments. The themes of its abundant sculptural decoration, the work of various Saxon sculptors of the pre-Zwinger generation, are primarily taken from antiquity. The magnificent double flight of steps on both sides of the building is an indication that the design of the palace was influenced entirely by the conception of the garden.

A garden developed from an overall plan can only be properly appreciated when viewed from above; the *parterre* with its ornamental hedges and flowers has a design of great complexity and imagination that is best looked at from the top of the stairs.

Eight houses mark out the inner garden. Originally used as accommodation for the king's guests when he held his sumptuous festivals, such as the Venus festival of 1719, they were later occasionally used to house the royal collections of antiquities. The German archaeologist and art historian Johann Joachim Winckelmann (1717–68) recorded having seen them here.

Extensions: What has been described above is to some extent the ideal state of the Great Garden. It is possible to picture it as it once was, since in spite of the

Horseback visitors.

repeated damage inflicted on it (in 1760 by Frederick the Great, in 1813 by Napoleon and in 1945 during the bombing of Dresden) it has survived, and has changed little in outline. Sections of the park were separated off, in 1863 for the Zoological Gardens, the oldest zoo in the former GDR, and in 1882 for the Botanical Gardens, which have a total area of 7.4 acres (3 hectares) and contain around 9,000 different species of plant.

When the Bürgerwiese, a park to the south-west, was redesigned by Peter Joseph Lenné (1789–1866) it was joined on to the Great Garden, thus increasing its total area. There was a further extension in the north-east; this section was designed in the English style as a landscaped garden with winding paths.

Today the Great Garden is the largest park in Saxony, with an area of 500 acres (200 hectares). Even during the Biedermeier epoch the people of Dresden came here to relax and enjoy the fresh air, and this large green space still has a beneficial effect on the climate of the city. Restaurants and cafés have been built within its confines and in 1887 a horticultural exhibition was staged here.

The **Carolasee**, a lake with boats and a restaurant, is situated on the south side of the Great Garden. A 3½-mile (5.6-km) narrow-gauge railway runs across the whole park, which carries over half a million passengers during the season, from April to October. It was originally run by a "young pioneers" collective of 340 boys and girls who were supervised by experienced railwaymen. The Sonnenhäusel puppet theatre, the old open-air park theatre, hidden behind shrubbery near the palace, and the new open-air stage Junge Garde are now the main venues of park festivals.

The damage which was inflicted on the Great Garden's trees during the war is no longer visible, but in this park as in many others the general level of environmental pollution of the modern world is sadly taking its toll.

Rowing on the Carolasee.

DRESDEN NEUSTADT

The Elbe divides Dresden into the Altstadt (Old Town) and the Neustadt (New Town). It is all perfectly simple; the names say it all. Or do they?

Before taking a look at the Neustadt it is important to understand the origins of its name, and for this it is necessary to go right back to the very beginning, before Dresden had ever been thought of. The river of course was there, as it had always been, and the old trade route from east to west meant that somehow or other people had to cross it.

There was a good crossing-point where the city stands today and simple settlements appeared on both sides of the water. It was not long before a bridge was built, and in 1287 replaced with the first more permanent stone structure. At first today's Neustadt bore the name of "Altendresden", or Old Dresden; it received a charter in 1403, but lost it again in 1549. In order to put an end to "such and similar aberrations and weaknesses resulting in unneighbourly attitudes and tedious justifications", Elector Moritz decided that the two towns on either side of the Elbe should become a single community with respect to councils, guilds, army campaigns, seals and other matters. The ostensible reason for unification was a dispute over brewing rights.

Old becomes new: In the year 1685 Altendresden was devastated by fire. Augustus the Strong had it rebuilt by the head state architect Wolf Caspar von Klengel (1630–91) and from then on it was known as Neue Königsstadt (New Royal Town). This was gradually simplified to **Neustadt**, which was not only easier to say, but also in keeping with the subsequent political changes. The former Neudresden was now known as the **Altstadt**.

To enter the Neustadt, cross the Elbe on the **Augustusbrücke** and take the subway under the wide, busy road at the end of the bridge to the large square on the other side – at the entrance of which is a plan of the Neustadt in sandstone. Although this open space was actually caused by the bombing, some of the old features of the area have been retained and it still manages to look like a self-contained ensemble.

Back in its original place, the focal point of a group of new buildings arranged like a convex lens, is the **Goldener Reiter** (Golden Horseman), the monument to Augustus the Strong who is portrayed in keeping with the absolutism of his day; as the Elector Frederick Augustus I of Saxony and King Augustus II of Poland, here he is dressed up in the guise of a Roman emperor. The statue was erected in 1736, three years after the ruler's death. It was damaged in the war, restored in 1954 and newly gilded in 1956.

In spite of numerous alterations to detail, the basic structure of the **Innere Neustadt** (Inner New Town) has remained as it was when designed as the Neue Königsstadt. It is encircled by the

Preceding pages: basket-maker on the Strasse der Befreiung. **Left**, Pfunds Dairy, a work of art in the Bautzner Strasse. **Right**, Neustadt idyll.

Äussere Neustadt (Outer New Town), which was built in the 19th century during the reign of King Anton (1827–36). The original name of Antonstadt has been changed to the rather more prosaic but geographically logical name of **Dresden Nord** (north).

Classic promenade: The wide straight street which starts at the square and gradually becomes narrower is the **Hauptstrasse** (Main Street), the name of which was changed in 1945 to "Strasse der Befreiung" (Liberation Street). It is now a pedestrian precinct shaded by old plane trees (formerly lime trees) and decorated with flowerbeds and historic sandstone statues. Shops and restaurants of all kinds line both sides and it has become the favourite promenade of citizens and visitors alike – by contrast with the once famous Prager Strasse in the Altstadt, which has since been completely spoiled.

The fountains marking the beginning of the Hauptstrasse once stood in front of the Neustadt **town hall**. All that re-mained of this after the war was the cellar (under the buildings on the left-hand corner), now the location of an atmospheric restaurant, the **Meissner Weinkeller**. The new buildings on either side of the street soon give way to a number of old houses which survived the war. The beautiful baroque facades have been restored and brighten up the whole precinct.

Free port of art: On one of these houses, in gold letters, are written the words: *An Gottes Segen is alles gelegen* (all blessings come from God). This was the home of the painter Gerhard von Kügelgen (1772–1820), well-known for his portraits of Schiller and Goethe but above all for his work *Jugenderinner-ungen eines alten Mannes* (Recollections of an Old Man).

On the second floor of this same house is the **Museum zur Dresdner Früh-romantik** (Museum of Early Romanticism in Dresden), documenting the emergence of Romanticism in around 1800, the broad-based arts movement **Neustadt art.**

that was to change cultural and intellectual history.

Famous names from the worlds of philosophy, literature, art and music were in Dresden at this time and frequented these rooms. Among them were the artists Caspar David Friedrich, Carl Gustav Carus, Philipp Otto Runge and Johan Christian Dahl, the writers Ludwig Tieck and Heinrich von Kleist, the composer Carl Maria von Weber and later Robert Schumann and Richard Wagner. One room is devoted to the Körner family, whose house stood nearby on the site of the present Hotel Bellevue. In the park, between the hotel and the Japanisches Palais (Japanese Palace) a stele with the insignia of this "Free port of knowledge and art" commemorates this meeting place of great intellects. Mozart, Schiller, Goethe, Herder, the Humboldt and Schlegel brothers, Novalis, Graff, Arndt, and Stein were among the many guests at the Kügelgen house.

Continue along the Hauptstrasse to the **Dreikönigskirche** (Church of the Epiphany). This building, completed between 1732 and 1739 by Matthaeus Daniel Pöppelmann and George Bähr, was the third church on this site. It was gutted in 1945 and is currently being restored, although only a part of the nave will be reconstructed as a church, while the rest will be a community centre. The Saxon State Parliament is meeting here until it has a new building. On the way to **Bautzner Platz** ("Platz der Einheit"), it is impossible to overlook the white marble memorial to Schiller by Selmar Werner (1914), a highly idealistic work in a mixture of neo-classical and art nouveau styles.

Baroque Königsstrasse: From the large circle (dating from 1811) at the centre of Bautzner Platz, the design of Neustadt becomes apparent: it is star-shaped with 12 roads radiating out in all directions from this central point. The grandest of these are the Königsstrasse (King Street, formerly Friedrich-Engels-Strasse) which leads to the Japanese Palace and

Literally, "love and imagination can do anything".

the Hauptstrasse (Strasse der Befreiung) which leads to the Blockhaus and the Golden Horseman statue. The city's original fortifications extended to this point, with the Bautzen/Lausitz road beginning here at the Schwarzes Tor (Black Gate); until 1732 this was also the site of the gallows.

Continue along the Königsstrasse (1,100 ft or 340 metres long and 100 ft or 30 metres wide) in the direction of the Japanese Palace. The street is lined with magnificent baroque houses which survived the war intact but are now urgently in need of renovation. The houses in Nieritzstrasse off to the right are all from the Biedermeier period while the Rähnitzgasse on the left has buildings from the 18th century.

The Königsstrasse leads to the square in front of the **Japanese Palace**, which acquired its name in 1732. From 1727 to 1736 the palace was remodelled by Matthaeus Daniel Pöppelmann, Zacharias Longuelune and Jean de Bodt: as the roofs suggest, it was intended for the display of Chinese, Japanese and in particular Meissen porcelain. From 1786 to 1945 it housed the Royal Electoral/Saxon Library and at times also the antiquities and the coin cabinet. It was badly damaged during the war, and since its restoration has been provisionally housing the **Museen für Völkerkunde und Vorgeschichte** (Ethnological and Prehistorical Museums), but the rooms are really more storerooms than exhibition rooms.

Another Augustus: Next to the Japanese Palace is the monument to Augustus the Strong as the Elector Frederick Augustus I; opposite is what was originally one of the two gatehouses of the **Leipziger Tor** (Leipzig Gate), built in 1829 by Gottlob Friedrich Thormeyer in the neo-classical style. Today it is a registry office.

Continue in the direction of the Golden Horseman, past the **Hotel Bellevue** (note the baroque palace facade incorporated into the hotel building) and the **Blockhaus**, until recently the "Haus der Freundschaft" (House of Friendship)

Café in front of Kügelen's house, today a museum of Romanticism. Right, measuring air pollution.

ENVIRONMENTAL ISSUES

From the environmental point of view, Dresden is paradise compared to such ecological former East German disaster areas as Buna or Bitterfeld. Pollution in this city has been steadily decreasing since 1989.

A few miles further up the Elbe, though, some areas are almost as heavily polluted as Bitterfeld. The environmental report issued by the GDR only a few months before it ceased to exist used the term "Pirna Syndrome" to describe a rather complex syndrome resulting from sulphur dioxide air pollution. Long-term observations by the regional sanitation department in Pirna had established a connection between emission of contaminants by the cellulose industry and an increase in symptoms such as headaches, aching limbs, apathy and general exhaustion.

The cellulose industry does not only pollute the air, it also contributes to what is the worst environmental problem of the Dresden region: the pollution of the Elbe. Unprocessed waste from factories and municipalities is being released directly into the river and poisoning it. Once there were 57 different species of fish in the Elbe: now only 18 survive.

In Pirna, environmentalists connected the discharge pipe of the United Cellulose Works to its tap-water intake pipe with the aid of a tube, and raised a Greenpeace banner. The staff of the pharmaceutical works in Radebeul were served samples of poisoned water in cocktail glasses.

The city of Dresden is not only suffering from the pollution of the Elbe – it is doing a lot of the polluting itself. A sewage treatment plant with septic tank towers and a fermentation gas installation, designed to serve 600,000 inhabitants, was built in 1910 in Dresden-Kaditz, and at the time it was the most modern in Europe. It has been closed since 1987 and since that time 47 million gallons (180 million litres) of almost completely untreated sewage have been flowing from Dresden into the Elbe daily. The Dresden sewer system is so dilapidated that a large amount of the city's sewage, as well as a substantial quantity of its drinking water, is just seeping away into the ground.

Dresden's partner city of Hamburg had DM 3 million at the ready in the autumn of 1989 in order to buy a sewer-pipe cleaning machine, but it turned out that the machine only functioned properly in systems that were regularly maintained – not the case in Dresden. There are grounds for optimism, however: the first agreement under international law entered into by reunited Germany and Czechoslovakia in October 1990 involved protecting the Elbe.

In Rossendorf, 9 miles (15 km) away from the centre of Dresden, lies a nuclear research institute with three reactors designed in the 1950s and '60s. Radioactive isotopes for medical and industrial use are also produced here, and radioactive waste is processed within the institute.

The level of radioactivity is very high and whenever helicopters flew over Rossendorf the local inhabitants suspected that a cloud of radioactivity had escaped and was having to be dispersed from the air. They demanded that the entire installation be closed down.

German reunification has brought new environmental problems in its wake. The GDR's exemplary refuse processing system has ground to a halt, while the amount of refuse produced by the new consumer society has doubled within a very short space of time. Meanwhile, the number of private cars has also increased drastically: in the early 1990s, 200 new cars a day were being registered in Dresden, with a noticeable effect on the quality of the air.

Ecological thinking is something of a Dresden tradition, however. The Protestant church's ecological study group recently celebrated its 10th anniversary. With its discussion evenings, tree-planting sessions and question-and-answer services in the Kreuzkirche, the group had been active long before the Wall came down. Its greatest success was when it managed to block the construction (planned for 1989) of a silicon works.

The Wall has come down, but the ecological study group is still continuing with its efforts: "It's not the state we're working against, it's man's destructive effect on nature," they say.

restaurant and now nameless, to the **Jägerhof**. This long low building, all that remains of the original structure dating from 1568–70, is now surrounded by much taller new buildings but still stands out with elegant simplicity. Since 1913 it has been the home of the **Museum für Sächsische Volkskunst** (Saxon Folklore Museum), and includes a delightful display of toys from the Seiffersdorf area and an exhibition of typical Advent novelties from the Erzgebirge such as the pyramids of hand-carved figures that rotate when the candles on the bottom layer are lit.

The Ministries on the Elbe: Avoiding the roads, follow the right-hand bank of the Elbe upstream through the gardens of the **Königsufer** (Royal Bank). They were laid out in 1934, and culminate in a splendid rose garden. The path is lined with ministerial buildings of monstrous size – though doubtless not too large for the administration of Saxony. Follow the river bank to the point where the Priessnitz flows into the Elbe. The rather ordinary-looking Holzhofgasse does not immediately suggest historic significance, but it was here that E.T.A. Hoffmann wrote his novella *Der goldene Topf* and Carl Maria von Weber composed parts of the opera *Freischütz* and the first act of the opera *Undine*.

Palatial dairy: Walk down the Wolfsgasse to the Bautzner Strasse, where the first thing that catches the eye is a **shop** that started selling dairy products in 1892 (formerly the Pfunds Dairy). The contrast between the interior of this shop and its dismal surroundings is an indication of what this city was once really like. Its designers set out to make it beautiful in every detail in the fashion of the time. Everyday culture is the humus for works of artistic genius: even great palaces have their origins here. The salesroom of this dairy is decorated from floor to ceiling with tiles. Putti demonstrate in a series of pictures the various ways of processing milk and each scene is framed with a colourful Renaissance border. Whether this is **Kügelgen's studio.**

kitsch or not is a question of taste, but if so, it is of a most delightful variety. Unfortunately the shop was closed after the events of 1989, and the front is boarded up at the time of going to press so that it is not even possible to admire it through the window. The original owners, to whom the building was returned, fear speculators.

Melancholy Jewish Cemetery: Follow the Pulsnitzer Strasse round to the right, across Martin-Luther-Platz past the neo-Romanesque **Luther-Kirche** (1883–87), to a concealed cemetery which has not been used for 120 years. It is rare that the gate is even open – this is the former burial place of the Jewish community, which was allotted the site in 1751. Before then, the Jews of Dresden had been forced to bury their dead beyond Saxony's borders, in Teplice in Bohemia. Just a glimpse over the wall is enough to demonstrate what ephemerality really means; there can be few places in Dresden that exude such a sombre, melancholic atmosphere as this,

The Neustadt is popular amongst young people and artists.

whatever the time of year, whether it's raining or shining. The cemetery's state of oblivion was such that it even avoided destruction by the Nazis.

A few minutes away from this thought-provoking place, at Zittauerstrasse number 12, is another of Dresden's rare treasures which survived the successive destructions: **Kühl**'s, an art dealer's which specialises mainly in contemporary art. Here the old atmosphere of the art world has been preserved, a rarity today when most art dealing establishments are more like banks.

The Äussere Neustadt is surrounded by a ring of **barracks**, which ironically survived the war and are still used for their original purpose. Soviet and German soldiers currently continue to share the buildings of the former garrison town built during the reign of King Albert (1873–1902). One of the barracks in this military complex, however, accommodates the **Sächsische Landesbibliothek** (Saxon Library), epitomising the powerless mind surrounded by

mindless power. The book museum is worth a visit.

Halting the decline: In spite of the original intention merely to describe the main features to be seen on a walk through the Neustadt, there have been many historical deviations. The reason is that during the war the Neustadt, by contrast with the Altstadt, was not so extensively damaged and it is easier to reconstruct the city's past here. In the 1970s and '80s the redevelopment of the whole area was embarked on with great enthusiasm, which nevertheless ran out after only a single street (Strasse der Befreiung) had been completed.

A start was made on the area around **Martin-Luther-Platz**, but the degeneration of the old buildings was proceeding at a faster rate than that of the reconstruction. The houses were in official terminology "lived in free", a state of affairs made possible by the new housing estates on the periphery of Dresden. This was the final blow for buildings which were already at risk.

Many flats and an even larger number of houses stand empty, if they have not already collapsed or been pulled down; the decline of most of them began with something as simple as a broken gutter. The question is whether this district can still be saved.

Bunte Republik: In spite of all, however, the Äussere Neustadt lives on. As well as housing many old people, who still make up 40 percent of the population, it has become a magnet for students, artists, poets, musicians, actors and starry-eyed idealists of every hue; but also for the lonely and for people with alcohol or social problems.

To live in the Äussere Neustadt is to be part of the Dresden scene. Recently a few of the inhabitants founded – with a certain humour – the "Bunte Republik Neustadt" (Multicoloured Republic of Neustadt). The aim of this dedicated group, supported by large sectors of the population, is to preserve the special culture that has been gradually developing in this part of the city.

The "Goldener Reiter" (Golden Horseman) statue of Augustus the Strong.

HEINRICH VON KLEIST

Students of German literature who are familiar with Heinrich von Kleist (1777–1811) as *the* Prussian poet may be surprised to learn of his associations with Dresden. Initially only there as a visitor, he subsequently lived in the city for almost two years (1807–09), a long time in a short life.

Kleist's Dresden years were in addition a highly productive period of his life. The house he lived in was in the suburb of Pirna, in a street by the name of Äussere Rampische Gasse that is now the Pillnitzer Strasse. Not one of the houses in this street survived the bombs of the war. Only in the Museum zur Dresdner Frühromantik (Museum of Early Romanticism in Dresden) are there any references to Kleist's life in the city.

What, however, can books displayed in a glass case tell us by comparison with the actual place where he lived? We can therefore only learn about Kleist's life in Dresden indirectly, from the people he associated with, from his letters, from the existence of the journal of which he was a co-founder, and even more indirectly from the individual works he wrote during this period.

The novella *Michael Kohlhaas*, for example, was influenced by the situation in Dresden and contains some references to the Saxon electors as allies of Napoleon against the Prussians, while in the play *Käthchen von Heilbronn* the atmosphere and scenery is not that of Heilbronn, but of Dresden.

Kleist described his visit in Dresden in 1801 in a letter to his fiancée as follows: "I doubt whether there is another city where it is so easy and pleasant to amuse oneself as it is in Dresden. I have never been able to forget the dull world of the intellect as totally as I have amongst all the works of art here in this city. The art gallery, the sculptures, the antiquities cabinet, the cabinet of engravings, the church music in the Catholic church, all these are pleasures which do not involve the intellect, only the senses and emotions."

In 1803 Kleist paid a second visit to Dresden. During this stay he worked on his plays *Der*  *zerbrochene Krug* and *Robert Guiskard*, and drafted *Amphitryon*, which appeared in May 1807 in the Arnold bookshop in Dresden. He saw his old Potsdam friends Ernst von Pfuel and Johann Jacob Otto August Rühle von Lilienstern again, and made the acquaintance of the Councillor of the Consistorial Court Christian Gottfried Körner, and the painters Dora Stock, Ferdinand Hartmann, Gerhard von Kügelgen and Caspar David Friedrich.

It was the Berlin academic and writer Adam Heinrich Müller, however, who became a particular friend of Kleist's, and it was with him that he embarked on a productive venture. Together they decided to found a "book, card and art shop" by the name of "Phönix", because "publishers earn six times as much as authors".

When this plan was foiled by the established booksellers of Dresden they had a second idea: to found a magazine embracing "all the written and visual arts". However, all the people they invited to contribute refused: Goethe, Wieland, Jean Paul, Tieck and Schlegel, to name only a few, and Kleist and Müller were obliged to fill the magazine almost entirely with their own contributions.

A selection of the texts which Kleist contributed included an "organic Fragment" from the tragedy *Penthesilea*, the story *Marquise von O*, a fragment from *Der zerbrochene Krug*, one from *Robert Guiskard*, two from *Käthchen von Heilbronn*, one from *Michael Kohlhaas* and the idyll *Der Schrecken*. But the "Phönix" was too ambitious a project, and soon got into difficulties. The publishers were not journalists and the level of content was too intellectual to appeal to a wide public. The twelfth number of the journal, issued in February 1809, was its last.

However, for a long time Kleist had had greater things in mind. In April 1809 he confessed in a letter: "I too find that one must become fully involved, however great or small the contribution one can make, in the events of the time." He communicated secretly with the Prussian Reformers, siding with them against Napoleon in the Wars of Liberation – while Saxony was allied with Napoleon.

NEUSTADT'S MULTI-COLOURED REPUBLIC

Since 1990 Saxony has been allowed to call itself a "free state" again, but within this state is another, even freer: the "Bunte Republik Neustadt", the Multicoloured Republic of Neustadt (BRN).

The Republic was proclaimed in June 1990, and the celebrations in the streets and squares of the Outer Neustadt district between Alaunplatz and Bautzner Strasse lasted three days. In order to enjoy their festivities undisturbed, the citizens of this "Bunte Republik" simply sealed off their state territory and for those three days even circulated their own currency. A "Regular Provisional Government of the Bunte Republik Neustadt" met, and decided to intervene as little as possible in the affairs of the citizens of Neustadt.

A resident was appointed head of state: Gunther Neustadt. A "party-political, regional and biased" newspaper was issued called *Schild* (the well-known German newspaper *Bild* had just opened an office in Dresden), dated the first day of the first year of the Republic. It explained that the government was not prepared to take responsibility for anything or anyone but contained a useful map on which several new official buildings were marked.

Alternative forms of survival: The following statement was issued: "To make the Bunte Republik as colourful as its name, the provisional government has decreed that flags are to be flown on the occasion of the anti-state celebrations. You are reminded that the BRN flag has Mickey Mouse framed in a garland against a black, red and yellow background, with the 'swords to ploughshares' symbol on the reverse side".

Was all this just a joke, another example of how much the people of Saxony love celebrating? Not for the organisers from the Neustadt "scene" – their festivals are a symbol of the struggle for survival of an alternative culture.

A meeting place for squatters.

Under the communists the dilapidated houses of the Äussere Neustadt (Outer Neustadt), most of them empty, became a refuge for many dropouts, artists and critics of the regime. After the events of 1989 it was revealed how much creative potential had accumulated here. Brightly painted banners now fluttered from occupied houses and improvised galleries and cafés sprang up like mushrooms.

A say in redevelopment: The Äussere Neustadt has now been declared a redevelopment area, which both pleases and alarms its residents. Many are afraid that the planned measures will destroy the local culture that has developed here, as happened in the 1970s and 1980s in West German cities. The active residents are thus demanding a greater say than normal in what happens to their district.

The Äussere Neustadt still has a bad reputation within Dresden. Formerly it was a poor area, and today it is commonly identified with negative headlines which report yet another brawl between left-wing squatters and neo-Nazis. Is it, however, the fault of the Neustadt residents that they have become the target of young right-wing radicals from the dormitory towns? Their first priority is therefore to speak out, to get themselves noticed and show that in the midst of all the dilapidation there is a thriving local culture. Imaginative campaigns drawing attention to their situation are their only weapon. On the first anniversary of the republic therefore, they once again summoned the population to take part in elaborate festivities.

"We hereby announce that there are people who like living in Neustadt; people who are not going to be easily driven away and who also want to contribute to the preservation of this district; that in spite of the problems, we enjoy life and are not going to let it be spoiled by politicians and bankers etc., who think they can tell us what to do; that there are still people who dream of a free, united and just world, a world without weapons, pollution and consumer mania! Welcome to our festival!"

Black, red and gold and Mickey Mouse, mascot of the provisional government of the "Bunte Republik".

THE JEWISH CEMETERY

In the twilight zone between oblivion and dilapidation it continues its anonymous and sad existence in a small Neustadt street connecting the Pulsnitzerstrasse with the Priessnitzstrasse. Until January 1991 there was no indication either on the blackened sandstone wall or the entrance gate as to what lay hidden behind. The people of the neighbourhood used it as a rubbish dump.

The action group "Äussere Neustadt" (Outer Neustadt) then put up a plaque next to the entrance detailing the history of the place and soon the cemetery became a target for graffiti artists. A very obvious star of David is emblazoned on the wall, with "rest in peace" written beneath it. So it is no longer forgotten, no longer overlooked – and this in itself has generated new fears. It was its state of oblivion that preserved this cemetery from destruction by the Nazis.

Unhallowed ground: This cemetery was originally "On the Sands" – this at any rate was the name of the area that the Dresden Jews were allotted to bury their dead way beyond the city gates, after persistent negotiations with the city council and the monarch in 1751. The only other people who were buried here were criminals and suicides who had no right to a grave in Christian soil. Until then the Jews had had to take their dead to Teplice, and were frequently attacked on the way.

Augustus the Strong, who was very generous with those of other faiths when it was a question of expanding his own wealth and power, was also more liberal with the Jews than his predecessors. Although he intervened on numerous occasions, however, he could not persuade the council to give the Jews a cemetery. It was Count Brühl who finally succeeded.

Expensive burials: The Jewish community paid the city 1,000 talers for the cemetery. At the beginning they were not allowed to have a building on the land, the attendant had to be a Christian, and they were not permitted to hunt or collect wood in the forest. Twelve talers were charged for the burial of an adult and five for a child, while gravestones, at first prohibited, cost 20 talers. The dead were good business. The mourners at the burial ceremonies had to be silent, in order not to disturb Dresden citizens out walking on the heath. The first burial took place on 25 April 1751 – the deceased were a Jewish prisoner, who was killed during the building of the fortress, and the widow of the money-lender Isaak Meyer.

Later on the Dresdeners were still rejecting their fellow-citizens, the Jews, and in 1861 the inhabitants of the street bordering the cemetery pressed for its name to be changed from Judengasse (Jews' Alley) to Pulsnitzer Strasse. Eight years later the cemetery was closed; the heath surrounding it had become a new city district and a garrison, and the cemetery could no longer be extended.

However, in 1867 the community was assigned a new burial ground on Blasewitzer Strasse, and by then also had a synagogue again, which was built in 1840 by Gottfried Semper and destroyed in the pogrom of 1938.

Dresden initiatives: Today the old cemetery is a peaceful place overgrown with ivy. The stones are beginning to crumble. Surrounded by houses in "Gründerzeit" (late 19th century) and art nouveau style, it is an integral part of a fascinating world. Young architects and sculptors rescued one of the neighbouring houses that was about to be pulled down, and, together with friends from Hamburg, embarked on its reconstruction. It is now the meeting place of the Jewish History and Culture Society. In this area especially the state imposed numerous restrictions, and it is the aim of the group to tackle the many feelings these constraints produced. It hopes that through its work Jewish history will be prevented from slipping into oblivion again in this part of the world.

The Jewish Cemetery sank into oblivion long before the Nazis arrived.

LOSCHWITZ

The slopes of Pillnitz, Lössnitz and Meissen, with their ideal climate, are one of the northernmost wine-growing areas in the world; visitors are surprised to find themselves in the midst of a sunny, almost southern landscape.

In 1864 British writer James Boswell described it in his *Journal*: "This day I had a pleasant drive between Meissen and Dresden. We went along the side of the Elbe. On each side of the river were beautiful rising grounds covered with vines. Pray may we not have the same in Scotland? Surely our climate differs little from that of Saxony. I saw too, here and there, old castles, Heerschaften's houses, seats of gentlemen. It pleased me. It was Scottish."

Elegant living: Dresden's villa suburb of **Loschwitz** is on a broad bend in the River Elbe. Today it makes a popular weekend excursion for Dresdeners.

The city's patricians owned vineyards in Loschwitz as long ago as the 15th century. From the 17th century onwards, the buyers of vineyards were primarily aristocratic and bourgeois court officials. Everyone dreamed of having a second home here, including the court Kapellmeister Heinrich Schütz and Augustus the Strong's goldsmith, Johann Melchior Dinglinger, whose vineyard house (Schevenstrasse 59) has been preserved.

In his *Jugenderinnerungen eines alten Mannes* (Recollections of an Old Man), the Dresden painter and author Wilhelm von Kügelgen (1802–67) describes how his family spent the summer in a Loschwitz vineyard cottage: "From the top floor you looked on to a vine terrace and from there into the distance through the old walnut trees that protected the vines from the midday sun. It was a wonderful position, around three hundred feet above the Elbe, from which there was a splendid view of the colourful landscape, like something out of a dream. At least four miles of river were visible, together with the wide Elbe valley with the distant capital and hundreds of villages, churches and gleaming country seats, and finally, in the far distance, the ridges of the Erzgebirge and the mountains of Bohemia. Our father [the painter Gerhard von Kügelgen, 1772–1820] came with us to this heavenly place so that he could complete a number of unfinished pictures at his leisure."

The Councillor of the Consistorial Court, Dr Christian Gottfried Körner and his family, entertained their literary friends at their Dresden home and Loschwitz vineyard house (Körnerweg 6), where their generous hospitality, wise counsel and stimulating conversation were legendary. They gave financial assistance to Friedrich Schiller, who wrote *Don Carlos* in the Körners' vineyard summerhouse, in what today is Schillerstrasse.

In 1834 Loschwitz had a population of 1,500 and was the largest village in the Dresden area; in the 19th century it

became industrialised – primarily as a result of the establishment of the Leonhardi ink factory, which in 1901 had a workforce of over 500.

Loschwitz was connected with Dresden by the Elbe ferry to Blasewitz. The warehousing for the ferry, consisting of half-timbered buildings from the 17th century, is still standing today on the banks of the river. In 1893 the government architect Claus Köpcke built the remarkable **suspension bridge** from Blasewitz to Loschwitz, which for its time was an outstanding technical achievement. Its blue paint earned it the nickname "Blaues Wunder" (blue marvel – also the German expression for a surprise), a name it has kept ever since. The horse-drawn tram ran across the bridge to Königsplatz; this was replaced in 1896 by the electric tram.

Also at a very early stage, in 1895, a **funicular railway** was built from Körnerplatz to the top of the hill, a quick route from Loschwitz to the Weisser Hirsch. The cable railway, which also starts at Körnerplatz and goes to Oberloschwitz, was the first of its kind in the world, starting in 1901. it was initially steam-driven, but it has been powered by electricity since 1909.

The beautiful Loschwitz countryside also began to attract numerous painters, musicians and writers: Richard Wagner, Otto Ludwig and the music pedagogue Friedrich Wieck, following the marriage of his daughter Clara to Robert Schumann. The land became increasingly built up after the vine pest that ravaged the area from 1886 to 1889 had put an end to vineyards in Loschwitz.

Best villages: After World War I, it was decided that 20 further villages should be incorporated into the city of Dresden, but the city fathers would agree to this only on condition that Blasewitz, Loschwitz and Weisser Hirsch, which were taxed at a lower rate, were also included. Many of the citizens flew symbolic black flags, or flags at half-mast – all to no avail.

Beyond the top station of the railway,

Loschwitz, with elegant villas dating from the end of the 19th century.

on Zeppelinstrasse and the Plattleite is the research institute of Manfred von Ardenne which has a staff of 450.

The village of **Weisser Hirsch**, high up on the edge of the Dresdner Heide (Dresden Heath) next to Loschwitz, is located on Bautzner Landstrasse where it crosses a narrow valley on the bridge known as the Mordgrundbrücke and rises steeply to the plateau.

The visitor hearing the names Mordgrund and Stechgrund ("murder valley" and "stabbing valley") for the first time might be forgiven for thinking that Weisser Hirsch is a dangerous area. However, the name "Mordgrund", recorded as long ago as 1420, is probably derived from the Sorbian word "mokry" (wet), while Stechgrund was originally "Steggrund" ("Steg" meaning bridge).

The swiftly-moving stream which flows through the Mordgrund originates in the Bühlauer Waldgärten and soon joins up with the Elbe; at Weisser Hirsch it already cuts deep into the woods.

In 1686 the electoral Kapellmeister Christoph Bernhardi, a pupil of Heinrich Schütz, had a restaurant built on Bautzner Landstrasse, which received a licence in 1688 and was called the "Weisser Hirsch" after the albino or white deer shot by hunters on the Dresdner Heide in 1563. The restaurant served not just as a road-house for horse-drawn vehicles, but also as a meeting point for deer hunters.

When the water from the neighbouring heath was discovered to contain iron, people came here to take medicinal baths and cures. In 1873–74 the Dresden soap manufacturer Ludwig Küntzelmann bought the restaurant, added side wings to it and turned it into a proper sanatorium.

However, Weisser Hirsch only started to become a world-famous health spa when the young doctor Heinrich Lahmann bought the Frida Bath and opened his "Physiatric Sanatorium" in 1888. Here patients were treated by means of various health-promoting measures: baths, a low-fat diet, physical work-outs

Left, the Leonhardi Museum. **Right**, having a rest in the "Weisser Hirsch" district.

MANFRED, BARON VON ARDENNE

Baron von Ardenne lives in Zeppelinstrasse – even the street name denotes a happy state of suspension. "My life has proceeded like a Beethoven symphony, the Eroica, for example," said the Baron in his autobiography, written in 1987 when he reached the age of 80.

Von Ardenne works in a number of scientific fields, as a chemist, mathematician, astronomer, doctor and biologist, and accordingly has numerous doctorates, but they are all honorary ones.

At the age of 16 he received his first patent, at 17 he wrote his first book, and he has now written 34 books and published 678 scientific papers, while his patents number over 600. At the age of 30 he developed the scanning electron microscope and was responsible for the first electronic television broadcasts. At 40 he was working in the Soviet Union on the industrial isotopic separation process in order to obtain nuclear fission products, or in other words on the development of the atom bomb. With his earnings from this work and the Stalin Prize, which he was awarded in 1953, he founded the research institute which is named after him. In the most profitable period of its existence it had 500 employees, and produced new technologies in the fields of electronics, plasma physics and vacuum technology.

At the age of 60 von Ardenne shifted the focus of his research to the fields of medicine and biology and began to work for new methods of combating cancer. He is best known for the therapy by means of which the low oxygen content in the arterial blood of older people is restored to normal levels. On several occasions he has been awarded the Soviet state prize and the GDR national prize. He was a member of the Kulturbund (Cultural Union) group in the People's Chamber (the GDR parliament).

"Today people often speak of major achievements, when these are no more than normal technological developments," he said, criticising the "state of our economy" and morale in the GDR.

One problem that has preoccupied von Ardenne in particular is the role of the scientist in society. It is significant that, as he records in words and photographs in his autobiography, he was familiar with "many of the key figures in society", "actively supported the communist system", and was even "closely connected with our state". He almost certainly acted with an eye to procuring greater freedom and more money, since research is an expensive undertaking. "The responsibility of the scientist in the modern age", the title of one of his lectures, is undisputed, but so too are the limitations of scientific activity. The rather strange pronouncement by Johannes R. Becher, who wrote the words of the GDR national anthem, that "The opposite of a mistake is another mistake", is perhaps applicable to von Ardenne: has someone like him who was so closely connected with the last regime still got a chance?

"Take advantage of what the present has to offer," was always Manfred von Ardenne's advice to young people. This is what he himself has spent all his life doing, and in this way he has survived all the political and economic systems: the bourgeois, the fascist, the regimes of Stalin and Honecker. When Honecker was toppled, von Ardenne immediately supported Egon Krenz.

Since the demise of the communists' planned economy, he has been an advocate of the market economy and appears rather often in the company of the Minister President of Saxony, Kurt Biedenkopf, CDU, an "import" from the West. In 1985 he did strongly advise the former Central Committee member Egon Krenz to make certain changes designed to boost the market economy, but to no effect.

After the events of 1989 the von Ardenne institute was divided into three limited companies: 250 staff have already been dismissed. Professor von Ardenne is in charge of the medical section.

The palatial building in Weisser Hirsch, high above the city, is his home, and also contains the library, conference room, management office and most of the medical laboratories. Perhaps within its walls this scientist was rather too far removed from the realities of communism to have known how it really affected the people.

in the fresh air, communal living and psychotherapy.

By 1893 the sanatorium already had a total of over 1,000 guests, of whom around half came from abroad. It also included 10 villas in which the patients lived. Here the rule-breakers amongst them could easily adapt the rather austere cure to suit their requirements. If cabbage had been on the menu yet again, they ate outside the sanatorium as well to put some proper food in their stomachs, and here no-one could stop them smoking.

In 1927 a mineral spring rich in calcium hydrocarbonate was discovered. It was christened the "Paradise Spring" or "Weisser Hirsch Mineral Spring", and a series of pipes laid in 1928 carried the water to a pump room on Konzertplatz where it can be sampled today.

After World War II, when the Soviet Union commissioned the German-Soviet joint-stock company Wismut to mine uranium for its bombs, a "night sanatorium" was founded on these premises. Here the miners received medical treatment in the evenings, spent the night in the clinic and during the daytime exposed themselves once again to the radiation inside the mountain.

The Dresden Heath: This deciduous forest is the city's most important recreational area, but a long time ago sections of the large forested area consisting of the Dresdner Heide (Dresden Heath), Junger Heide and Friedewald were appropriated for military purposes, in particular from 1873 onwards, when a garrison town was built here.

The geological foundation of the forest area is granite and heath sand. The numerous streams are the most attractive feature of the Dresden Heath, in particular the Priessnitz, with its valleys cutting deep into the hilly landscape. In past centuries the heath was primarily used by the court for hunting, and from the mid-19th century on the forest was also commercially exploited.

The oldest network of paths across the heath dates from the 16th century

and lacks any specific pattern. More recent is the systematic network designed by Heinrich Cotta (1763–1844) and his son August, a system which was imitated all over the world.

The **Seifersdorfer Tal** valley in its beautiful setting with springs, ponds, a small cave in the rocks and an oak tree (no longer in existence) to commemorate the "Liberators of Germany" was once owned by an aristocratic family who used it to indulge their sentimental passion for nature. In the age of Romanticism and English-style landscaping, Countess Christina von Brühl and her husband Moritz landscaped the deep valley of the Grosse Röder that ran for a little over a mile (about 2 km) from the Grundmühle to the Marienmühle and beyond.

On an idyllic park meadow lively summer parties were held and birthdays celebrated, and there was a small semicircular open-air stage for amateur performances and musical events. Contemporary figures – Johann Gottfried Herder, Laura, Naumann, the singer of the valley – were honoured with temples, memorial stones, statues, busts and altars, and antiquity, which influenced the thinking of the day, was also commemorated: there was a Pythagoras lodge, an Amor memorial and a Petrarca lodge. Memorials were also erected to virtue, truth, friendship and the memory of good people.

North-west of Radeberg was one of the country estates of the ruling officials and officers, the **Seifersdorf manor**. This estate was acquired by the Saxon Prime Minister Count Brühl in 1747 when at the height of his power. The moated palace, built in 1531 in the Renaissance style, was redesigned by Karl Friedrich Schinkel from 1817 to 1822 in neo-Gothic fashion.

Today the romanticism of the Seifersdorfer Valley is a thing of the past, as the heavy pollution of the Grosse Röder by the industries around Radeberg takes its toll on the beautiful surroundings with their cultural monuments.

Below, picnic on the slopes above the Elbe, Schloss Albrechtsburg in the background. Right, rococo dancers from the Puppet Theatre Collection.

HOHENHAUSEN PUPPETS

On the window ledge of the lecture room in Radebeul perches the dainty figure of a woman. She is dressed in a tail coat and on her head is a top hat. From the overgrown garden a mellow green light falls on her white gloves, shirt front and soft features as she sits motionless, one hand in her lap. Her face is half turned towards the window, and her eyes with their heavy black lashes are lowered; her smiling red lips meet the curve of her painted black moustache at the corners of her mouth.

Out of the woman's back protrudes a yard-long stick; other inhabitants of the Puppentheatersammlung (Puppet Theatre Collection) are hollow and are moved by wires or dangle from strings. Beneath the ceiling of the entrance hall the clown riding on a winged dragon was once the star of a film. Death bares his teeth from a glass case, a gruesome figure made by a soldier in World War I.

An illustrious society has gathered in this house, including some familiar German puppet figures: Kasperl (the equivalent of Punch) and the robber, the grandmother, wizard and devil. There are marionettes produced by the Bauhaus, rococo-style dancing couples and their equivalents from the rock'n'roll era, a red-cheeked princess in Peking opera costume, Indonesian stick puppets and a jazz band that jiggles amusingly when a button is pressed. And under the roof, where several thousand puppets are crammed into crates and cases, a skater in a blue dress hangs on a nail: Katarina Witt, the skating star of the former GDR, as a puppet.

The house in the midst of the vineyards, with marionettes sprawling on the stairs, window ledges and old furniture, is known as the "Hohenhaus". It looks like one of the grand villas from the end of the 19th century, but under the white plastering the walls are made of felsite and go back 500 years. The Bishop of Meissen once resided here and at a later date the poet Gerhart Hauptmann and his brothers were frequent visitors to the house, marrying three of the five daughters of the then owner, the rich wool merchant Berthold Thienemann from Kötschenbroda. From that time on Gerhart was free of financial worries and was able to devote himself without pressure to the writing for which he became famous.

After the death of Thienemann in 1885 the house was rebuilt by its new owners in typical end-of-century German style – no other house in the whole of the former GDR has such a well-preserved interior from this epoch. It is not really a suitable place for exhibiting and storing the puppet collection, as it is already a museum in itself.

In the neo-baroque "White Drawing Room" there is only space for a few paper theatres, which are so small that they fit into a suitcase. The dark tea room with its marquetry can only just accommodate two glass cases of puppets from Asia.

"We have 37,000 exhibits in the collection," says the deputy director, "and can show only 400. Although we have puppets from every culture, our speciality is the complete history of the puppet show in Saxony from the 18th century onwards. Practically none of this can be shown."

The house is more than just a museum: it specialises in the theory and practice of producing a puppet show. There is a specialised library covering every aspect of the subject; people come here to research their doctorates and for 30 years the Hohenhaus has published its own academic journal.

Teachers come with their pupils to seek advice. The staff of the museum go on visits to demonstrate theatre techniques and invite puppeteers to the museum. Between May and October there is a family day with a puppet show on the last Sunday of the month.

Once a year, on a Sunday in autumn, the Hohenhaus (Barkengasse 6, tel: 74373) organises a "Kasperiade". The garden is decorated with garlands and coloured scraps of cloth, and large puppets are perched on the walls and stone sculptures. There is coffee, cakes and Meissen wine. The deputy director demonstrates 19th-century marionettes which perform circus tricks and a number of puppet theatre groups set up their stages under trees a hundred years old. The children squeal as the dragon appears behind Kasper's back and boo the witch, while their elders look on nostalgically.

WEBER AND WAGNER

Carl Maria von Weber and Richard Wagner, two important figures in the history of Dresden, made Dresden's opera and orchestra famous all over the world and gave both the musical life of Dresden and German opera a new national significance. *Freischütz*, *Tannhäuser* and *Lohengrin* were composed in Dresden and the city's beautiful surrounding countryside, and introduced a new folklore element involving a wide range of hitherto untapped sources.

In around 1820 Weber lived and worked in Hosterwitz, and in 1846 Wagner had a home in Graupa near Dresden-Pillnitz. Both houses are now evocative museums. They are also the only preserved residences of the two masters in the eastern part of Germany and a mecca for anyone interested in music, professional or amateur.

Carl Maria von Weber (1786–1826) is probably best known as the composer of the German folk and national opera *Der Freischütz*, a work of enduring popularity. Today the opening of the aria, *Durch die Wälder, durch die Auen*, is the signature tune of Saxon Radio Dresden.

German national opera: When Weber became Kapellmeister to the Saxon King Frederick Augustus I in 1817, the songs he wrote after the Napoleonic Wars of 1813–14, especially *Lutzows wilder, verwegener Jagd*, based on a text by the liberation poet Theodor Körner, established him as the nation's song-writer and he was soon a popular figure throughout Germany.

During his time in Dresden and up until his death he concentrated on his own personal mission: the creation of a German national opera. The material for *Freischütz* was drawn from German legends and the main roles are played by the German forest, peasants and hunters. Even the score is in the spirit of folk music, although the composer does not use or imitate folk themes directly. Initial moves in this direction had already been made by Mozart with *The Magic Flute* and Beethoven with *Fidelio*, but it was Weber who in fact created the first purely German opera, *Der Freischütz*.

It was on account of *Freischütz* that Weber fell out with his old friend, the lawyer Friedrich Kind, who wrote the libretto. Instead of the tranquil initial scene suggested by Kind, Weber, on the recommendation of his wife, began the opera with a folk scene of great dramatic effect.

Battles with Italians: At the court theatre Weber was forced to maintain his position against his Italian colleague Francesco Morlacchi, and initially even had to fight for equal status as court Kapellmeister. In those days Dresden was the bastion of "Italianism". Morlacchi ordered rehearsals at times reserved for Weber or engaged musicians from the latter's ensemble. The king, together with his entire court, often demonstrated his low opinion of Weber by

staying away from performances organised by him, took back commissions for compositions, such as the music ordered for the wedding of the prince who, as Frederick Augustus II, subsequently became Wagner's employer, and on the birth of Weber's first daughter insulted him by sending only a valet and lady's maid to congratulate him instead of the chamberlain and a lady-in-waiting. It is typical of the attitude towards him that the operas he wrote in Dresden were premiered not at the Royal Saxon Opera House, but in Berlin, Vienna and London.

Inventor of the baton: Weber experienced his greatest difficulties when he tried to improve the seating arrangement of the orchestra. As conductor, he wanted to be able to see all the players, but the king rejected the new arrangement. However, the orchestra supported Weber and he eventually had his way, since his idea was also more practical.

Weber was the first to use the baton in order to demonstrate to the orchestra what he actually wanted. Previously the most important entries were given on the piano, and otherwise the musicians followed the leader of the orchestra. The constant quarrels were particularly detrimental to Weber's health, which had not been good since his youth.

A new source of hope was unexpectedly provided when the Webers discovered the charming vineyard house in **Klein-Hosterwitz** while out walking in June 1818. For the whole of each summer, when the work in the vineyard was in full swing, the couple subsequently rented several rooms on the first floor; here Weber had all the time he needed to work, go for walks and receive visitors.

Among his guests were the composer Louis Spohr, the young Heinrich Marschner, members of the Italian opera company including the castrato Sassaroli, and the banker Abraham Mendelssohn, who sometimes brought his 10-year-old son Felix with him to the house in the vineyard.

In the nearby Keppgrund Weber rolled up his sleeves and played skittles with the valets, lieutenants and villagers, and it was on the piano of the local Keppmühle restaurant that he first played his *Invitation to the Waltz* to his friends; this was dedicated to his wife, whom he had met in Prague and who supported him faithfully to the end of his days.

Creative phase: In this peaceful, happy atmosphere Weber completed the overture for the king's 50th jubilee, then went on to compose some of his most beautiful romantic songs, large sections of the operas *Freischütz* and *Euryanthe* and the first part of *Oberon*. In May 1820 he completed *Freischütz*, which was first performed in the Berlin Schauspielhaus in June of the following year. It was an immediate triumph, and the most memorable of its melodies became popular hits.

Much care has been devoted to the arrangement of the rooms in the **Weber Museum** of Hosterwitz with its treasure of documents illustrating the life and work of the master.

After Weber's death, the high standard of the Dresdner Kapelle and the theatre was maintained by Heinrich Marschner and Carl Gottlieb Reissiger. They were followed by Richard Wagner, who was full of ambitious ideas: although his historicising opera *Rienzi* had been persistently rejected at the Paris Grand Opera, by the time he arrived in Dresden in April 1842 preparations for a production were already in full swing. It was first performed in October 1842 in the court opera house of Gottfried Semper, which had just been completed, and was his greatest success during his lifetime.

High expectations: Wagner became court Kapellmeister and seemed to be established. However, the premières of the operas *The Flying Dutchman* and *Tannhäuser* met with only qualified success, and even the singers – top performers from all over Germany – had difficulty singing the works the way the master wanted.

His life was further complicated by

frustrations of a quite different nature. His repeated "Memorandum concerning the Royal Orchestra" proposed a rise in the wages and number of the musicians in order to improve the social status of this famous institution, which, with great reverence, he described as the "wonder harp". However, all his efforts met with the resistance of the central management.

He also had continual financial problems, and he was pursued by former creditors from Magdeburg, Königsberg and Riga. On more than one occasion his friend and doctor Anton Pusinelli had to help him through the worst of his debts.

Retreat to Graupa: Thus, after a "repulsive winter" (1845–46) Wagner decided to take a holiday in rural seclusion in order to recuperate physically and mentally. In mid-May 1846 he moved beyond Hosterwitz to Gross-Graupa by the Borsberg. He was the first city-dweller to live at the large farm belonging to the Schäfers, and the children of the family formed a guard of honour as court Kapellmeister Wagner and his wife Minna moved into their lodgings on the first floor.

He was inspired by the Bastei in Saxon Switzerland to write *Lohengrin*, which he drafted in Graupa. His friends visited him frequently and music sessions often took place in the hallway of the house.

In 1843 he performed the *Liebesmahl der Apostel* in the Frauenkirche with Saxon male-voice choirs; later the mystical echoes produced in this church with its huge dome inspired him to create the work of his old age, *Parsifal*.

German legends: In 1847, after moving into the Marcolinische Palais in Friedrichstadt (now the district hospital), he immersed himself in the re-translation of German legends and a study of ancient dramatic art, primarily that of Aeschylus, and conceived the "intoxicating image of an Attic day of tragedy".

On the basis of this he developed his idea of reviving the theatrical Gesamt-

Carl Maria von Weber fled city life to this house in Klein-Hosterwitz.

kunstwerk (whereby all the arts are united in one work) and recreating it in the spirit of his age. The ideas for all the work Wagner produced after 1849 were first formulated in Dresden.

The high point of his administrative endeavours was his draft plan for a reform of the theatre in Saxony, including the establishment of a festival theatre and an educational institution for young musicians, which he submitted in 1848. When this too was rejected and he became increasingly isolated, he felt that only a revolution would make his work acceptable. What he had in mind, however, was radical, intellectual and moral change rather than bloodshed.

He therefore published anonymous articles, made stirring speeches to the Dresden Fatherland Society and, when the May uprising began, risked his life distributing leaflets, stuck posters demanding reconciliation on the barricades and, from the tower of the Kreuzkirche, where he was exposed to Prussian sniper fire from the lantern of the Frauenkirche,

sent signals informing the provisional government (which included the Russian anarchist Bakunin) in the town hall of approaching volunteer troops.

In flight: Wagner narrowly escaped being taken prisoner while accompanying revolutionary troops, by fleeing through the back door. After the May uprising was crushed he took his wife Minna to relatives in Chemnitz and fled, first to Franz Liszt in Weimar and then, when the authorities started looking for him, to Zurich. Here he continued to develop the ideas of his Dresden years.

The fascinating subject of Richard Wagner and Dresden is covered in detail in the Richard Wagner Museum in Graupa with its many valuable memorabilia and documents. Portraits and theatre programmes, letters and manuscripts are a mine of information about the first generation of Wagner interpreters and their successors, and about Wagner's friends and sponsors, with the inevitable curio corner providing a final humorous touch.

Left, the "Church in the Vineyard" was built by Pöppelmann in 1723. Below, ferry quay near Pillnitz.

DRESDEN CAKE

One of Dresden's major claims to fame the world over is its *Christstollen*, or Christmas cake. For years now, in many different countries, Christmas without it would be like Easter without chocolate Easter eggs.

The *Stollen* season begins in early autumn in Dresden, and way before any of the country's housewives have even started thinking about what to bake for Christmas, many *Christstollen* are already wending their way overseas from more than 20 different Dresden bakeries, in order to arrive on time for their recipients in Africa, Japan or America, or to give the crews on German ships the world over a taste of home.

The *Stollen* was first mentioned in a document dated 1486. Popular only in Dresden at first, it soon started getting sent to destinations all over Germany, and was first sent abroad at the end of the 19th century.

There are only very few countries left in the world now where a *Dresdner Christstollen* isn't proudly sliced at Christmastime. Neither World War II, when Dresden virtually died under Allied bombings, nor the gloom of socialism after 1945 have managed to erase this particular East German speciality.

The secret of the *Stollen*'s international success? If you try to track down the traditional recipe in Dresden you'll be given evasive answers; nobody wants to give away any secrets. Of course, they'll happily tell you what every baker knows – that the *Stollen*'s dough contains exotic spices as well as the normal mixture of flour, milk, butter and carefully selected raisins and almonds. They'll also tell you in unison that the correct choice of ingredients and above all the way you make it is absolutely crucial.

No other cake needs such careful preparation as a *Christstollen*. Its makers need to be strong, thoroughly trained and used to a punishing routine. It's a matter of honour and tradition for Dresden bakers that the dough be laboriously kneaded, shaped, and then finally buttered and sugared by hand – which amounts to quite a bit of work if you consider that five million kilos of *Stollen* are produced annually.

In this age of foil wrappers and refrigeration systems one wonders how such a perishable commodity as this managed to survive what were often weeks of being transported across the world. In the olden days, the *Stollen* which were destined for tropical countries and the US were placed inside welded metal cases, which in turn were packed inside wooden crates.

An account by one of the oldest producers of Dresdner *Christstollen* reveals that: "Every evening Herr Fiedler, the plumber who lived in the Zahngasse, used to come and weld shut the cases we used to prepare daily, and his visit was usually accompanied by a lengthy chat... We children always used to marvel at the addresses, and would pull out our atlas to look for the strange places on the map. We would picture the black porters carrying *Christstollen* through the jungle – something that actually happened quite often."

Social life in the Kingdom of Saxony was noted for its high level of culture and sophistication. The patrician families used to keep a clean house, and they ate excellent food. This meant in turn that the bakeries had high demands placed upon them. No wonder that, from 1871 onwards, Dresden developed its own flourishing chocolate and confectionery industry. Saxons are famous for their sweet tooth; in the old days if a father wanted to give his children a special treat he would take them on an outing to one of the city's famous bakery-cafés.

In recent years, bakers from outside the city and industrial bakeries have taken advantage of the cake's growing popularity to develop their own so-called *Dresdner Stollen* using their own individual recipes.

It's not hard to understand why the 20 businesses that make up the bakery business in Dresden founded the "League for the Protection of *Dresdner Stollen*", and has had the name *Dresdner Stollen* registered at the patent office. The aim of this legal protection is to ensure that, in future, the proper *Dresdner Stollen* can only be produced in bakeries located in the Saxon capital and its surrounding areas.

PILLNITZ PALACE

In the midst of a landscape dotted with traditional Saxon villages, the royal summer residence of **Pillnitz** is a highly exotic phenomenon. It is the creation of Augustus the Strong who was inspired with the idea of building an "Indian summer residence" here on the banks of the Elbe 7½ miles (12 km) south-east of Dresden and furnishing it with articles imported from Turkey and Persia.

The old palace: The complex was built in 1720 alongside the old palace of Pillnitz, a late Renaissance building which – suitably distant from the royal capital – had served both Augustus the Strong and his predecessor Elector Johann Georg as a country seat for their mistresses. These beautiful women both met with tragic ends: one died at the age of 18 in 1694 from smallpox; the other, Augustus's mistress Anna Constantia von Cosel, was imprisoned in 1716 at the age of 36 in the inhospitable Burg Stolpen for her involvement in political intrigues.

The baroque palace: Pillnitz is the work of a team of architects. Most of it was designed by Matthaeus Daniel Pöppelmann, the imaginative creator of the Dresden Zwinger, while the elements of French neo-classicism with their restful two-dimensionality and clarity, particularly evident in the outline and the facade, were introduced by the court architect Zacharias Longuelune. In 1720 the prince, with his penchant for grandiose projects, had already started issuing instructions from his Warsaw residence concerning a "major plan" for an enormous area between the river and the Elbe heights. The final result in 1724 after four years of building took up only about a sixth of this area and consisted of the present pleasance (secluded garden) and the central pavilions of the Water and Hill Palace.

The most immediately noticeable features of Pillnitz are the strange form of its roofs and its attractive setting on the river. Court architecture in the late baroque age frequently tended towards the exotic, and today Pillnitz is the most important architectural example of the fashion for all things Chinese that first made its appearance in the mid-17th century. The curved "pagoda roofs", the chimneys shaped like lanterns and the decorative Chinese scenes on facades and cavettos are all examples of chinoiserie, which in this case was obviously influenced by the decorations found on East Asian porcelain.

Dreams of Venice: Since it was to be sited on the river, the architects decided to design the Water Palace with its front facing the Elbe. Here, where the complex opens out with a wide flight of steps and a small gondola harbour, the magnificent architecture is seen to its best advantage. In front of the south facade a double flight of steps leads up to the main floor of the palace, where the doors of the banqueting hall were once flung wide to receive the prince's

guests as they alighted from the ceremonial gondolas. These were copies of the Venetian gondolas: Augustus wanted to turn the river into a second Grand Canal, and was soon holding Venetian-style festivals on the Elbe featuring magnificent displays of fireworks, masquerades and water music.

Between 1788 and 1791, four long wings roofed with copper were added to both baroque palaces by the architect Christian Traugott Weinlig. The extensions were built to accommodate the numerous court officials who came to Pillnitz when its status was raised to that of electoral summer residence.

Colourful stucco decoration in the post 1790 "Zopfstil" (the rather stiff transitional style between rococo and neo-classicism in Germany) has been preserved in some of the ground-floor rooms of the Hill Palace.

The 1791 Pillnitz Convention: The new palace wings were dedicated in 1791 with a political event of European dimensions, when the rulers of Prussia, Austria and Saxony met to draw up a joint plan of action for combating the revolutionary regime in France. This is the background to the somewhat enigmatic pronouncement of Napoleon on his visit to Pillnitz in 1812 that he "was born here".

The new palace, a square building on the east side of the pleasance, was built exactly 100 years after the two baroque palaces. The architects were able to make a fresh start after a fire reduced the old Renaissance palace to ruins in 1818, and the new complex with its central banqueting hall and Catholic palace chapel blends in well with the older buildings. The interior is in the contemporary neo-classical style.

The domed hall and chapel were decorated by the Saxon Nazarene Carl Vogel von Vogelstein, who, though the court artist, was not blessed with overwhelming talent.

"The excellent palace park" was praised as such by a connoisseur of the place as long ago as 1741. It contained,

The oldest camellia in Europe is protected from frost by its own house.

in addition to "precious oriental art and ornamental buildings, many different types of entertainment for whiling away the time, roundabouts, running at the ring, and all manner of interesting contraptions for the enjoyment of the guest."

Today the richly varied park is a splendid illustration of the changing styles and tastes in the history of landscape gardening.

The geometric form of the baroque garden is represented by both the pleasance between the Hill and Water Palaces and the hedge gardens running to the east. The English park with its winding paths and artificial island in an artificial lake, which mirrors a small round temple, dates back to the sentimental age after 1778.

In accordance with contemporary fashions the park was extended into the surrounding countryside, and paths of a similarly sentimental design featuring artificial waterfalls, grottoes and a ruin were laid out in the Friedrichsgrund and up to the Borsberg.

The Chinese Pavilion, built in 1804 in the northern Chinese Garden, ranks as the best imitation of an East Asian building in Europe.

Nature and art together: Finally there are the areas of the park that reflect the botanic interests of certain of the princes: the Dutch Garden collects exotic plants from the former Dutch Cape Colony in South Africa.

As long ago as 1770, what is now the oldest and **largest camellia in Europe** was brought to Pillnitz from Japan. It is now a massive tree 26 feet (8 metres) high and many visitors come to Pillnitz just to see it, especially in early spring, a riot of light red blossom.

Today people come to Pillnitz Palace for its art and the relaxing atmosphere of its charming surroundings. The Hill and Water Palaces are the location of the **Museum für Kunsthandwerk** (Museum of Arts and Crafts) with an exhibition of precious objects beginning with the Gothic age and continuing to the present day.

THE GARDEN CITY OF HELLERAU

"Fifty years ago everyone knew what Hellerau was and what it signified", says writer Peter de Mendelsohn. Today the progressive settlement, built around the turn of the century and modelled on the "garden cities" of England, is far from being the famous place he remembers. Anyone unfamiliar with the term "garden city" might be forgiven for associating it with allotments, but nothing could be further from the truth: the idea on which it was originally based is a comprehensive concept reflecting a whole philosophy of life.

What was planned at Hellerau and what was actually achieved is described with a certain amount of cynicism in the last GDR Dresden guide published by the VEB-Tourist-Verlag in 1989: "This was a typical bourgeois reform movement, the purpose of which was to gradually remove certain 'inadequacies' of capitalism such as exorbitant rents, poor housing and inhumane working conditions by means of model businesses in which the workers participated in the management, but above all by means of houses built on a cooperative basis in green surroundings and a natural, healthy way of life and culture."

It would have been paradise for the citizens of the German communist state, but its leaders allowed this alternative to both capitalist and communist town planning to fall into ruin, since the Utopian reform project contradicted official ideology. At the beginning of the century both the dream and the reality went even further than the above description: the settlement developed to become a forward-looking artists' colony, attracting visitors from all over Europe. Hellerau offered a humanistic alternative to the crowded industrial landscape of the late 19th century.

Pioneering ideas: To reach Hellerau, leave Dresden on Königsbrücker Strasse (still Otto-Buchwitz-Strasse) in author

Erich Kästner's home district; after a few kilometres the road enters the pleasant, pine-studded landscape of the Dresdner Heide and signs point the way to the settlement, which was incorporated in the city of Dresden in 1950.

The pioneering idea of creating a self-contained settlement built according to particular architectural principles is based on the theories put forward by the Englishman Ebenezer Howard (creator of Welwyn Garden City) in 1898 in his book *Garden Cities of Tomorrow* and became reality through the endeavours of the cabinet-maker Karl Schmidt (1873–1948). A man of taste and imagination who was aware of the range of his craft and familiar with the English reformist spirit, Schmidt developed his inner-city workshop into a highly successful business, thereby earning for himself the nickname of "Holz-Goethe" (Wood Goethe).

In search of further means of expansion outside the city he acquired the land between Klotzsche and Rähnitz,

then an agricultural area, and commissioned the Munich architect Richard Riemerschmid (1868–1957) to do the basic planning. The mixture of architectural styles that characterised the settlement of Hellerau ranged from the country-house cosiness of Riemerschmid to the objective formal severity of Heinrich Tessenow (1876–1950) and the "English" style of Hermann Muthesius (1861–1927). They designed the area of small houses and the villa quarter, the welfare facilities and the factories.

Humane production: The factories were the most urgently needed of all the facilities and here Riemerschmid produced something resembling a huge manor estate where the working quarters were grouped around a self-contained farmstead. Instead of the usual dull factory building he created a lively industrial complex which blended in with its surroundings and also provided an extremely healthy working environment. By 1910 the factory complex was ready for use. Next to it Riemerschmid

built the area of small houses known as "Am grünen Zipfel" with its rural air and attractively varied streets featuring small groups of low terraced houses, front gardens, green shutters, jutting corners and art nouveau door handles. In 1911 Riemerschmid completed the spacious market square with its small businesses and shops.

Two further contributors also left their mark on the settlement. The Berliner Muthesius built 14 groups of terraced houses in the English country-house style, more austere and less idyllic than the other buildings. Hellerau thus became an "island of salvation from the tenement house", and the "first completely valid example of a model settlement on German soil" (Muthesius), but also a homely workers' settlement with a vibrant atmosphere.

The alternative: The contribution of Dr Wolf Dohrn (1878–1914), an energetic, sensitive and sophisticated young man from an academic family, was of a cultural nature: his dream was to turn

Terraced housing in English style built by Muthesius.

Hellerau into a metropolis of alternatives. With the founder of the settlement Karl Schmidt he went to a performance by the Geneva dance teacher Émile Jaques-Dalcroze (1865–1950), who made a lasting impression on both of them. Dalcroze saw music as a force which ennobled human existence on the intellectual, spiritual and physical plane; instead of the conventional gymnastic drill he trained his dancers to express musical rhythms through bodily movements. Dohrn engaged Dalcroze at Hellerau in order to promote his ideas to the "level of a social institution". In addition he commissioned Tessenow, after his successful work on the housing settlement, to build a festival theatre, surrounded by a widely spaced ring of guest houses.

Place of pilgrimage for artists: Soon an illustrious society of artists had gathered at Hellerau, and there was even a publishing house, founded by Jakob Hegner of Vienna. In October 1913, the medieval miracle play *L'Annonce fait à Marie* by Paul Claudel (1868–1955) was performed in the new festival theatre to a select public that included such famous names as Gerhart Hauptmann, Max Reinhardt, Oskar Kokoschka, Rainer Maria Rilke, Franz Kafka and even George Bernard Shaw. The Russian theatre reformer Stanislavski worked here, and Mary Wigman acquired one of the first diplomas in dance.

However, after the sudden death in an accident of Wolf Dohrn in February 1914 the colony collapsed. The festival theatre had one last moment of glory in 1920 when Alexander Sutherland Neill, the Summerhill pedagogue, presented his repression-free education.

Since 1937 Hellerau has been a barracks. The recently founded "Förderverein Hellerau" is now hoping to revive the world reputation of the derelict complex, so that it will once again be as Lanny, hero of the novel *World's End* (1940) by the North American writer Upton Sinclair described it: "The most wonderful place I have ever been to."

Sunday is wash day in Hellerau.

In the chapters that follow, the key uniting figure is Augustus the Strong. The first chapter features one of the places – Haus Hoflössnitz, near Radebeul – that Augustus confiscated, just as he did everything that he felt would somehow suit his philosophy of life. Wine festivals were definitely part of court life, and Hoflössnitz was just the place. For bigger events Augustus made use of the Moritzburg – the favourite spare-time destination of Dresdeners – in order to have homage paid to himself and his absolutist power. And as for Meissen: well, it all had to be financed somehow. Since nothing more could be squeezed out of the farmers, he was banking on artificial gold produced by alchemists. In fact, the result was porcelain. Not bad, considering.

The following chapters could actually all come under the heading: "A trip round Dresden with Augustus the Strong". It was only a few miles from Pirna that Augustus completed the baroque pleasure garden of Grosssedlitz, which had formerly belonged to the Count of Wackerbarth.

Naturally, Augustus was more than familiar with the Sächsische Schweiz – "Saxon Switzerland". One of the tourist attractions, the 250,000-litre barrel of wine in the fortress of Königstein, was only ever filled to the brim once. By whom? Augustus, of course. Burg Stolpen, however, is one of the darker chapters in Augustus's life. It was in that forbidding castle that he left his mistress and confidante of many years, Constantia von Cosel, without paying the slightest attention to the unswerving fidelity she showed him.

Limiting the area around Dresden to Augustus alone, however, would be somewhat short-sighted. Goethe was here too, of course. In the long letter he wrote to his wife, Christiane, he shows that gift of precise observation with regard to social life that always provided him with subject matter and gives us a vivid impression of daily life in the Meissen of the day.

In the following pages, Bernd Arnold, eastern Germany's best-known climber, describes how people in Saxon Switzerland have developed and retained their own special climbing methods (see *Rock Climbing*). This region is also the home – astonishingly enough – of the "Moravian Brotherhood", a religious community famous throughout the world for its missionary activities.

And finally there are the Sorbs, rather better known to the majority of people as the only Slav minority in Germany. Like many people in Saxony, they are hoping for a lively, yet properly controlled development in tourism – which will provide their income while leaving nature in presentable condition at the same time.

Preceding pages: the Bastei in Saxon Switzerland in the wintertime; the rooftops of Meissen; Schloss Moritzburg. **Left**, Sorbian Easter traditions.

Dresden and Environs

4 km / 2.5 miles

Großdobritz

Naunhof

Radeburg

Steinbach

Bärwalde

Zehren

Diera

Berbisdorf

Gröbem

Winkwitz

Niederau

Meisatal

Weinböhla

Moritzburg Palace

Cathedral

Auer

Moritzburg

Market

B.

Meissen

Porcelain
Manufactory

Korbitz

Jahna-
Löthain

Sieben-
eichen

Coswig

Garsebach

Reichenbach

Scharfen

Brockwitz

Elbe

Zitzschewig

Reichenberg

Kötzschen-Broda

Gauernitz

Radebeul

Lössnitz

Sönitz

Röhrsdorf

Heynitz

Taubenheim

Weistropp

Kaditz

Mobschatz

Mickten

Burkhardswalde-
Munzig

Klipphausen

Brabschütz

Briesnitz

Limbach

Wilsdruff

Gompitz

Tanneberg

Löbtau
Resterwitz

Triebisch

Grumbach

Helbigsdorf

Braunsdorf

Cosc

Neukirchen

Niederhermsdorf

Saalhausen

Döhlen

Mohorn

Freital

Dittmannsdorf

Grossopitz

Tharandt

Schweinsdorf

Kurort
Hartha

Weißeritz

Bobritzsch

Hetzdorf

Niederschöna

Rabenau

Poise
häuse

Grillenburg

Karsdo

Conradsdorf

Naundorf

Dorfhain

Höckendorf

Seifersdorf

196

Gr. Röder

roß-
nns-
dorf

Ottendorf

Medingen

Okrilla

Höckendorf

Oberlichtenau

Großnaundorf

Friedersdorf

LAUSITZ

HILLS

Pulsnitz

Lomnitz

Ohorn

Hermsdorf

Lichtenberg

Wachau

rsdorf

Weixdorf

Bretnig

Langebrück

Liegau-Augustusbad

Gross-Röhrsdorf

Friedrichstal

Klotzsche

Radeberg

Hellerau

Arnsdorf

Seeligstadt

eschen

Ullersdorf

Großerkmannsdorf

Weißer Hirsch

Loschwitz

Weißig

Wilschdorf

per
ra Hause
Zwinger

Blasewitz

Frauenkirche
Ruins

Tolkewitz

Schönfeld

Rosienendörfchen

Helmsdorf

Dresden

en

Mockritz

Dürrröhrsdorf

Strehlen

Laubegast

Palace

Zschachwitz

Pillnitz

Liebethal

annewitz

Niedersedlitz

Söbrigen

Graupa

Lohmen

Rippien

Lockwitz

Mügeln

Birkwitz-
Pratzschwitz

Hintercopitz

Possendorf

Heidenau

Borthen

Dorf Wehlen

to Bautzen

to Stolpen

to "Saxon Switzerland"

Brandmühle

Dohna

Market

Kreischa

Baroque
Garden

Groß-
sedlitz

Pirna

Elbe

Elbe

RADEBEUL AND MEISSEN

North-east of Dresden are three destinations popular with both the residents of the city and its visitors: Radebeul, Moritzburg and Meissen. A day can easily be spent in each of the three with their numerous attractions: Gothic and Saxon baroque architecture, Indian peace pipes, Indonesian stick puppets, old vineyards and peaceful lakes.

Meissen is best reached by S-Bahn, or, if time allows, by steamer down the Elbe, while Radebeul is on the tram network. Tram number 4 passes the Zwinger, the opera house and the Goldener Reiter and turns into Leipziger Strasse, an arterial road that follows an interesting route for several miles through some of the outlying districts of Dresden. At the Mickten tram depot it is worth alighting briefly to have a look at the old trams stationed here.

Radebeul is joined on to Dresden.

Created in 1924 through the combination of 10 country communities, and with a current population of 35,000, this town has no proper centre. The tram passes through several old village centres, and between them villas and gardens with greenhouses alternate with factories. In the south the town is bordered by the Elbe, in the north it fans out across the vineyard slopes of Lössnitz. Its landmarks are particular buildings that stand out along the vineyard ridge, especially the yellow Spitzhaus (today a restaurant) and the observatory on the Ebenberge, which has a small planetarium attached to it.

The tram stop by the old country restaurant **Weisses Ross** is a good place to alight and continue exploring on foot. At this point it is also possible to change on to the small local train to **Moritzburg**. It is an easy walk to the top of the vineyard ridge, past old wine-growing estates dating back to the 16th century. The Spitzhaus is reached by a flight of steps designed by the Zwinger architect Matthaeus Daniel Pöppelmann and popularly known as the Jahrestreppe (Year Steps), as there is a landing after every seven steps. From the top there is a panoramic view of Dresden.

Wine-growing: At the bottom of the Jahrestreppe is the **Weinbaumuseum** (Wine-Growing Museum) in the Haus Hoflössnitz, a "Hill and Excursion House" built in 1650 for Elector Johann Georg I. During the grape-picking season there were court excursions to this house, and Augustus the Strong organised wine festivals and wine-growers' processions. The people in charge of the museum in Haus Hoflössnitz are trying to revive this tradition and hold a wine festival every autumn.

The ceilings and walls of the half-timbered top floor are completely covered with paintings of birds and allegorical female figures; these frescoes date from the 17th century and are well worth seeing. A charming little exhibition illustrates the history of wine-growing on the warm southern slopes of the

Elbe valley. The first vines were planted by monks in the Middle Ages. An example of the vine pest that completely destroyed the vineyards in 1885 can be examined under a microscope. Since 1920 the barren slopes have been planted again, this time with pest-resistant American vines.

Thanks in particular to the efforts of the many amateur wine-growers, every year a few more square yards of disused vineyard land are planted. The grapes are pressed by the Sächsische Winzergenossenschaft (Saxon Wine-Growers' Cooperative) and the private growers receive a few bottles as payment in kind.

Even in the past, the farmers were not able to live from wine-growing alone: every third year the harvest fails and only every 10th year is a good wine year. Wine from Meissen and Radebeul is a rarity and in recent years almost the only place where it was to be found was at formal state receptions of the GDR government.

The Schloss Wackerbarth champagne company in Radebeul, which was originally government-owned, processes blended wine, most of it imported; the name is taken from a palace built in 1728–29 and set in a baroque park at the foot of the vineyards.

Indians and puppets: The **Karl May Museum** in the last home of this writer, the Villa Shatterhand, named after the hero of his stories about the Red Indians, draws up to 250,000 visitors a year to Radebeul. The Indian museum in the log cabin behind the villa has the largest collection in Europe of exhibits illustrating the life of the North American Indians.

With his gripping tales of lands and people he had never seen, Karl May was Germany's answer to Henry Rider Haggard. But up until 1984 his name was ostracised in the GDR. His books were out of print until somehow he was rehabilitated as, in the official wording, a "communicator of high humanistic moral concepts". The popular interpretation is that Karl May was made re-

Meeting of the prairie Indians. Right, Karl May's work was never appreciated during his lifetime.

KARL MAY

A reader once wrote to Karl May: "I am a missionary – and so are you; my most treasured possessions here in the heart of Africa are the Word of God and your books." Heroes, adventurers and Christianity are the essential ingredients of Karl May's novels and imagined (travel) writing: no sex, no drugs, no rock'n'roll. How did he ever arrive at such an exotic fantasy world, especially since he did not even see Arabia and America until he was quite old? He was called a "splendid liar" all his life – and that was by those who were favourably disposed to him.

A psychologist would look for the answer in the author's early childhood, and in the case of May this would be precisely the right place to look. In his autobiography he writes: "Times were hard in the Erzgebirge. At midday we asked our neighbour for his potato peelings to make soup with and from the mill we got a few handfuls of flour dust and husks. We picked orache (edible shrubs) from the rubbish dumps, adder's-tongue from the banks and prickly lettuce from the fences to fill our stomachs."

Karl May's mother worked as a midwife, his father tried his luck dealing in pigeons, got through a small inheritance, and later set Karl to work copying prayer books and antique natural histories.

As a boy, Karl was fascinated by his grandmother's stories, and in particular by his godfather, who had travelled all over the world as a journeyman. "Everything he told us came alive and made a lasting impression on us, he had the special skill of making his figures say precisely what it would be good for us to hear."

He got to the teacher training college with the help of the village clergyman, where he was recorded as "a lout of good average achievement", but then stole six candles for his family at Christmas and was expelled. He asked to be pardoned and was taken back, passed his exams and became an assistant teacher, but this lasted only two weeks: during this period the 19-year-old was accused by his landlord of "trying to entice his wife away and have his wicked way with her".

Karl May became locked into a pattern of minor misdemeanours that continually got him into trouble. He also lost his next post after he was supposed to have taken a watch, and was sent to prison for six weeks. Less successful thefts – he had furs shown to him in a hotel and disappeared with them, but was soon caught – resulted in four years in the workhouse. "Scarcely was I back with my parents in Ernstthal than the temptations began again." This time he tried robbery and skilfully exploited the Saxons' faith in authority. As a "secret policeman" he went into shops and asked to look at banknotes, which he then declared to be forgeries and confiscated: four years in prison.

These experiences, however, by no means subdued him, and he began to create a fantasy world of increasing complexity, laying the foundations for his pastiche novels and subsequent (invented) travel novels, which were serialised in magazines.

Karl May's fantasies were so successful that the writer Peter Rossegger wrote: "This story about Egypt is so clever and exciting that the author must be a man of great experience who has lived in the Orient for a long time."

This was precisely what gave Karl May so many problems: the more successful he became, the more he claimed publicly to have experienced everything exactly as he described it in his works.

He called his villa in Radebeul near Dresden the "Villa Shatterhand" and furnished it with "souvenirs" from North America.

In his endeavours to present himself as a person of the calibre of his heroes, Old Shatterhand and Kara Ben Nemsi, he denied the sins of his youth and spun a web of lies around himself which even the trips he made to the Orient and later to North America were unable to make good. The hostility and derision of which he was the target, but above all the disputes over the copyright of his earlier works, resulted in exhausting court cases which went on for years. In 1912 he died of a heart attack. Berta von Suttner, the pacifist, said in his defence: "Anyone who has seen this handsome old man, solemn, passionate and full of high thoughts, must feel that in this soul burns the fire of goodness."

spectable again "so that the people could learn from Old Shatterhand how to love their red brothers".

Both exhibitions are rather sterile, and not really the best that Radebeul has to offer. In the interests of the many visitors it is to be hoped that they will soon be appropriately modernised.

Probably more fascinating – especially for children – than the Karl May house with its crowds of tourists is the **Puppentheatersammlung** (Puppet Theatre Collection) in the Hohenhaus, which has very few visitors. Like the Karl May Museum it cannot be missed from the tram, since the shelters at the tram stops have been painted by children with Indian and puppet figures.

The Hohenhaus in the midst of the vineyards was once the residence of the Bishop of Meissen, and it was here too that the poet Gerhart Hauptmann met his wife. No other house in the former GDR has such a well-preserved late 19th-century interior. The atmosphere of the rooms with their luxurious furniture, from which all stuffiness is removed by the marionettes, theatres and theatre programmes on display, is overwhelming. The old house is full of life: teachers come here with their pupils for advice and the museum staff go on visits to demonstrate old techniques and invite puppeteers to the museum. During the season, from May to October, there is a family day on the last Sunday of the month with a puppet show. The season ends with a big children's festival in the autumn, the "Kasperiade". To visit the collection it is necessary to make an appointment first.

Moritzburg: Everyone who goes to Moritzburg, the Dresdeners' favourite place for an outing, must make the journey at least once by train; the narrow-gauge railway was built in 1884 and is under a preservation order. The old railway carriages are pulled by a real steam locomotive, which is not one of the largest in existence, but compensates for that with the amount of smoke it produces and whistles constantly so that

Coach-ride in Moritzburg.

it is impossible to ignore. It wails through the woods like an aging ghost and is the acoustic symbol of the district. It is, of course, forbidden to stand on the platform at the end of the carriages to breathe in the mixture of forest air and engine smoke and admire the panorama of vineyards, villas, orchards, sheep, meadows and lakes. And people, of course, do it anyway, while the guard in historic costume obligingly looks the other way.

Moritzburg is connected with Dresden by a straight avenue of poplars. This is also the main street of the village and leads directly to the dam which crosses a lake full of reeds to the hunting seat of Moritzburg.

On the way, you come across the **Moritzburg Church**, an interesting architectural mix combining the baroque style of the palace and the art nouveau style fashionable when the church was built (1902–04). On the door is a note describing how the building, visible for miles around, narrowly escaped being blown up by the SS in 1945.

Schloss Moritzburg was used during the last ten years of Augustus the Strong's rule (1723–33) as a prestigious setting for feudal hunting parties. Around 100 aristocratic guests could be accommodated and lavishly feasted in the building with its four distinctive round yellow towers. The Schloss is named after Elector Moritz, who had a hunting lodge built on this spot in the mid-16th century.

After the death of Augustus his original plan to redesign the land around the Schloss was not completed; money was short and other projects were more important. The Schloss itself remained unaltered for the same reason and has been preserved as an impressive example of absolutist splendour. In recent years parts of the facade have been gradually restored, as far as the meagre funds have allowed. The current plan is to renovate the Schloss by 1994, at the cost of millions of marks – provided, of course, that sponsors can be found.

No better location could be imagined

Schloss Hoflössnitz near Radebeul.

GOETHE IN MEISSEN

In the spring of 1813 Johann Wolfgang von Goethe travelled via Leipzig, Wurzen, Oschatz and Meissen to Dresden. He described his experiences and impressions – as always on his journeys – in a letter to his wife Christiane. As usual for this observant author, no detail escaped him.

"We saw the beautiful Elbe Valley ahead of us glowing in the warm light of the evening sun and reached our quarters in the 'Ring' in Meissen on time. A widow with two daughters is running the inn in these hard times, and the youngest daughter with her happy disposition reminded me of you. She described the burning of the bridge very calmly and said how beautiful the flames had looked in the night. The collapsing bridge was carried away on the surface of the river still burning and landed at the wood yard, but since there was not a breath of wind, the flames were gradually extinguished.

"Tuesday 20th was a very pleasant and informative day. We went mainly to the castle and looked first at the porcelain factory, or rather at the stockrooms. It is strange and almost unbelievable that one finds very little there that one would like to have in one's own home. The problem is that they had too many workers (20 years ago there were over 700), and wanted to keep them occupied, so had large supplies made of everything that happened to be in fashion.

"Fashions changed, and they were left with the supplies. They did not dare auction these articles or send them to countries on the other side of the world for a very low price, so everything stayed here. It is the most fantastic exhibition of everything that is no longer popular and could never be popular again, and there are not just individual examples of each article but hundreds and even thousands of them. There are now just over 300 workers.

"For a number of reasons the cathedral is not attractive from the outside, but inside it is the most slender and beautiful building of its time that I have ever seen, not darkened by any monuments nor spoiled by an altar or pulpit, painted a yellowish colour and lit by clear glass panes, with only the one middle window of the choir made of stained glass. What I particularly noticed and was new to me, also in the choir, was the stone baldachin over the seats of the canons. Chapels and castles float in the air and religion alternates with the secular world of the knights. The decoration is most suitable, bearing in mind that the canons were descended from the knights of old. I made a drawing of it straightaway which conveys the whole idea in a way that cannot be done in words.

"At midday we ate carp in Polish sauce, which we had already particularly enjoyed the evening before. I went to see the piers of the burned bridge and left at 12.30. The sky was cloudy and the air cool but the sun came out frequently, so that we had a very pleasant trip.

We crossed the new pontoon bridge and then drove along the right-hand bank of the Elbe, which is unbelievably built up; at first there are just isolated houses, then for several hours they are continuous, forming an endless suburb.

"In the Neustadt we found everything in its familiar place, with the metal king still galloping intact on the same spot. In Weimar he lost an arm through the explosion of the bridge arch.

"While still half an hour away from the city we met many people out walking, even a lady reading, but on the bridge the third day of the holiday was really in full swing, with numerous ladies and gentlemen strolling up and down. The two arches of the bridge that were blown up have been replaced with a wooden framework, but this is not the same height as the stone bridge, so that it is necessary to ride down and then up again. The reason for this inconvenience is a mystery. The city itself was also full of life. There were Russians in Moritzstrasse waiting for a good billet.

"Captain Verlohren accommodated us on the first floor of his house, with Herrn Hofrath von Burgsdorf. It is extremely comfortable here, we are served well, and are eating splendidly and not too expensively in a nearby restaurant; our wine is still in good condition, the arrak, of course too… Now – I wish you well and hope to send further reports".

for the **baroque Museum**, which was accommodated here after the dispossession of the Wettin family in 1945. On display are – to quote the guide – "the biggest collection of red deer antlers in the world", furniture, paintings, porcelain and pottery. For all the twirls and flourishes of the baroque style, the rooms and exhibits never look showy – on the contrary, the overall impression is one of extreme elegance. On leather wallpaper that is very hard to preserve in its original state are mythological scenes featuring the goddess of hunting, Diana, and the ladies of the court and the royal mistresses are immortalised in a picture gallery. Augustus's hunting seat was known to his contemporaries as the "Dianenburg".

Käthe Kollwitz spent the last year of her life in Moritzburg and died on 22 April 1945 in Rüdenhof. There is a small exhibition in memory of this graphic artist and sculptress in the Schloss, and the house where she died has also been opened to the public.

The countryside around the Schloss with its numerous lakes and great variety of rare plants and birds is now a nature reserve. Footpaths lead to a stud farm, a game enclosure and the pheasantry, and there is also a little rococo palace containing an exhibition of stuffed birds, on the roof of which storks nest in the spring.

China town: The name **Meissen** is automatically associated with the world-famous porcelain with its hallmark of crossed swords. The town greets its visitors with a rather unattractive station, a bridge across the Elbe that rattles alarmingly, and conspicuous signs of dilapidation in the old town with its winding alleys.

Around 600 buildings are under a preservation order, but two-thirds of the houses in the **Altstadt** (Old Town) are in a deplorable condition. Meissen, the cathedral town with a thousand years of history, the birthplace of Saxony and one of the few historic towns in Germany that was not destroyed in the war,

Left, Goethe, unimpressed by the manufactory in Meissen. **Below left**, wine bar in the old town. **Below right**, alley in the old town.

was almost completely ruined by the centralistic building policy of the GDR.

People soon began to protest against what was happening: when, in 1987, Berlin was cleaned up for its 750th anniversary celebrations by building workers commandeered from all over the country, hand-painted cardboard signs were displayed on the local Trabants proclaiming "1058 years of Meissen".

In the meantime a committee has been formed to save Meissen and here and there modern scaffolding from the West adds a touch of colour to the town.

Most of the buildings round the **Marktplatz** (Market Square) date back to the Middle Ages, such as the late Gothic Rathaus (town hall) built in 1472 and the Frauenkirche (Church of Our Lady), a medieval building with an intimate atmosphere.

The first porcelain carillon in the world, with 37 bells, was installed in the tower in 1929. After two centuries of unsuccessful attempts to produce an operable carillon, this was finally achieved in time for the 1,000-year celebrations. In a half-timbered house next to the church is the wine restaurant **Vinzenz Richter**, which is in fact half restaurant, half museum (including a torture chamber).

Steps and steep alleyways lead up to the **Albrechtsburg**, which dominates the town. Next to it is the mighty Gothic **Cathedral** with its 263 feet (81-metre) towers. There was already a castle on this site in 929; the existing building, however, was constructed between 1471 and 1525 as a Wettin residential palace during the reigns of Elector Ernst and Duke Albrecht. It was built as a symbol of royal prestige rather than for defence purposes, and clearly anticipates the Renaissance style.

The brick cell vault, built without ribs, is fascinating with its endless play of light and shade that makes the architecture come alive. The largest rooms were painted in the 19th century with historical monstrosities which have less

Below left, the interior of Meissen cathedral. Below right, on the marketplace in Meissen.

to do with the Middle Ages than the image the people of the last century had of this period.

The **Meissen Porcelain Manufactory**, the first in Europe, was accommodated in the Albrechtsburg from 1710 to 1863. Its first director was Johann Friedrich Böttger, who invented European hard-fired porcelain as an emergency solution. A pharmacist's apprentice who had fled from Berlin, he was held at the court of Augustus the Strong and commissioned by him to make gold in order to improve the state finances, which were in a bad way as a result of his extravagant lifestyle. When the alchemy experiments failed, Böttger kept his head in more ways than one by inventing the "white gold".

In order to keep the formula secret, Augustus the Strong transferred production to the castle. Since there was not enough room for it even in these spacious premises, it moved in 1863 into the Triebischtal. In 1916 the firm opened its own **Porcelain Museum**, with an adjacent open workshop where visitors can admire the craftsmanship of the porcelain makers. Basic training takes four years to complete, and specialised training up to 10 years. Today the manufactory is a limited company and belongs to Saxony.

Even more fragile than the porcelain is the special sweet pastry known as the Meissner Fummel, the inside of which consists primarily of air. Augustus the Strong apparently had it made in order to ensure that the coachmen who transported the precious porcelain from Meissen to Dresden drove carefully. With every delivery of porcelain they had to bring Meissner Fummel undamaged to Dresden or face certain punishment.

Meissen wine, Meissen porcelain, Meissner Fummel: the people of this town have sophisticated tastes. It is thanks to their aesthetic sense that the charming atmosphere of the town has not been lost in spite of the dilapidation, for which the citizens of Meissen were not after all responsible.

Getting away from Meissen men.

IN THE EASTERN ERZGEBIRGE

A little off the beaten track and somewhat eclipsed by the famous sights of Dresden are the Eastern Erzgebirge, named after the tin "Erz" (ore) that has been mined here for centuries. The hills rise gradually to an average height of 2,743 feet (844 metres). At most the visitor merely passes through the area on the way to Bohemia or Prague; its reputation is not a very inviting one. The pollution damage to the trees is considerable and on the ridges of the hills the woods have disappeared altogether, although lower down the situation looks a little better. The Altenberg-Zinnwald district with its unreal lunar landscape is not necessarily an essential part of every tourist itinerary.

Nevertheless, the visitor who is not too put off by the sight of environmental damage will find that this area also has interesting things to offer. The "Pinge" in **Altenberg** is a particular curiosity: a giant crater like a wound in the landscape, man-made but the work of centuries. The mountain that had been hollowed out by the tin mines collapsed in 1500 with a tremendous crash which was heard in Dresden. From then on until recently the stone with its tin ore content was taken in easily obtainable quantities from the base of the crater, so that it is constantly being enlarged in circumference and depth.

The low tin content and the fall in the price of tin on the world market made the mine uneconomical, and it has now been forced to close. Around DM50 million had already been spent on its modernisation and expansion. The display section also had to close and it will take years to renovate the museum, but there is still a tin mining exhibition at **Huthaus Zinnwald** near the Czechoslovakian border.

It seems rather ironic that 30 acres (12.5 hectares) of land in the midst of the damaged landscape should have been designated a nature reserve. Approximately 1¼ miles (2 km) south-west of Altenberg on the F 170 in the direction of the border and diagonally opposite the Grenzensteinhof restaurant, a signposted footpath leads up to the **Georgenfelder high moor**, where a 4,000-ft (1,200-metre) log road has been constructed to provide access to visiting vehicles.

The moor was once also a source of peat, but it was primarily a mining area. An artificial channel leads to a reservoir, the Grosser Galgenteich of Altenberg, which dates back to the 16th century and was used to operate the waterworks of the mine. Mountain pine, marsh tea, cotton grass, sundew and cranberries and in particular heather and lichens are to be found here. From May to October there are daily guided tours of the high moor.

For the visitor who is more interested in castles, palaces or museums than in nature the Eastern Erzgebirge also have much to offer. Two of the many sights

Preceding pages: wooden toys from the Erzgebirge. Left, woodcarving was done by miners. Right, nutcrackers being prepared for Advent.

should on no account be missed: Schloss Kuckuckstein near Liebstadt south of Pirna and the toy museum in the spa town of Seiffen (F 171 near the Czechoslovakian border).

The first castle on the site at **Kuckuckstein** near Liebstadt was built in the 10th century and was reconstructed in the 14th century. In its present form, in the west wing with its hunting, court and Napoleon rooms, the building is reminiscent of the era of Carl Adolf von Carlowitz (1771–1837) owner of Kuckuckstein castle when it was a bastion of freemasonry.

Today the reputation of the industrious mountain area is based less on its mineral resources than on its **toy industry** with its 300 years of history, which is of course more a history of a home-based craft than one of industrial manufacture. In the **Erzgebirgische Spielzeugmuseum** (toy museum) at **Seiffen** a well-preserved toy-maker's workshop illustrates working and living conditions in around 1900. The visitor can admire everything that was produced here and also buy much of what is on display, since these objects have lost their importance as a GDR export.

The toys are varied, imaginative and have a natural beauty. December is a particularly good time to visit the museum, since this folk art has its origins in the Christmas festivities. There are pyramids with figures which revolve by convection when candles are lit at the base, Christmas lanterns in the form of miner's lamps, and hollow wooden figures with pipes in their mouths which "smoke" when a lighted incense cone is placed inside the body and angels. The Dresden painter and poet Ludwig Richter (1803–84) drew many scenes from this attractive landscape, which also provided him with the inspiration for his picture *Genoveva*.

The visitor interested in the history of technology should not miss the **Frohnauer Hammer** at Annaberg-Buchholz. Built in 1436 as a grain mill, it was equipped in 1621 as a silver hammer

Tin mining has been practised for centuries in the Erzgebirge.

works and rebuilt in 1657 as an iron hammer. It still functions and demonstrations are given. The largest of the three hammers can deliver a force of 2,950 newtons and operates at a speed of 20 to 40 blows a minute. The home of the last masters of the mill is next door.

The Eastern Erzgebirge boasts a good network of roads and paths and is easily accessible by car. Given the area's environmental problems, however, it would be more reasonable to take the passenger train which goes from Dresden via Heidenau through the Müglitz valley to Altenberg-Geising. Or perhaps enjoy the pleasures of a romantic trip on the **narrow-gauge railway** from **Freital-Hainsberg** to the spa of **Kipsdorf**. Through tunnels and over bridges the railway follows the Rabenauer Grund, a winding valley 2.1 miles (3.5 km) long with steep cliffs, through which the Rote Weisseritz flows.

Dying trees: Why is it so important to take the train just here? By the 1960s the Erzgebirge no longer had any healthy trees. The Technical University of Dresden almost succeeded in introducing sulphur-dioxide-resistant woods; initial experiments of this nature were conducted in the middle of the last century by Adolf Stöckhardt, head of the former Saxon Academy of Forestry, when it first became apparent in England that the vegetation in the immediate surroundings of industrial complexes was being seriously damaged.

In the early days of the GDR economy the main interest was in the effects of sulphur dioxide. Species were planted that had proved particularly resistant to this gas in the university's experiments: Serbian spruce, blue spruce, black pine, beeches, also mountain maple and mountain ash.

In the meantime, the harmful substances have changed and it is the hydrocarbons and nitric oxide from car exhausts that are doing the damage. It is, unfortunately, precisely the sulphur-dioxide-resistant trees that are most sensitive to the new tree killers, the cars.

PIRNA AND SURROUNDINGS

With a medieval town, a massive castle perched on a cliff and a baroque pleasance, the immediate surroundings of Dresden are full of contrast. The best view of the 750-year-old town of **Pirna**, which today has a population of around 47,000, is obtained from the bridge over the Elbe. From here the visitor can look across to the towers of the Marienkirche (St Mary's Church), the Rathaus (town hall) and the monastery church with the Sonnenstein Fortress towering above them and the honeycomb blocks of a new estate in the background.

Canaletto's view of the marketplace: The bridge across the Elbe was crucial for the development of the town, and in the late Middle Ages Pirna became an important trading centre. Its former prosperity is still evident in its fine bourgeois architecture but the old town is in a very dilapidated state and in urgent need of renovation.

"Pirna is not a bad little place," wrote the "Pirna monk", who spent 50 years in the town's Dominican monastery, 400 years ago. The Swedes in the Thirty Years' War, on the other hand, were undoubtedly bad – the legendary "Pirna Misery" is a reference to their burning of the town. It was thanks to a courageous pharmacist, Jacobäer, that the worst was avoided: at night, he rode through the enemy camp outside the town to Dresden and returned with a letter of intercession from a princess related to the Swedish royal family.

A tour of the old town is best begun with the **monastery ruins**. The monastery church, rebuilt after 1945, is one of the few existing Gothic churches with two naves. In the little streets leading from the Karl-Marx-Strasse (pedestrian precinct) to the market are bourgeois houses featuring Gothic portals with seats, gables, Renaissance and baroque ornamentation. At the end of the Schuhgasse is the famous view of the **market-place**, dominated by its imposing **town hall**, that was painted by Canaletto in 1750. The town hall unites the styles of five centuries and features on its elegant tower an ornamental clock dating from 1612. Beneath a gold and black moon and the clockface itself are two ruby-coloured lions standing by a pear tree – the coat of arms of the town.

The most striking of the houses on the square is the **Canaletto house** (Markt 7), a Renaissance house (1520) with a steep decorative gable. Not neon signs but house symbols draw the eye to some of the other buildings: a lion with a mortar on the **Apotheke zum Löwen** (Lion Apothecary, Markt 17), a swan on the **Weisser Schwan** (White Swan) restaurant (Markt 19). The baroque double portal of **house no. 9** features Corinthian columns embellished with fruit motifs – a reference to the activity of the market, the noise of which drowns out the splashing of the three fountains.

Witty Gothic style: East of the town's "inner courtyard" is the **Stadtkirche St**

Marien (St Mary's Town Church). This massive late Gothic church was consecrated in 1546 and has remained in the same form ever since, untouched by either war or fire. The interior has impressive ribwork which, at the point where it traces the outline of the choir, takes on a life of its own with curlicues, loops and other patterns.

The ceiling frescoes, some of which are painted across the ribs, are also unorthodox, with the ladies depicted revealing an astonishing amount of leg and bosom. Four medallions contain symbols of the Reformation, including the "Lutheran rose" and the coat of arms of Melanchthon.

The corner house behind the church, the "Deutsches Haus" hotel, is one of the most important Renaissance buildings in Pirna; the architect inserted a portrait of himself in the magnificent portal. From this street a flight of steps leads up to the former fortress of **Sonnenstein** (literally "Sunny Stone"), which is also accessible by car and worth a visit primarily for the view of the town obtainable from here. Although the history of Sonnenstein goes back to the Middle Ages, the present building was only put up in the 19th century. Its name is also deceptive, since its recent past is sinister rather than sunny. Formerly a renowned institution for the care of the mentally ill, its purpose during the Third Reich was changed from caring for the disadvantaged to the elimination of "lives not worth living".

Garden of sensual pleasures: Those of a romantic disposition will be delighted by **Grosssedlitz** (follow the signs to the "Barockgarten" approximately 3 miles/ 5 km from Pirna). A walk in this baroque garden with its elegant stairways, fountains and sensuous statues is a stroll in a bygone age.

The secluded garden was begun by Graf Wackerbarth in 1719 and acquired in 1723 by Augustus the Strong, who commissioned the best architects of Dresden, including Matthaeus Daniel Pöppelmann, to complete it in the ba-

Augustus the Strong purchased the baroque gardens of Grosssedlitz from Count Wackerbarth.

roque style. Used primarily for the sumptuous parties of the Saxon royal household, it was later commandeered by Frederick the Great during the Seven Years' War (1756–63), in which he fought against the Austria of Maria Theresa and her allies France and Russia for supremacy in Europe.

The most famous part of the garden is the **Stille Musik** (silent music) opposite the 325-feet-long (100-metre) orangery: a stairway with curved balustrades named after its decorative groups of putti playing musical instruments. Summer concerts are once again held in front of the orangery, and the hall of mirrors in the small 19th-century palace of the Friedrichschlösschen is a popular place for stylish wedding breakfasts.

Weesenstein, the "Pearl of the Müglitztal", also has a sophisticated French park. The village clusters round a massive fortress on a spur of rock above the narrow wooded valley, which had its origins in around 1200. The slender, oval tower rises from the oldest part of the castle, which was built from top to bottom. In 1879 Theodor Gampe described it thus: "To get to the *bel étage* one goes down from the palace courtyard; the stables are on the third floor, the cellars on the fifth and a former ice cellar on the sixth floor."

The date 1575 is inscribed on a Renaissance portal; a path in the rock leads to the upper vaults. The lower residential tract of the castle is today a **tapestry and wallpaper museum**, its rooms furnished with historic wall coverings made of fabric and paper, plus a valuable gold leather exhibit from France which was made in 1790.

The castle was the favourite country seat of the Saxon King Johann (1801–73), an educated man who made extensive studies of both the humanities and the sciences. He was particularly interested in linguistics, at the time a new discipline, and at Weesenstein he himself produced a translation of Dante's *Divine Comedy*, using the pseudonym of Philalethes.

A view towards Saxon Switzerland.

SAXON SWITZERLAND

Saxon Switzerland is the name given to a large area of the Elbsandsteingebirge (Elbe Sandstone Mountains), which run between the Erzgebirge and Oberlausitz and were once known as the Meissner Hochland. The highest mountains, the **Grosse Zschirnstein** and the **Grosse Winterberg**, incorporate the word "large" in their names, but at a mere 1,823 and 1,794 feet (561 and 552 metres) they by no means measure up to Swiss peaks.

Nevertherless, Saxon Switzerland is impressively mountainous. In this area, consisting primarily of chalky sandstone, the rock was worn away by the elements to form high cliffs and peaks. In between them are deep valleys and gorges, where the stone was washed away by the Elbe and its tributaries. Isolated table mountains tower above wooded valleys and the Elbe describes two large loops through the middle, hence the official name of these mountains, Elbsandsteingebirge, which also applies to those mountains located in Czechoslovakia.

Pioneers of Romanticism: Although the comparison with Switzerland is not very appropriate, the name Saxon Switzerland, which appears in the literature on the area from 1790 on, was in fact coined by two Swiss, Adrian Zingg (1734–1816) and Anton Graff (1736–1813) who were both painters at the Dresden Art Academy and whose walks in this region filled them with nostalgia for their homeland. In addition to the guidebooks and travel accounts in which it featured, the rocky landscape was popularised more than anything by the pictures painted here. Important Romantic artists such as Caspar David Friedrich and Ludwig Richter walked the "Artists' Route", as the usual, three- to four-day hiking trail through Saxon Switzerland was called. Aristocratic or well-off citizens, on the other hand, had themselves carried through this mountain world in sedan-chairs.

In those days the boats on the Elbe were also still moved by manpower; up to 40 men, known as "Bomätscher", pulled a barge from the towpath upstream, sometimes with the assistance of horses or oxen. It was only when the first steamships were introduced in 1837 and the railway line through the Elbe Valley was completed in 1851 that mass tourism began. Guest houses, restaurants and hotels sprang up in the villages, hiking trails were marked out and observation towers built.

Not even the sheer rock faces escaped the invasion of nature enthusiasts; since the 1860s the crags have been the province of climbers. During the communist regime this mountain region had to take the place of Switzerland and the Alps for GDR citizens who were keen hikers, with the result that 2½ to 3 million holidaymakers came every year to the nature reserve of Saxon Switzerland, which has an area of 142 sq. miles (368 sq.

Preceding pages: storm in Saxon Switzerland with Königstein on the left and Lilienstein on the right. **Left**, the Bohemia fortress of Königstein has had many inmates. **Right**, the crags of Saxon Switzerland.

km). Today some of the rock faces can no longer be climbed: the stone is beginning to crumble through exposure to the environmental pollution of the nearby industrial areas.

The Elbe route: For the visitor who is not in too much of a hurry there is still no better way of travelling to this area than on one of the **paddle steamers** which ply the Elbe, and have a draught adapted to the shallow water of the river. The 30-mile (50-km) journey from Dresden to Schmilka on the Czech border takes six-and-a-half hours upstream and around four hours downstream. At the 14 stops the mooring procedure is a skill in itself: a long wooden pole is used, as the ships have no bow thruster.

For centuries the Elbe was an important route between Bohemia and Meissen, used for transporting not only Bohemian goods but also sandstone and wood from Saxon Switzerland. However, the wooded, rocky characteristics of the landscape on either side of the Upper Elbe in Saxony have been re-tained in spite of the quarrying. The importance of the quarries, which are now no longer in operation, for the population of the whole region, was recorded by a chronicler in the 18th century. "It is only when the quarrymen have work that the boatmen are required, and the locksmiths, smiths, sailmakers and even the shoemakers and tailors are occupied, otherwise there is poverty and need in the land."

After Pirna, the gateway to Saxon Switzerland, signs of industry are rare and houses isolated. Sheep graze in the wide meadows and sometimes break into a run, as if trying to beat the steamer to its next stop. The attractions of a trip on the Elbe, by comparison with the classic Rhine trip between Mainz and Coblenz, is that the Elbe is smaller, calmer and not on such a grand scale.

Rock balcony: The scenery between the town of **Wehlen** – the nickname "Wehstädtel", which diminishes it, is much more apt – and the spa of Rathen is particularly spectacular: to the right **The Elbe Valley.**

are the Bären and the Rauenstein mountains; to the left, close to the river, is the famous group of peaks known as the **Bastei**. From the platform known as the "balcony of Saxon Switzerland", there is an unparalleled view of the bizarre labyrinth of rocks with the Elbe winding through it. In 1851 the impressive 247-ft (76-metre) stone **Bastei Bridge** was built across the Mardertelle Gorge, past the massive peak known as the Steinschleuder.

It is an easy walk up the gentle slope from the town of Wehlen on to the Bastei. The shortest climb from the Elbe Valley, involving a height difference of 617 feet (190 metres) begins in the spa of **Rathen** (Basteiweg). The top section squeezes through the steep **Felsengasse**, which is part of the Neurathen Castle complex, a former stronghold of Bohemian knights dating from the early 13th century. A path, made safe for walkers, has been built through the reconstructed remains, which crosses daring bridges and leads on to rocky promontories with

a view over the Wehlgrund and the massifs of the Grosse and Kleine Gans which are popular with climbers. The peaks in the Bastei area were christened by the local people and include the Lokomotive, Talwächter, Mönch and Höllenhund (Locomotive, Guard of the Valley, Monk and Hell-Hound).

Since the Bastei can also be reached from Dresden by car via Lohmen (around 15 miles or 25 km), it is flooded with visitors. Opposite the panorama restaurant, which replaced the old restaurant in 1979, a hotel is being constructed. The subsidiary buildings and car parks extend far into the hinterland.

To go back down to Rathen, take the path through the **Schwedenlöcher** or Swedish holes, used by the population as hiding places during times of war. This labyrinth of rocks is a lesson in geology, with the structure and layering of the Elbe sandstone clearly visible. The path becomes steps leading down into the **Amselgrund**, a valley with an artificial lake, the Amselsee, 1,600 ft

A view from the Bastei.

(500 metres) long, where there are rowing boats for hire. Where the houses of Rathen start a little further up the Wehlgrund is the entrance to the famous stage in the rocks, an open-air theatre seating over 2,000 people. From mid-May to mid-September the **Landesbühnen Sachsen** (Saxon regional theatres) put on almost daily performances of plays, operas and operettas appropriate for the picturesque rocky setting, including *Winnetou*, Weber's *Freischütz* and Humperdinck's *Hansel and Gretel* (tickets are available from the Dresden Information Office, Prager Strasse, and other advanced booking offices).

The spa of Rathen is a particularly good place for a rest cure, since there are no cars here. The rocky peaks rise up right behind the houses. It is connected by ferry with the Elbe's opposite bank.

Bastion and prison: After Rathen there is a large bend in the Elbe, which circles round the colossal sandstone peak known as the Lilienstein. On the opposite bank is the fortress of **Königstein**, perched at a height of 1,170 feet (360 metres). First recorded as a Bohemian royal castle in 1241, it came under the control of the Meissen Marches in 1459 through the Treaty of Eger.

From the village of Königstein, squeezed into the narrow area between cliff and river, the bastion can be reached on foot via the Palmschänke or on the old castle road. There is also a lift in the sandstone cliff which takes only seconds to ascend the 162 feet (50 metres) to the top. From here there is an excellent view of Saxon Switzerland.

The extension of the fortress was begun in 1589 under Elector Christian I. The plateau was surrounded by a ring of walls with a walkway on top. One of the oldest buildings is the **Magdalenenburg**, which from 1428 on, was the location of the brewery. The giant wine vats were kept in its cellar until 1891, including the largest vat in the world, which had a capacity of 55,000 gallons (250,000 litres), but was filled only once. The Friedrichsburg was converted by **A steamer on the river.**

Augustus the Strong into a baroque summer residence in 1731, where he held intimate parties, but the complex was also used for celebrations on a larger scale. In times of emergency Königstein served as a place of refuge for the Saxon court and a safe place for the state treasures, such as the art collections, which were stored in underground casemates.

The fortress also had a rather less illustrious role as a state prison: among those held here were Johann Friedrich Böttger, the man who could allegedly make gold and the subsequent inventor of European porcelain, the Russian anarchist Mikhail Bakunin who took part in the May uprising of 1849 and August Bebel, the father of social democracy.

Since 1955 the castle has been open to the public: points of interest include a well 152 metres (485 ft) deep, an army museum in the arsenals and a Böttger memorial. The valley of the River Biela, which flows into the Elbe southwest of Königstein, is an attractive hiking and climbing area.

Spas: After the stop at **Prossen** – the name comes from the Sorbian word *bróda*, meaning a ford – the steamer passes under the Brücke der Einheit (Bridge of Unity), originally built in 1874–76 as the Königin Carola Brücke (Queen Carola Bridge), and **Bad Schandau**, "the heart of Saxon Switzerland", with its waterfront restaurant comes into view. Travelling hawkers, in particular Vietnamese, wait on the promenade for disembarking passengers. The coat of arms of Bad Schandau (population 4,500) features a sailing boat: this little town was once an important Elbe trading centre.

Since the discovery of springs containing iron in the Kirnitzschtal in 1730 it has become the most important spa in Saxon Switzerland; "Bad" or spa was added to its name in 1920. Worth seeing is the market square with the 17th-century **Church of St John**, which was rebuilt after the town fire of 1704. It has a baroque pulpit carved out of sandstone and the famous Renaissance altar

The Elbe and the town of Königstein.

by Johannes Walter (1579), which stood in the Kreuzkirche in Dresden until 1760. Also on the market square is the former **brewery** ("Ernst-Thälmann-Haus") which has a Renaissance portal. A lift, financed by a hotelier in 1904, goes up the cliff to the district of **Ostrau**: from here there is a splendid view of the Schrammsteine.

Visitors interested in hiking are recommended to take the Kirnitzschtalbahn, an old tram built in 1898 which is still going strong; after a 5-mile (8.3-km) trip through the romantic Kirnitzschtal (valley) it arrives at the artificial Lichtenhainer waterfall where the popular ascent to the **Kuhstall** ("cow-shed") begins. This imposing rock gateway is 36 feet (11 metres) high, 55 feet (17 metres) wide and 88 feet (27 metres) deep and was once used as a natural shelter for animals, as its name suggests. With its restaurant, the Kuhstall is a popular place for Sunday outings.

Those less interested in leisurely beer-drinking can take one of the hiking trails to the scenic paradise of the **Grosser Winterberg**. Hikers with alpine experience should be warned against underestimating the peaks of Saxon Switzerland. Over-confidence is liable to be punished – in no time at all the hiker can lose his way and find himself perched at some dizzying height late in the afternoon, with the only means of descent being a ladder or iron pegs hammered into the rock. Once at the bottom he will discover that he has just negotiated the Wilde Hölle ("wild hell"). The weather too can be unpredictable.

Perilous stone: Bad Schandau is also a starting point for hikes across the rugged **Schrammsteine**. In Middle High German the word "schramen" means to tear open: climbers are thus warned of the dangers that await them when attempting these crags, which are particularly sharp.

One of the ascents starts in the **Postelwitz** district of Bad Schandau. The most famous of the attractive half-timbered houses in this old fishing vil-

The sandstone peak of Lilienstein.

lage are the **Sieben-Brüder-Häuser** ("seven brothers' houses") and the **Vaterhaus** ("parental house"), which the seven brothers left to start their own homes.

From Postelwitz the path leads via the Grosses Schrammtor and the Jägersteig to the Kammweg, with its impressive views. The highest of the Hintere Schrammsteine is the **Carolafelsen**, at 1,472 feet (453 metres).

Sidetrips home: Back on board the Elbe steamer for the final leg of the trip. The Weisse Flotte's last stop is **Schmilka**, just before the Czechoslovakian border. This place is also a popular summer resort and a starting point for hikes in the Schrammstein and Winterberg area as well as for visits to the nearby **Edmundsklamm**. This gorge was discovered in 1890 by the aristocrat Edmund Clary-Aldringen: here the water of the Kamnitz has been dammed up by a weir to form a boating lake.

The return trip to Dresden can also be made by train. Double-decker S-Bahn (suburban railway) trains run along the left-hand side of the Elbe, and provide another good view of the river.

Although the Elbe flows through the middle of Saxon Switzerland, it does not pass close to all the magnificent hiking areas. To reach Hohnstein, for example, it is necessary to go by car via **Lohmen**. This little town is located high above the Polenztal and is dominated by **Castle Hohnstein**, today one of the largest youth hostels in the eastern part of Germany. This castle was a notorious prison for centuries and from 1933–34 on was one of the first Nazi concentration camps – memorial plaques remind visitors of this period of its history. Lohmen has an attractive market square with a baroque church and several half-timbered houses, including the town hall and a pharmacist's.

The **Paul-Mai-Weg** is a nature trail leading into the **Polenztal**. Around 60 notices along the way explain the geology, flora and fauna of the area. The Polenztal is also worth a longer hike

with its mills and famous narcissi meadows. The Neuweg goes downhill to the Waltersdorfer Mühle (mill), where the valley is narrow with vertical sandstone walls. The Maimühle was once the official or castle mill, and is followed by the Russigmühle, Heeselichtmühle and Scheibenmühle.

From here a narrow path cut in the rock winds along the hillside above the River Polenz. Shortly before the **Bockmühle** the trail enters the nature reserve with the largest area of wild narcissi in Saxony. The Bockmühle burned down almost completely in 1926 and was never rebuilt. In the convenient restaurant nearby, hikers can stoke up in preparation for the walk back.

The ascent of the Brand is shorter but much steeper; hikers are rewarded with a splendid view and a hilltop restaurant at a height of 1,030 feet (317 metres). From here the Bastei area, the Schrammsteine, and on a clear day even the Erzgebirge and the Bohemian mountains are visible.

The paddle-steamer journeys 30 miles from Dresden to the border town of Schmilka.

ROCK CLIMBING

The sandstone in the various districts of Saxon Switzerland, especially where it has been shaped into a variety of forms by exposure to the elements, offers the climber the opportunity to practise every technique that has ever been developed. Here is everything from wide chimneys to straddle across, from body-width crevices to cracks the width of a finger, from walls with "jugs" to those with the minutest ledges for desperate fingertip holds, from climbing faces with maximum friction to those requiring a feat of balance for several yards. Versatility is thus essential, since a single climbing route can include all these features.

Mountaineering centre: For Dresden, which has around 7,000 active climbers, this is an important sport. In the "Golden Twenties", Dresden ranked with Munich and Vienna as one of the main mountaineering centres in the German-speaking world and still enjoys the same status today.

The increasing numbers of visitors naturally poses a problem, and climbing had to be forbidden on some of the rock faces because they were crumbling under the mass invasion. Large areas of Saxon Switzerland have been turned into a national park in order to preserve this region for future generations of holidaymakers and climbers.

Established principles: It is of course not possible just to climb any way you can; simply as everywhere else, there are certain climbing rules which have to be followed. In this part of the world these were formulated in 1913 by Rudolf Fehrmann. Sportsmen continue to follow these principles today, which state that climbers must rely solely on their own physical strength and natural holds in the rock surface to resist the force of gravity.

The climber is protected by attaching himself to "nuts" that he places into suitable cracks at regular intervals, or pegs that he drives into narrower fissures. These pegs, approximately 8 inches (20 centimetres) long, are put in by the first climber, so that climbing routes are principally created from below. He is belayed from below by his "second" who is secured by a rope sling often placed over a rock spike. The evaluation of climbs according to degree of difficulty is therefore an open-ended process; currently there are ten grades of difficulty.

Local restrictions: The use of chalk to aid friction between the hands and the rock is prohibited, whereas in other regions it is allowed. These self-imposed restrictions are unique to climbing in Saxony. They guarantee that a climb here will be an adventure that stretches the climber's physical and mental powers to the full.

The people of the region have always had a special relationship with this landscape of rocks. The Elbe and its tributaries cut into the table mountains, creating deep gorges, and it is the combination of steep cliffs, extensive forest and over a thousand separate peaks that makes this area so unusual. In the Middle Ages castles were built on the peaks and in time of war people sought protection in inaccessible gorges.

In 1864, gymnasts from Schandau tackled the Falkenstein. But they used artificial climbing aids; the first time such aids were consciously abandoned was in the climbing of the Mönchstein as long ago as 1874 and since then the art of free climbing has become an end in itself.

Climbers of the Saxon school soon had major achievements to their names: the Schüsselkarspitze was first climbed in 1894 by Oscar Schulte, the Campanile Basso in 1908 by Rudolf Fehrmann; the first man to get to the top of the north wall of Monte Pelmo was Felix Simon in 1924, while Fritz Wiesner mastered the 28,250-ft (8,611-metre) K2 in 1939 and Dietrich Hasse and Lothar Brandler, finally, were the first to climb the north wall of the Grosse Zinne, in 1958.

Bernd Arnold, author of this chapter, free climbing.

BURG STOLPEN AND BAUTZEN

The town of Bautzen, over 1,000 years old, is situated on the Spree approximately 35 miles (53 km) from Dresden. It is best reached via trunk road No. 6, from which a detour can also be made to Stolpen. Visible from a long way off is a 1,137-ft (350-metre) high basalt hump which broke through the Lausitz granite in prehistoric times: crowning this extinct volcano is the old Burg Stolpen (Castle Stolpen), best known as the prison of Countess Cosel, the "Saxon Pompadour".

Stony ground: During the 15th century the small town of **Stolpen** gradually spread over the north flank of the castle hill; it features a steeply sloping market square with 18th- and 19th-century town houses. In the vicinity of the castle is an imposing natural monument in the form of slim, five- to eight-sided pillars made of blue-black Stolpen basalt and popularly known as the **Stolpen organ pipes**.

The hard stone was an ideal foundation for the massive castle, which dates back to 1100. For over 300 years **Castle Stolpen** belonged to the bishops of Meissen, and most of the existing buildings are early 16th century. In 1559 the Reformation came to Stolpen and castle and town became the property of the electors. Later in its history it was occupied by Napoleonic troops: after their defeat in the Battle of the Nations at Leipzig in 1813 they retreated to France, but blew up many of the buildings before they left. The oldest sections of the castle became increasingly dilapidated. Since 1877 the complex, now partly in ruins, has been a museum.

Castle Stolpen consists of four courtyards. After the granary, the first building on the right is the main guard house, in which there is an exhibition of historic weapons. Opposite this are the royal stables. A model of the Stolpen "waterworks" is on display here, the equipment that was invented for pumping water on to the hill. Behind the stables is the torture chamber, with an exhibition of torture instruments and stocks illustrating the cruel methods of interrogation and punishment that existed in feudal times.

In the upper part of the castle is the **Schösserturm**, (the Tax Collectors' Tower) with its distinctive cupola. This was where the castle tax collector (bailiff) officiated: a crack in the thick wall enabled him to listen in secret to the conversations of the people waiting outside the gate. A Gothic portal led from the outer ward to the courtroom in the lower tower, the **Johannisturm**. From here condemned prisoners were thrown straight into the dark dungeon below, and were left to starve to death in this "hunger hole".

Countess Cosel's prison: From the third courtyard a winding staircase leads to the rooms in the Johannisturm where Countess Anna Constantia von Cosel spent 21 years of her 49 years as a "prisoner of the state" in Stolpen. After

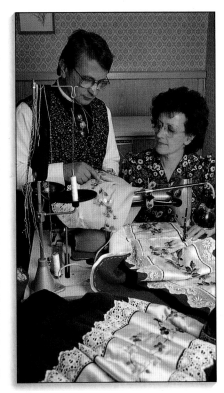

Left, Ortenburg Castle was built as a border outpost during Germany's expansion eastwards. Right, making traditional costumes.

THE MORAVIAN CHURCH

For those unaware of its history, the village of Herrnhut in Saxony (near Löbau), a little place of around 2,000 souls, is full of surprises. What are imposing baroque town houses, and even a museum of ethnology with a collection of exotica, doing here? Most surprising of all is the church: the parishioners sit on pews that are arranged across the "hall" and painted white like the rest of the elegant interior. There are no pictures, no altar and no pulpit; the sermon is delivered from a simple "liturgy table". And the members of the congregation, finally, address one another as "brother" and "sister".

The Moravian Church (Herrnhut Brüdergemeinde), which is today a Protestant Free Church, dates back to 1722 when the pious Count Nikolaus von Zinzendorf took in a group of Bohemian-Moravian religious refugees and founded a settlement for them.

Together with these refugees he formed a community which was dedicated to the service of Christ. A special kind of piety developed which was peculiar to Herrnhut, and appealed in particular to the emotions. Moving church festivals were introduced, among them the impressive "Easter morning". On Easter Sunday before dawn the community, accompanied by the trombone band, goes to "God's acre" (the cemetery), and as the sun comes up celebrates the resurrection of Christ.

In this cemetery there is a striking absence of crosses and showy monuments. The deceased brothers and sisters lie in simple individual graves marked only by flat stone slabs, symbolising the equality of all human beings in death.

The Christian community of Herrnhut was not concerned solely with spiritual matters, but was also politically, socially and economically organised. A council of elders was elected to regulate its affairs. The "corps system" was devised to help the community to fulfil its aims and enable its members to lead a more intensive religious life and disseminate the Christian doctrine.

The unmarried men formed the "corps of brothers" and lived in a community house which was not just a residential home but also a workplace and training centre for craftsmen – later also for missionaries, who were sent all over the world. There was a sisters' house for the young girls, and widows and widowers also formed their own "corps". Married people lived in their own houses: members of the community were not required to lead celibate lives.

Herrnhut and the considerable number of other settlements founded in the 18th and 19th centuries by the Moravian Church in Central Europe, the British Isles and also America and Africa as a result of mission work, were primarily craftsmen's colonies.

The "brothers and sisters" were not encouraged to feel tied to their particular community like farmers to their land, but always had to be prepared to take "postings" in the service of the church, whether in the Königsfeld community in the Black Forest or as missionaries with negro slaves in the Caribbean, the Eskimos in Greenland or Maroons in Surinam. One group emigrated to America as long ago as 1733, and in 1741 founded Bethlehem in Pennsylvania to devote themselves to converting the Indians. (The exhibits in the Herrnhut Ethnological Museum were brought back by the missionaries.)

In Germany the self-contained communities of the Moravian Church with their alternative way of life survived until 1870. It was not until then that the strict rules governing the communities began to be relaxed. Most of the settlements themselves, which are all laid out according to the same pattern, have been preserved – there are six in the former GDR alone, including, in addition to Herrnhut, Niesky in Oberlausitz, Kleinwelka near Bautzen and Gnadau in the Magdeburg district.

In the western part of Germany one of the municipal districts of Neuwied on the Rhine also has the typical characteristics of a Moravian Church settlement. And amongst the "brothers" and "sisters" living scattered outside these centres, who are bound by their common history, their education in a Moravian Church boarding school, meetings and magazines, there is still a surprisingly strong spirit of solidarity.

nine scintillating years at the court of Augustus the Strong, by whom she had three children, the powerful mistress lost her position as a result of intrigues and at the age of 36 was banished to Stolpen. From 1716 until her death in 1765 she was held prisoner without an official sentence; all her many appeals for mercy and attempts to escape were in vain.

Countess Cosel was an unusually beautiful and intelligent woman with a ready wit, and the king's equal at shooting and riding. He loved her passion and cleverness, but would not tolerate her interference in politics. Through the intrigues of his courtiers she fell out of favour with him and he broke his secret promise to marry her. To prevent this from becoming generally known and damaging his reputation, Augustus removed her from public life and she remained in the tower for a further 30 years after his death.

In the fourth castle courtyard is the 286-ft (82-metre) well which was "sunk"

Left, Church of the Moravian Brotherhood. **Right**, rape fields near Bautzen.

inch by inch into the basalt. The hard stone was heated with large pieces of wood, and then chilled with water so that it cracked.

Sorbian centre: From the bridge over the River Spree the old castle of **Bautzen** perched on its granite cliff looks as massive as Stolpen. The name of this town is also associated with a prison: many thousands of GDR opponents are familiar with the inside of the "yellow marvel", widely feared as the "yellow misery camp". Bautzen, however, is far more than a prison.

The town with its splendid towers, first recorded in official documents in 1002, is often called the Saxon Rothenburg. In addition Bautzen ("Budysin" in Sorbian) is the centre of the Sorbs in Oberlausitz, who for centuries have kept alive their separate and distinctive language and culture. Their national organisation, the *Domowina-Heimat*, has its headquarters here.

In the old town some of the elegant streets are becoming increasingly di-

lapidated; the splendid baroque facades of the town houses in the Reichenstrasse, however, were restored in 1981. There is a good view of this lively pedestrian precinct from the **Reichenturm**, the "leaning tower" of Bautzen. Number 12 Reichenstrasse, built between 1634 and 1709, is particularly attractive with its stucco work flower garlands; number 14, which has a Hebrew inscription, was once the property of a Jewish merchant. Reichenstrasse opens into the **Altmarkt** (Old Market), the centre of municipal life with the **town hall**. In its present, simple form this building dates back to the 1830s, and the people of Bautzen have no excuse for being late – on its slim tower there are three clocks.

The east and west sides of the market square are lined with imposing patrician houses. Hauptmarkt number 7 has a particularly beautiful baroque facade dating from 1730. Next to it is the house known as the "Handtuch" (literally hand towel), only two windows wide and dating from the 15th century.

Peacefully divided church: A narrow alley leads off to the right past the town hall to the **Fleischmarkt**. Tours of the town start at the "Bautzen Information" located on this square, which is dominated by the massive **Petridom** (St Peter's Cathedral): its tower is almost 276 feet (85 metres) high.

Since the Reformation, which was particularly welcome in Bautzen where there had been a strong reaction against the selling of indulgences, the Cathedral has been used by both Catholics and Protestants, and is accordingly divided in two by a grille. However, the two congregations never had to sing against one another and came to a peaceful agreement over the times of the services. The oldest part of the Cathedral is the west door, which contains 13th-century Romanesque elements.

The Nikolaipforte is one of the town's five gateway towers, all of which have been preserved. Outside the town walls, by the ruin of the **Nikolaikirche** (Church of St Nicholas) which burned down

The Moravians demand a simple life style.

during the Thirty Years' War, is a Catholic-Sorbian cemetery. From here there is a good view of the district of Seidau in the Spree valley, which was once a Sorbian settlement.

Ruins: The oldest district of Bautzen is centred around the castle, but is now so dilapidated that it is almost uninhabited. Above the entrance to the **Ortenburg**, the castle that was once the seat of the landowners, is the striking monument to the Hungarian-Bohemian King Matthias Corvinus, who had the ruins of the previous castle removed and built the present one in its place in 1483–86. On the left-hand side of the curved entry are the heads of a man and a woman, popularly believed to represent a monk and a nun who were walled in alive. The castle buildings will probably be covered in scaffolding for some time to come as restoration proceeds: so far the former salt store, which was used as the court building, has been completed, and now accommodates the "Serbskij Muzej", the **Sorbian Museum** (open 1–4 p.m.).

Concerts are held in the former court room with its frescoes in the style of the Dresden Opera House.

Along the town wall from here is the Mühltor, the gate which leads to Michaeliskirchplatz. The choir of the **Michaeliskirche** (the Church of St Michael), the church of the Protestant Sorbs, originated as a chapel as long ago as 1429. Opposite is the **Alte Wasserkunst** (old waterworks), the symbol of Bautzen, which pumped water from the Spree to supply the town. Today the tower, which was also part of the town's defence system, houses the **Technical Museum**.

From the adjoining terrace there is another delightful view of the narrow streets down in the Spree Valley, where there is still an old fisherman's cottage, known as the "Hexenhäusel" (Witch's House). It survived several fires in the neighbourhood as if bewitched; more such magic is needed today if large areas of the old town are to be saved from ruin.

One of the last red flags in Eastern Germany.

THE SORBS

The Sorbs are a unique minority. By contrast, for example, with the Danes living as an ethnic minority in Schleswig-Holstein, this Slavic people has no motherland across the border, but in spite of this have managed to keep their language and culture intact with astonishing perseverance to the present day. The area bounded by the towns of Bautzen, Hoyerswerda and Kamenz has remained largely Sorbian: the total population of Sorbs or Wends is now approximately 60,000. They first began settling the region between the Oder and Saale, Spreewald and Erzgebirge in the 5th century, and in 1884 there were still 164,000 Sorbs in Lausitz.

Red sauce: In the final years of the GDR it was the marketable, folklore element of the Sorbian culture that was primarily promoted. During Advent, for example, it is not Santa Claus who tra-ditionally brings the presents, but a young girl in Sorbian costume, her face veiled with lace. On 25 January, Ptaci Kwas, the traditional "bird wedding" is celebrated: this is primarily a festival for children who caper along in bird masks behind a stork, and is a lively occasion also featuring street music and traditional dances. At Easter the men ride two-by-two in a long line through the villages in top hat and tails, cakes are distributed from large trays and the Easter eggs are decorated with traditional patterns. This picture of a people who do nothing but celebrate is not, however, a very accurate one. "In the days of the GDR," says Jan Malink, a spokesman for the Sorbs, "everything was smothered in red sauce. Officially there were Sorbian folk festivals, but on the street people who spoke Sorbian were treated with hostility."

A forbidden language: This was not the first time. As with other ethnic minorities, their more powerful neighbours tried to prohibit their language. In a **Easter arrival in Marienstern.**

238

report to the Frankfurt government in 1818, Superintendant Botzenthal of Cottbus wrote: "The Wendish or Sorbian language is an obstacle to national education, and the education of the Wends would also be improved if the language were to be gradually abolished." The Nazis dissolved the Sorbian national association *Domowina-Heimat* which was founded in 1912 and Heinrich Himmler labelled them a "leaderless working-class people". The patriots were imprisoned in concentration camps and once again the Sorbian language was prohibited.

Immediately after World War II the Sorbs applied without success to the Soviet military government for independent status, and the SED, the ruling party in the GDR, took over the leadership of this people. There was a Sorbian radio station, the state-subsidised daily newspaper *Nowa doba* and Christian weekly magazines, bilingual road signs and a 10-class Sorbian school system, but the price of all this was subordina-

The Sorb minority is held together by closely-knit village communities and deep religious convictions.

tion to the GDR regime and all that it stood for.

The Stasi, the secret police, had a special department for monitoring the Sorbs. This modern colonialisation is summed up by the Bautzen doctor Hans-Eberhard Kaulfürst: "The worst blow struck against this small national group was the brown coal mining which systematically destroyed their traditional home area, forcing them to leave around 60 villages in Lausitz and move to the new housing areas of Weisswasser, Spremberg and Hoyerswerda."

Since the Berlin Wall came down, the society formed to assist threatened national groups has been establishing contact between Sorbs and other cultural minorities in Europe. Tourism now provides some of the Sorbs with a living. Like the gondoliers in Venice, they punt visitors through the Spreewald in flat boats holding 25 people, using 13-ft (4-metre) poles. Tours through this enchanting area start from Lehde and last four to seven hours.

AETERNITATI
IVSTICIS ET SVMTIBVS
FRIDERICI AVGVSTI
POLON REGIS ET ELECTOR SAX
RINCIPIS OPTIMI PATRIAEQVE PATRIS
INCOMPARABILIS
MOLES ISTHAEC ARDVA
PONTE ANNO M DCC XVII RESCISSO
EX ANNO M DCC XXVII AD TANTVM DECVS
AB MERIS SAXIS QVADRATIS
FELICI SVCCESSV
SVRREXIT
VELVT REGIAE AE PRICIPALIS
MVNIFICENTIAE
MONVMENTVM PVBLICVM

TRAVEL TIPS

GETTING THERE

Currently the state capital of Dresden is undergoing rapid change. New shops, department stores and offices spring up daily. A state parliament and a new democratically-elected administration of the federal state of Saxony and the city of Dresden have been set up. New names for streets and squares, new business hours and procedures are introduced by the hour. Consequently the following information is only a snapshot of present conditions. In putting together this guide the editorial staff have kept the information as up-to-date as possible but some of it may already have become somewhat obsolete. Both old and new street names are given below as the former are still more familiar to native Dresdeners, and may help when asking directions. When in doubt, a good idea is to ring the place you intend to visit and enquire as to their business hours, prices, etc.

A current calendar of events and list of addresses is included in the monthly editions of the city magazines *SAX* and *Dresdner* easily available at streetside newsagents.

BY AIR

Several European and non-European airline companies offer flights to Dresden, from the following airports: Amsterdam, Athens, Budapest, Dortmund, Frankfurt am Main, Hamburg, Kiev, Cologne, Moscow, Munich, Paderborn, Sofia, Stuttgart, and Zurich. There are no direct flights from Gret Britain. The quicker alternative is flying to Frankfurt and then taking the train onwards. Dresden Airport is approximately 7 km (4 miles) north of the city centre and can be reached by shuttlebus leaving either from Dresden Main Railway Station, Ho-Chi-Minh-Strasse, 120 minutes prior to anticipated flight departure, or the Dresden-Neustädter Railway Station on Friedrich-Wolf-Platz, 105 minutes prior to anticipated flight departure.

Dresden-Klotzsche Airport, Karl-Marx-Strasse, O-8080 Dresden. Tel: 58 31 41, Telex: 2 66 36.
Lufthansa, Hotel Bellevue, Köpke Strasse 15, O-8060 Dresden. Tel: 57 08 52. Hours: 8.30am–12.30pm and 1pm–5pm Monday–Friday.

BY RAIL

Trains operated by the German Railways (DB) are divided into the following categories:
IC = Inter City = 6DM supplementary charge
EX = Express Train = 5DM supplementary charge
D = Train = 3DM supplementary charge
IEX = Inter-Express = 3DM supplementary charge
E = Fast Train = 2DM supplementary charge
P = Passenger Train = no supplementary charge

If there are no particular stipulations noted on the ticket, you are free to break your journey within the period of validity specified. As a rule it is necessary to make seat reservations on all international trains. It's also a good idea to book your return passage before leaving your hometown as it could save a lengthy wait at one of the station ticket offices later. If you find yourself without a seat reservation on a train requiring themone be prepared to endure the trip standing up. The railway traffic between Dresden and Eastern European countries is generally much busier than that between Dresden and the West. There are a number of brand-new direct connections with cities like Hamburg, Düsseldorf, Frankfurt am Main, Stuttgart and Munich. The *Vindebona* starting in Vienna passes through Dresden daily. Remember that not all long-distance trains depart from the main railway station; some leave from the Dresden Neustadt Station.

Main office for seat reservations:
O-1130 Berlin, Weitlingstrasse 22. Tel: 5 25 20 00, Telex: ZRES–DR–11 24 40.

There are two main railway stations located in Dresden:
Main Railway Station, Am Leninplatz 4, O-8010 Dresden. Tel: 47 96 06 or 46 13 54, Telex: 261 51-328. Information: Open daily 6am–9.45pm. Tel: 47 06 00 and 47 15 02.
Dresden Neustadt Railway Station, Dr-Friedrich-Wolf-Platz, O-8060 Dresden. Tel: 51 185. Information: 6am–8pm Monday–Friday, 7am–8pm Saturday and Sunday.

All railway stations have connections to the public transport system (trams, buses, trains). Both main railway stations are connected to each other by train.

BY ROAD

Since 3 October 1990 the entry policies of the Federal Republic of Germany apply to what was formerly known as East Germany. In addition to a national driver's license and car registration papers, a nationality sticker, warning triangle and first-aid kit are mandatory.

Dresden is easily accessible via motorway from just about all points located within the German-speaking sphere. The one exception to this is if you are travelling from Austria. In the this case it is best to either go through Prague and from there get on the "euroroute" E 55, or to use the route that leads via Nürnberg/Hof.

THE COLOUR OF LIFE.

A holiday may last just a week or so, but the memories of those happy, colourful days will last forever, because together you and Kodak Ektachrome films will capture, as large as life, the wondrous sights, the breathtaking scenery and the magical moments. For you to relive over and over again.

The Kodak Ektachrome range of slide films offers a choice of light source, speed and colour rendition and features extremely fine grain, very high sharpness and high resolving power.

Take home the real colour of life with Kodak Ektachrome films.

LIKE THIS?

OR LIKE THIS?

A KODAK FUN PANORAMIC CAMERA BROADENS YOUR VIEW

The holiday you and your camera have been looking forward to all year; and a stunning panoramic view appears. "Fabulous", you think to yourself, "must take that one".

Unfortunately, your lens is just not wide enough. And three-in-a-row is a poor substitute.

That's when you take out your pocket-size, 'single use' Kodak Fun Panoramic Camera. A film and a camera, all in one, and it works miracles. You won't need to focus, you don't need special lenses. Just aim, click

and... it's all yours. The total picture. You take twelve panoramic pictures with one Kodak Fun Panoramic Camera. Then put the camera in for developing and printing.

Each print is 25 by 9 centimetres. Excellent depth of field. True Kodak Gold colours.

The Kodak Fun Panoramic Camera itself goes back to the factory, to be recycled. So that others too can capture one of those spectacular phooooooooooootoooooooooooooos.

Although the roadway network in Dresden is quite extensive, road conditions often leave much to be desired. At the present time there is quite a bit of road construction going on which, combined with increased traffic, makes very slow progress.

Distances from various (German, Austrian, Swiss) cities to Dresden:

Berlin: 180 km (110 miles)
Bern: 1,000 km (625 miles) (via Nuremberg)
Düsseldorf: 650 km (410 miles)
Frankfurt am Main: 500 km (310 miles)
Hamburg: 470 km (295 miles)
Hanover: 370 km (230 miles)
Cologne: 680 km (425 miles)
Leipzig: 120 km (75 miles)
Munich: 550 km (345 miles)
Nuremberg: 400 km (250 miles)
Stuttgart: 620 km (390 miles)
Vienna: 600 km (375 miles) (via Prague)

Traffic regulations and signs correspond to those commonly used internationally. Throughout former East Germany it is strictly forbidden to drive while under the influence of any amount of alcohol.

Maximum speed limits:

Motorways: 100 km/h (about 62 mph)
Secondary roads: 80 km/h (50 mph)
Within city limits: 50 km/h (30 mph)

TRAVEL ESSENTIALS

VISAS & PASSPORTS

Visas are not required for citizens of European Community countries; a valid personal identification card or passport are enough to ensure entry and exit. Holders of Australian, Canadian, Japanese, New Zealand, South African and US passports automatically get three month permits on crossing the border but visas are required for longer stays.

MONEY MATTERS

The unit of currency in Dresden is the German Mark (DM). There are 1, 2, 5, 10, 50 pfennig and 1, 2 and 5 mark coins; bills come in denominations of 5, 10, 20, 50, 100, 200, 500, and 1,000 marks. Foreign currency is not subject to any particular regulations. It is possible to exchange money at border-crossings, in hotels, travel agencies and banks.

Exchange offices in Dresden's city centre:
Dresden-Altstadt (Old Town), Rampische Strasse 2.

Tel: 495 21 98. Hours: 7.30am–7pm Monday–Thursday; 9.30am–7pm Friday; 8am–1pm Saturday and Sunday.
Dresdner Bank, Waisenhausstrasse, O-8010 Dresden. Tel: 495 10 02. Hours: 8.30am–12.30pm and 2–4pm Monday–Wednesday; 8.30am–12.30pm and 2–5pm Thursday; 8.30am–12.30pm Friday.

Apart from a small amount of cash, visitors are recommended to take traveller's cheques and credit cards with them. Rates for paying with Eurocheques are especially good, being accepted at most larger hotels, restaurants and shops to a maximum of 400DM per cheque. There are EC cash machines available; several are located on Prager Strasse.

WHAT TO WEAR

Dresden has a fairly mild climate, so a warm sweater may be necessary to ward off the chill of an occasional cool day. An umbrella is not a bad idea as it may rain at anytime of year.

CUSTOMS REGULATIONS

As of 3 October 1990 the customs regulations which once just applied to the Federal Republic of Germany now also apply to the country formerly known as East Germany. Bringing drugs and weapons into Germany is strictly prohibited. Visitors with questions about what may be taken out of the country on departure should enquire at the customs office:
Zollamt, Reichspietschufer, O-8060 Dresden.
Tel: 48 30.

GETTING ACQUAINTED

With a population totalling 523,000 inhabitants (from a census taken on 31 December 1984), Dresden is the third largest city in former East-Germany. It is also the capital city of the German state of Saxony. Its geographical position in a valley carved out by the Elbe River provided good conditions for its relatively early settlement. Over the past centuries the city has evolved into an industrial, scientific, technological and, above all, an artistic and cultural centre. Following the incorporation of a number of villages in the year 1956, Dresden presently covers a land area of 225 sq km (87 sq miles). The forest area of the Dresdener Heide (Dresden Heath) alone takes up 50 sq km (19 sq miles).

The River Elbe flows for a total of about 20 km (12.5 miles) through the city, dividing it into the Altstadt (Old Town) and Neustadt (New Town). Its water level is given at 105.7 metres (350 ft) above sea level. To the right of the river, on the Neustadt side, the landscape is characterised by steep slopes. To the left of the Elbe the land is composed of gently rising fertile fields and meadows. The Erzgebirge, Elbsandstein Gebirge (Elbe Sandstone Mountains) and the Lausitz Uplands make the broad Elbe Valley around Dresden a charmingly varied area.

The two halves of the city are connected to each other by 5 bridges and a ferry system.

TIME ZONE

The time in Dresden corresponds to Central European Standard Time, one hour ahead of Greenwich Mean Time. As is the case in many other countries, Daylight Saving Time is in effect in Germany from April until September. During this period, clocks are set either ahead or behind one full hour.

CLIMATE

Dresden has a temperate climate: summers are not unbearably hot nor are winters severe. Because it is situated in a valley, the climate is often moist and the air pollution significant. Due to these conditions, asthmatics frequently have difficulties. However in the nearby mountains surrounding Dresden the air is drier and cleaner. You can count on some rainfall at any time of year.

Average annual temperature: +10° C
Average annual precipitation: 700–800 mm
Coldest month: January, average -0.1° C
Warmest month: July, average +18.0° C
Weather Report: Telephone Information: 0163
Radio Weather Report: Every hour on the hour following the news report, Dresden Station (Sachsenradio), VHF 92.2.

WEIGHTS & MEASURES

The Metric System is used throughout Germany. Occasionally older people use pounds as a unit of weight; 1 pound = 0.45 kg.
Electrical supply: AC 220 volts

BUSINESS HOURS

Generally speaking shops are open for business between 9am and 6.30pm. Some shops, usually located in the outer sections of the city, close for lunch between noon and 2pm, or from 1 to 3pm. On Thursdays they remain open until 8.30pm.

HOLIDAYS

New Year's Day
Good Friday and Easter Monday
May Day
Ascension Day (Christi Himmelfahrt)
Whit Monday
The Feast of Corpus Christi (Fronleichnam); in Catholic states.
The Day of the Assumption of the Virgin Mary (Mariä Himmelfahrt)
Day of German Unity: 3 October
All Saints's Day (Allerheiligen); in Catholic States.
Day of Prayer and Repentance
Christmas Day and Boxing Day

FESTIVALS

Dresden has much to offer in the way of annual festivals and various other events. Here are some of the most important:
March: Young Peoples' Theatre Festival, featuring performances by foreign theatre ensembles.
1 May: A Folk Festival which takes place in the streets and at various squares throughout the city.
May: Dixieland Festival including performances by international musicians. The festival is brought to a spectacular conclusion by literally hundreds of enthusiastic fans accompanying Dixieland bands as they parade playing music through the city centre.
May/June: International Dresden Music Festival. A variety of opera and concert performances take place at the city's many facilities devoted to culture.
June: International Dance Competition.
July/August: Cinema Summer.
September: Contemporary Music Festival.

RELIGIOUS CONGREGATIONS

In addition to Protestant and Catholic congregations, there are a host of other religious communities of different denominations in Dresden.

SERVICES

The Protestant-Lutheran Kreuzkirche (Church of the Holy Cross) is the home of the famous Dresden Kreuzchor. The choir can be heard singing every Sunday evening at vespers at 6pm. On Christmas Eve at 2.15pm and again at 4.30pm the church is brimming over with people who have come to listen to the choir singing Christmas carols. On Maundy Thursday and Good Friday the choir performs St John's or St Matthew's Passion by Johann Sebastian Bach. Regular services are held Sundays at 9.30am. Special services are conducted on religious holidays, at the end of the year and on New Year's Day. Masses are held daily in the cathedral, formerly the Catholic Hofkirche (court church): Saturday at 6pm, Sunday at 7.30am, 9am, 10.30am and 6pm. A late afternoon service with organ music is held Saturdays at 4pm.

Saxony Regional Church Headquarters (Protestant/Lutheran), Lukasstrasse 6, O-8077 Dresden. Tel: 475 841.

St Peter's Cathedral Chapter, Käthe-Kollwitz-Ufer 84, O-8053 Dresden. Tel: 341 61.

Reform-Protestant Congregation, Brühlscher Garten 4, O-8010 Dresden. Tel: 495 13 02.

Jewish Congregation, Bautzner Strasse 20, O-8060 Dresden. Tel: 554 91.

Russian-Orthodox Church, Juri-Gagarin-Strasse 19, O-8027 Dresden. Tel: 47 94 14.

Moravian Brotherhood, Community Centre, Oschatzer Strasse 41, O-8023 Dresden. Tel: 57 74 41.

Church of Jesus Christ of the Latter Day Saints, Dr-Kurt-Fischer-Allee 1a, O-8060 Dresden. Tel: 537 02.

Protestant-Methodist Church,, Wiener Strasse 56, O-8020 Dresden. Tel: 47 74 41.

COMMUNICATIONS

All national daily newspapers and many foreign papers are available in the city. For those competent in German and wanting to keep abreast of news in Dresden and Saxony, pick up a copy of the *Sächsische Zeitung*, the *Union*, or the *Dresdner Neueste Nachrichten*. The city magazines *SAX* and *Dresdner* are published monthly. In addition to an extensive calendar of events and list of addresses they both include articles dealing with local politics, culture and art. The best collection of tips for tourists is found in the information brochure *Dresden*, put out by Dresden-Information. It includes a calendar of the current month's events, museum hours and a list of useful addresses, available from kiosks and information centres, price 1.20DM.

MEDIA

The radio station *Sachsenradio* focuses its broadcasts on issues and information relating to Dresden and Saxony. Broadcasting time: 5.05am–1pm Monday–Friday, 6.05am–1pm Saturday and Sunday. Information includes events, traffic conditions, the weather, sports results, etc. Tune into VHF 92.2.

POSTAL SERVICES

In general, post offices are open from 8am to 6pm. The following post offices maintain longer business hours:

Post Office 1, Am Queckbrunnen, O-8010 Dresden. Tel: 495 30 17. Hours: 8am–7pm Monday–Friday.

Post Office 25, Neustädter Railway Station. Tel: 53 886. Hours: 6am–8pm Monday–Friday; 8am–noon and 1–6pm Saturday; 8am–noon Sunday.

Post Office 72, Leningraderstrasse 26 (entrance on Prager Strasse), O-8010 Dresden. Tel: 495 41 65 or 495 25 75. Hours: 8am–7pm Monday–Friday; 9am–noon Saturday.

Post Office 73, Main Railway Station. Tel: 484 82 81. Hours: 6am–10pm Monday–Friday; 7am–noon and 1–9pm Saturday and Sunday.

Stamps may be purchased not only at post offices, but also at the newsagents' operated by the German Postal Service. Letter boxes are yellow and are emptied from one to three times a day. Some that are emptied on Sundays. Check the letter box itself for the scheduled mail pick-ups.

TELEPHONE

Telephone booths are yellow and it's not always apparent from the outside as to whether or not the phone is meant for domestic or foreign calls. Once inside the booth, however, you can tell which kind of a telephone it is by the coin slot; for local calls you'll need to put in three 10 pfennig coins, for long-distance calls you can use 50 pfennig or 1DM coins.

TELEPHONE RATES

Local Calls:	.30DM (with no time limit)	
Long-distance Calls:	**normal rate**	**cheap rate**
Zone I	.23DM	.23DM
Zone II	.69DM	.46DM
Zone III	1.38DM	.92DM

(in the region formerly known as East Germany) Calls to the region formerly known as West Germany and West Berlin cost 1.50DM per minute. Normal rates apply between 7am–5pm Monday–Friday and 7am–2pm Saturday. Cheap rates apply between 5pm–7am Monday–Friday; from 2pm Saturday, and on Sundays and holidays.

DIALLING CODES

The dialling code for calls placed from outside into what used to be East Germany is 037; the dialling code for the City of Dresden is 51. It is still necessary to use the 037 code when making a call from what was West Germany. If you want to place a call to former West Germany from Dresden first dial 07, then the city number (delete the 0), and finally the number you are trying to reach.

It is possible to place most long-distance calls within and outside of Germany without operator assistance. Dialling codes are found listed in the telephone books. If no telephone book is available, contact information: District Information (Saxony): 001 80, Long-distance Information: 001 81, International Information 001 17.

Operator-assisted Calls:
to European countries: 001 14
to non-European countries: 001 13
To send a telegram: Tel: 013
Time of Day: Tel: 019
Wake-up Service: Tel: 001 41

TELEX

Most hotels have telex connections which can be used by their guests. There are also telefax connections in both the hotels Bellevue and Dresdner Hof, at the disposal of hotel guests only.

EMERGENCIES

SECURITY & CRIME

Recently, among certain sections of the local population there has been a rise in animosity towards visitors to the city and especially foreigners. The crime rate has risen sharply. The causes of this unfortunate development have to do with social structure, unemployment, a general loss of identity and the problems of enforcing the new laws. The police are relatively powerless in the face of these changes and for the most part, are not accepted by the majority of the population due to their earlier connections with the secret police force (Stasi) of the former SED (Socialist Party) regime. Don't carry valuables and keep all money as close to your body as possible taking care not to leave your purse unattended. It's also important to watch out for traffic as the streets were not built to accommodate the increasing flow of cars; many drivers, accustomed to driving Trabants or Wartburgs, have not quite got the hang of manoeuvring safely through city streets in their new, relatively powerful Western-manufactured cars. If you should be involved in an accident, contact the police immediately.

Emergency: Police tel: 110
                 Fire Brigade tel: 112
Police Headquarters, Schiessgasse 7, O-8010 Dresden. Tel: 48 30

LOST & FOUND

Central Lost & Found of the City of Dresden, Bautzner Strasse 23, O-8060 Dresden. Tel: 534 84. Hours: 9am–noon and 1–5pm Monday, Wednesday and Friday; 9am–noon and 1–4pm Tuesday.

German State Railways Lost & Found, Dresden Main Railway Station. Hours: 7am–12.30pm and 1–3.30pm Monday, Wednesday, Thursday and Friday; 7am–12.30pm and 1–6pm Tuesday.
Lost & Found, Borsbergstrasse 14, O-8060 Dresden. Hours: 9.30am–noon and 1–6pm Monday–Friday.
Motor Traffic Lost & Found, Leninplatz, near the main railway station. Hours: 7am–noon and 1–3pm Monday–Friday.

In case of loosing your passport contact the **Police Registration Office**, Rampische Strasse 8, O-8010 Dresden. Tel: 483 21 59. Hours: 8am–noon and 1–3pm Monday and Friday; 8am–noon and 1–6pm Tuesday; 9am–noon and 1–3pm Wednesday; 8am–noon and 1–5pm Thursday.

MEDICAL AID

The same regulations that exist everywhere in Germany also apply to foreigners in Dresden. Members of other European Community countries are subject to the stipulations cited on the reciprocal health insurance agreement, for which appropriate forms are available at your usual health insurance office. Visitors from non-EC countries should enquire prior to their departure whether their medical insurance policy covers them while travelling in Germany. When in doubt, it's a good idea to take out a supplementary travel-abroad policy. At the present time there are still relatively few doctors with private practices. Medical treatment usually takes place in either hospitals or clinics.

Fast Medical Aid   tel: 522 51
Emergency   tel: 115 (no charge)
General Medical Emergency Service, Poliklinik Mickten Grossenhainer Strasse 25. Tel: 553 27. Hours: 7pm–7am Monday–Friday, 1pm Saturday–7am Monday.
Emergency Dental Aid, Leningrader Strasse 35, O-8010 Dresden. Tel: 495 41 41. Hours: 9am–midnight Monday–Friday; 1pm–midnight Saturday; 9am–midnight Sunday and holidays.
Emergency Medical Aid for Children, Poliklinik Friedrichstadt, Bräuergasse 7/9. Tel: 43 41 10. Hours: 7–11pm Monday–Friday; 1–11pm Saturday; 9am–11pm Sunday.

CHEMISTS

General business hours: 9am–6pm.
Day and night emergency duty: Apotheke Prager Strasse 5, O-8010 Dresden (located near the main railway station), tel: 495 13 20. Information regarding doctors and chemists on emergency duty is available on the telephone number 0160.

Getting Around

CITY MAPS

City maps can be purchased in just about every bookstore and at newspaper kiosks.

A bookshop specialising in travel literature is **Das Internationale Buch**, Kreuzstrasse 4, O-8010 Dresden. Tel: 495 41 90.

You can also find orientation maps which include some city information at hotels, travel agencies and in the Dresden-Information Office.

PUBLIC TRANSPORT

Dresden has a well-developed network of public transport system of trams and buses as well as a suspension railway and a cable railway operating in the Weisser Hirsch area. A special park train runs through the Grosser Garten (Great Garden) and even the ferries crossing the Elbe are part of the public transport system. Except on the mountain trains and ferries, which can be paid in cash, tickets are required for all journeys. They can be bought at public transport kiosks, newsagents and small shops and must be validated before travel.

FARES

Since 1 June 1991 public transport fares in Dresden have been subject to time limitations. Adults pay .50DM for 30 minutes, .75DM for 60 minutes and 1DM for 90 minutes. There are reduced prices for children. During this time, passengers can transfer in whatever direction and as often as they wish. The most recent tickets are multiple-journey tickets and can be used for any of the time zones. They are made up of 11 separate segments, each of which is the equivalent to one half the regular ticket price. This means that if you plan to be travelling more than 30 minutes, you'll need to cancel the second to the last section on your ticket in addition to the last. If you plan to be in transit for an hour, you'll need to cancel the third to the last as well, and for 90 minutes the fourth to last unit must also be stamped. These tickets may be purchased either in one of the public transport company's own or at one of the additional 700 independent ticket outlets. Another recent and convenient development is the Day Card, valid for 24 hours and costing 2DM (1DM for children).

TRAMS & BUSES

Trams are usually yellow and black, though there are a few red ones too. They run throughout the whole day at 7–15 minutes intervals. When travelling at night, consult an official schedule as they run much less frequently at this time. The main and Neustädter railway stations are connected by tram routes 3 and 11 and you can catch a bus or train heading in nearly any direction from the main railway station.

SUBURBAN TRAINS (S–BAHN)

The German State Railway System operates a passenger service to and from Dresden's suburbs for fast-train prices. Fares are divided into different categories from 1–5 and range from .30DM–2DM. Tickets are available at train station counters and from automatic ticket machines, and must be validated before any journey.

BUSES

The central point of departure and arrival for buses in Dresden is at the main railway station at Leninplatz. Tickets can be purchased at the traffic pavilion (Leninplatz, tel: 47 52 25) or from bus drivers directly. Hours: 5am–8pm Monday–Friday; 5.30am–8pm Saturday and Sunday. Information is available daily from 7–9am, 9.30am–noon and 12.30–4pm.

THE WHITE FLEET

White Fleet (Weisse Flotte) boats travel according to a prearranged schedule from April to October from Dresden to Bad Schandau and Schmilka on the Czechoslovakian border ("Saxon Switzerland") and back again. From May until September they also cruise to and from Meissen. The central mooring is located at Terrassenufer, just below the Brühlsche Terrasse. The boats do make numerous stops along the way, however. During the summer months special cruises take place continually on White Fleet boats (for example concert, senior citizen and lecture cruises). Advance notice for these events can be found in the daily press and on posters along the terrace bank. There are also special cruises into Czechoslovakia organised by a number of travel agencies. **Weisse Flotte**, Terrassenufer 2, O-8010 Dresden. Information: Tel: 43 72 41, Ex: 444. Reservations for short trips: Reisebüro-Zweigstelle (Travel Agency Branch Office), O-8060 Dresden. Tel: 5 28 01.

MOUNTAIN RAILWAYS

Tickets for the mountain railway cost 1DM and may be purchased directly from the conductor. A multiple-journey ticket valid for 20 trips costs 5DM. Prams, push-chairs and bicycles are permitted on board.

STANDSEILBAHN (FUNICULAR)

The funicular connects Loschwitz (located at Körnerplatz) to Weisser Hirsch and is counted amongst the oldest of its kind in Europe. Operating hours: 5.30am–11.15pm Monday–Friday; 6.30am–11.15pm Saturday and Sunday. Length of ride: 5 minutes.

SUSPENSION CABLE RAILWAY

This is the oldest suspension cable railway in the entire world and connects Dresden-Loschwitz (Pillnitzer Landstrasse) with Oberloschwitz. There is a good view from the top. Operating hours: 6am–8pm Monday–Friday; 6.45am–8pm Saturday; 9am–7pm Sunday. Length of ride: 3 minutes.

PARK RAILWAY IN THE GREAT GARDEN

This railway carries passengers from May until September. Both the first and final station on the route is at Fucikplatz, though the train stops along the way, for example at the zoo. A sightseeing tour of the entire park is possible too. Depart Fucikplatz: 1.30–5.30pm Monday–Saturday and 10am–5.30pm Sunday, every 15 minutes.

ELBE FERRIES

Ferries that cross the Elbe carry passengers, prams, strollers, bicycles and sometimes even motorcycles. The only ferry transporting cars runs between Kleinschachwitz and Pillnitz.
Ferry Routes:
Zschieren–Söbringen, 5am–8am and 2–6pm Monday–Friday.
Kleinschachwitz–Pillnitz, 24 hours a day.
Laubegast–Hosterwitz, 5am–6pm Monday–Friday.
Tolkewitz–Niederpoyritz, 4.30am–8pm Monday–Friday; 10am–6pm Saturday and Sunday.
Johannstadt–Neustadt, 10am– 6pm daily (from 6 April–7 October).
Schlachthof–Pieschner Winkel, 4.30am– 6pm Monday–Friday.
Some ferries do not run on Saturdays or Sundays and others are only in operation during the summertime.

NARROW-GAUGE RAILWAYS

Travelling through the charming countryside surrounding Dresden aboard a narrow-gauge train is an especially pleasurable experience. Trains run between the following destinations:
Freital/Hainsberg–Kurort Kipsdorf (Kipsdorf Health Resort), (via the Malter Dam)
Radebeul–Radeburg (via Moritzburg)
Zittau–Oybin/Jonsdorf (the Zittau Hills)
The Kirnitzsch Valley Railway operates between Bad Schandau and the Lichtenhain Waterfall.
Departure and arrival times are listed in the timetable put out by German State Railways (DB).

TAXIS

Unlike the GDR when you could count on waiting hours before finally managing to get a cab, nowadays you'll find plenty of them parked at the ready at special taxi stops and in front of the railway stations. Recently, several private taxi companies have come into being. Within the city limits a kilometre will cost you 1.60DM; outside the city the rate is 2DM per kilometre. There are no additional charges for night fares. There are still not very many taxi stops in the city so the best way to hail one is to simply wave it over, or to order one by telephone:
To order a taxi: Tel: 4312 (around the clock, immediate service). It's possible to order a cab up to 5 days in advance from 6am–9pm Monday–Friday.
Taxis for the physically disabled, tel: 435 32 42 and 453 32 36.
Taxi Co-operative Ltd. tel: 43 91 81 12.
Taxis for the transport of goods tel: 43 71 58 and 58 43 38.

CAR RENTALS

Nearly all the larger hotels operate a car rental service. Drivers must be at least 21 years of age and have been in possession of a valid driver's licence for a minimum of 2 years. Rental prices are based on car type and the number of kilometres driven. There are special discount fares offered at weekends.
Prominent car rental agencies in the city are:
Inter-Rent-Europcar, Liebstädter Strasse 5, O-8020 Dresden. Tel: 232 33 99
Herz Autovermietung GmbH, Köpckestrasse 15, O-8050 Dresden. Tel: 566 28 40. Hours: 7.30am–6pm Monday–Friday; 8am–noon Saturday.
Sächsische Taxi-und Fahrschule GmbH, Blüher Strasse 9, O-8010 Dresden. Tel: 495 12 08. (Transport trailers also available for rent.)
Autohaus, Bremer Strasse 5, O-8010 Dresden. Tel: 43 70 54
H.J. Dornig, Dohnaer Strasse 72, O-8020 Dresden. Tel: 47 70 62 and 47 99 89

LIFT-ARRANGING AGENCIES

Christopherus, Robert-Blum-Strasse 3, O-8010 Dresden. Tel: 5 54 93. Hours: 8am–5pm Monday–Friday.
Fast Car, Bischofsweg 66, O-8060 Dresden. Tel: 5 34 39. Hours: 4–7pm Monday–Friday; noon–2pm Saturday.
Friedrich-Engels-Strasse 10, O-8060 Dresden. Tel: 5 12 16. Hours: 9am–7 p.m Monday–Friday; 9am–2pm Saturday.
Studentische MFZ, Nürnberger Strasse 57, O-8027 Dresden. Tel: 463 60 60
Jungtourist, Wormser Strasse 15, O-8019 Dresden. Tel: 3 52 59

BY CAR

The German Automobile Association (ADAC) now has an office in Dresden and can (hopefully) answer any questions. Accident forms are available at their offices and the staff will be happy to advise and help. **ADAC Business Office**, Liebstädter Strasse 5, O-8020 Dresden. Tel: 232 33 00 and 232 33 01. Hours: 9am–6pm Monday–Friday; 9am–12.30pm Saturday.

In the case of a car accident, the first thing to do is stop immediately. The next step is to protect the site of the accident by appropriately placing a warning triangle, alert the police if there are any casualties (tel: 110), then write down the car licence numbers and addresses of any witnesses. Any accident must be reported within 24 hours of its occurrence. **Breakdown and towing services:** The ADAC and ACE "Golden Angels" are a fleet of mobile yellow cars prepared to come to your rescue if your vehicle has broken down on the motorway or in a large city. **Central Breakdown Service**, Dresden. Tel: 2 32 30, Telex: 014

ACE Breakdown Service, tel: 4 85 30. Hours: 8am–9pm.
ADAC Breakdown Service. Tel: 435 34 44. Hours: around the clock.
Towing Service, Cossebauder Strasse, O-8028 Dresden. Tel: 43 40 50
Towing Service, H.J. Dornig, Dohnaer Strasse 72, O-8020 Dresden. Tel: 47 70 62 or 47 99 89

PETROL STATIONS

Generally speaking, filling stations are open from 6am–10pm, although some close for an hour or two during lunchtime. Extra, Super, Regular, Mixed, Super/Regular and Diesel are all readily available. It's also becoming easier to find unleaded petrol. **Intertank**, at the corner of Wiener and Gerhart-Hauptmann-Strasse, O-8020 Dresden. Tel: 47 06 16. Open day and night, unleaded petrol available.
Intertank, Bautzner Strasse 93, O-8060 Dresden. Tel: 5 17 27. Open day and night.
Petrol Statio, Blüherstrasse 9, O-8010 Dresden. Tel: 495 60 31
Intertank, Wilsdrufferstrasse (on both sides of the motorway), O-8024 Dresden. Tel: (0294) 307. Open day and night, unleaded petrol available.
Petrol Station, Kesselsdorfer Strasse 49, O-8028 Dresden. Tel: 43 42 26
BP Petrol Station, Radeburger Strasse, O-8000 Dresden. Open day and night.

GARAGES

Hotel Bellevue. Tel: 56 626/616
Autoreparaturwerk, Liebstädter Strasse 5, O-8020 Dresden. Tel: 2 32 33 00
J. Zimmermann, Turnerweg 2, O-8060 Dresden. Tel: 5 30 30
F. Gröbel, Wilsdruffer Strasse 106, O-8210 Freital. Tel: 64 30 27

PARKING

When going out to explore the city, it's advisable to leave your car parked in the hotel garage, as finding a parking place can be quite difficult. Dresden has not yet managed to come to terms with its sudden and considerable increase of traffic. So far there are no multi-storey car-parks and underground parking lots are to be found only in hotels. You are required to pay a fee for most parking places on the streets.

CAR INSURANCE & THEFT

If your car is broken into, inform the police headquarters immediately.
Police Headquarters, Rampische Strasse 8, O-8010 Dresden. Tel: 483 21 59. Hours: 8am–noon, 1–3pm Monday and Friday; 8am–noon, 1–6pm Tuesday; 9am–noon, 1–3pm Wednesday; 8am–noon, 1–5pm Thursday.

Any insurance demands should be addressed to the car owner's insurance company. Car owners are obliged by law to divulge information about their insurance companies when the situation requires. If necessary, it's possible to find out where the car owner is insured by calling the Motor Vehicle Insurance Central Office.

WHERE TO STAY

ACCOMMODATION

This is likely to remain something of a problem for some time to come. For some comparatively few of the many hotels and pensions that existed in Dresden prior to the war survived the bombing in 1945 and later, the expropriation of property by the state made a difficult situation even worse. In the 1960s when Prager Strasse was undergoing extensive re-development, four new hotels were erected. Most recently two luxury-class hotels (the Bellevue and the Dresdner Hof) have been built with the support of Japanese and Swedish investors. However, the current supply of accommodation in the city does not by any means meet the demand. Frequently all the beds within a 20 or 30 km (12–20 mile) radius of Dresden are booked solid. Even the several boat-hotels located along the Elbe do not manage to alleviate the dire shortage of guest lodgings very much. Consequently, potential visitors to Dresden are strongly advised to choose a hotel and book a room far in advance of their projected date of arrival. If you're less interested in comfort than in getting into closer contact with native city-dwellers, lodging in private quarters may be just the thing. There are numerous private rooms available which can be reserved by telephone through Dresden-Information. Hotel rates vary depending upon how rooms are furnished and the services offered. In accordance with international custom, hotels are divided into 5 categories. Prices for private rooms have increased considerably recently, due to the general and acute shortage of lodgings in the city.

HOTELS

Accommodation can be reserved at the hotel directly or through:

Zentrale Zimmervermittlung für Interhotels, Prager Strasse 2, O-8010 Dresden. Tel: 485 66 66, Telex: 22 21.

Zentrale Zimmerreservierung, Hotel Bellevue, Köpcke Strasse, O-8060 Dresden. Tel: 566 20, Telex: 262 71.

	Double Room	Single Room
☆☆☆☆☆	270–380DM	180–270DM
☆☆☆☆	230–250DM	150–195DM
☆☆☆	85–210DM	70–140DM
☆☆	75–100DM	45–100DM
☆	ca. 50DM	ca. 22DM

☆☆☆☆☆

Hotel Bellevue, Köpckestrasse 15, O-8060 Dresden. Tel: 566 20, Telex: 26162. Single Room: 220–280DM, Double Room: 320–380DM. Rooms include bath, shower, WC, TV, radio, minibar and telephone.

Hotel Dresdner Hof, An der Frauenkirche 5, O-8010 Dresden. Tel: 4 84 10 , Telex: 24 88. Single Room: starting at 180DM, Double Room: starting at 270DM. Rooms include bath, WC, minibar and telephone.

☆☆☆☆

Hotel Newa, Leningrader Strasse, O-8010 Dresden. Tel: 4 96 71 12, Telex: 260 67. Single Room: 157–195DM, Rooms include shower, WC and TV.

☆☆☆

Hotel Lilienstein, Prager Strasse, O-8010 Dresden. Tel: 4 85 60, Telex: 261 65. Single Room: 107–144DM, Double Room: 119–160DM. Rooms include shower, WC, TV, telephone and minibar.

Hotel Königstein, Prager Strasse, O-8010 Dresden. Tel: 4 85 60, Telex: 261. Single Room: 103–140DM, Double Room: 114–155DM. Rooms include shower, WC, TV, telephone and minibar.

Motel Dresden, Münzmeisterstrasse, O-8020 Dresden. Tel: 47 58 51. Single Room: 120DM, Double

Room: 170DM. Rooms include shower, WC, TV, radio and telephone.

Hotel Astoria, Ernst-Thälmann-Platz, O-8020 Dresden. Tel: 47 51 71, Telex: 24 42. Single Room: 70–100DM, Double Room: 130–210DM. Rooms include shower, WC, radio and telephone.

Hotel Schloss Eckberg, Bautzner Strasse 134, O-8060 Dresden. Tel: 5 49 07, Telex: 21 20. Single Room: 90–105DM, Double Room: 120DM. Rooms include shower, WC and radio.

Hotel Gewandhaus, Ringstrasse, O-8010 Dresden. Tel: 4 95 61 80. Single Room: 85–110DM, Double Room: 85–170DM. Rooms include radio, telephone, TV (in some rooms), shower and WC.

☆ – ☆☆

Waldparkhotel, Prellstrasse 16, O-8053 Dresden. Tel: 3 44 41. Double Room: 55–70DM. Some rooms include bath/shower, telephone, radio and TV.

Parkhotel, Bautzner Landstrasse 17, O-8051 Dresden. Tel: 3 68 51/3 68 52. Double Room: 50–55DM. Rooms include washing facilities.

Hotel Stadt Rendsburg, Kamenzer Strasse 1, O-8060 Dresden. Single Room: 22.80DM. Rooms include washing facilities; shower and WC located on each floor.

Hotel Artushof, Fetscherstrasse 30, O-8019 Dresden. Tel: 6 34 96. Single Room: 39DM, Double Room: 55–85DM. Rooms include washing facilities; bath and WC located on each floor.

Hotel Rothenburger Hof, Rothenburger Strasse 17, O-8060 Dresden. Tel: 57 21 43. Single Room: 45DM, Double Room: 75–100DM. Rooms include TV, radio, WC and shower located on each floor, solarium and restaurant.

PENSIONS

Pensions, noted for their simplicity and individual service, are less expensive than hotels. Prospective guests can book rooms through Dresden-Information or directly at the pension itself.

Pension Bellmann, Kretschmerstrasse 16, O-8053 Dresden. Tel: 3 81 50. Single Room: 25DM, Double Room: 40DM. Rooms have washing facilities, shower and WC in the house, additional beds available, breakfast included.

Pension Magvas, Gondelweg 3, O-8046 Dresden. Tel: 2 23 60 84. Double Room: 40DM, Suite: 60–90DM. Additional beds available, WC and washing facilities on each floor, 2 suites with bathrooms, breakfast optional, dining-room.

Fremdenheim Lössnitzer Hof, Wilhelm-Pieck-Strasse 202, O-8122 Radebeul. Tel: 7 53 53. Single Room: 17.10DM, Double: 34.20DM. Rooms with washing facilities, WC on each floor, breakfast included.

Pension Bück, Wachwitzer Höhenweg 28, O-8054 Dresden. Tel: 3 63 36. Per bed: 15DM. Four apartments with shower, WC radio, TV, mini-kitchen and refrigerator.

THE KODAK GOLD GUIDE TO BETTER PICTURES.

Good photography is not difficult. Use these practical hints and Kodak Gold II Film: then notice the improvement.

Move in close. Get close enough to capture only the important elements.

Frame your Pictures. Look out for natural frames such as archways or tree branches to add an interesting foreground. Frames help create a sensation of depth and direct attention into the picture.

One centre of interest. Ensure you have one focus of interest and avoid distracting features that can confuse the viewer.

Use leading lines. Leading lines direct attention to your subject i.e. – a stream, a fence, a pathway; or the less obvious such as light beams or shadows.

Maintain activity. Pictures are more appealing if the subject is involved in some natural action.

Keep within the flash range. Ensure subject is within flash range for your camera (generally 4 metres). With groups make sure everyone is the same distance from the camera to receive the same amount of light.

Check the light direction. People tend to squint in bright direct light. Light from the side creates highlights and shadows that reveal texture and help to show the shapes of the subject. If shooting into direct sunlight fill-in flash can be effective to light the subject from the front.

CHOOSING YOUR KODAK GOLD II FILM.

Choosing the correct speed of colour print film for the type of photographs you will be taking is essential to achieve the best colourful results.

Basically the more intricate your needs in terms of capturing speed or low-light situations the higher speed film you require.

Kodak Gold II 100. Use in bright outdoor light or indoors with electronic flash. Fine grain, ideal for enlargements and close-ups. Ideal for beaches, snow scenes and posed shots.

Kodak Gold II 200. A multipurpose film for general lighting conditions and slow to moderate action. Recommended for automatic 35mm cameras. Ideal for walks, bike rides and parties.

Kodak Gold II 400. Provides the best colour accuracy as well as the richest, most saturated colours of any 400 speed film. Outstanding flash-taking capabilities for low-light and fast-action situations; excellent exposure latitude. Ideal for outdoor or well-lit indoor sports, stage shows or sunsets.

A P A
INSIGHT
GUIDES

Are Going Places:

Asia & Pacific
East Asia
South Asia
South East Asian Wildlife
South East Asia
★Marine Life
Australia
Great Barrier Reef
Melbourne
★★Sydney
★Bhutan
Burma/Myanmar
China
Beijing
India
Calcutta
Delhi, Jaipur, Agra
India's Western Himalaya
Indian Wildlife
★New Delhi
Rajasthan
South India
Indonesia
★★Bali
★Bali Bird Walks
Java
★Jakarta
★Yogyakarta
Korea
Japan
Tokyo
Malaysia
★Kuala Lumpur
★Malacca
★Penang
★★Nepal
Kathmandu
Kathmandu Bikes & Hikes
New Zealand
Pakistan
Philippines
★Sikkim
★★Singapore
Sri Lanka
Taiwan

Thailand
★★Bangkok
★Chiang Mai
★Phuket
★Tibet
Turkey
★★Istanbul
Turkish Coast
★Turquoise Coast
Vietnam

Africa
East African Wildlife
South Africa
Egypt
Cairo
The Nile
Israel
Jerusalem
Kenya
Morocco
Namibia
The Gambia & Senegal
Tunisia
Yemen

Europe
Austria
★★Vienna
Belgium
Brussels
Channel Islands
Continental Europe
Cyprus
Czechoslovakia
★★Prague
Denmark
Eastern Europe
Finland
France
★★Alsace
★★Brittany
★★Cote d'Azur
★★Loire Valley
★★Paris

Provence
Germany
★★Berlin
Cologne
Düsseldorf
Frankfurt
Hamburg
★★Munich
The Rhine
Great Britain
Edinburgh
Glasgow
★★Ireland
★★London
Oxford
Scotland
Wales
Greece
★★Athens
★★Crete
★Rhodes
Greek Islands
Hungary
★★Budapest
Iceland
Italy
Florence
★★Rome
★★Sardinia
★★Tuscany
Umbria
★★Venice
Netherlands
Amsterdam
Norway
Poland
Portugal
★Lisbon
Madeira
Spain
★★Barcelona
★Costa Blanca
★Costa Brava
★Costa del Sol/Marbella
Catalonia

Gran Canaria
★Ibiza
Madrid
Mallorca & Ibiza
★Mallorca
★Seville
Southern Spain
Tenerife
Sweden
Switzerland
(Ex) USSR
Moscow
St. Petersburg
Waterways of Europe
Yugoslavia
★Yugoslavia's Adriatic
Coast

The Americas
Bermuda
Canada
Montreal
Caribbean
Bahamas
Barbados
Jamaica
Trinidad & Tobago
Puerto Rico
Costa Rica
Mexico
Mexico City
South America
Argentina
Amazon Wildlife
Brazil
Buenos Aires
Chile
Ecuador
Peru
Rio

USA/Crossing America
Alaska
American Southwest
Boston
California
Chicago
Florida
Hawaii
Los Angeles
Miami
Native America
New England
New Orleans
★★New York City
New York State
Northern California
Pacific Northwest
★★San Francisco
Southern California
Texas
The Rockies
Washington D.C.

★★Also available as
Insight Pocket Guide

★Available as Insight
Pocket Guide only

INSIGHT
pocket
GUIDES

Ci Vedremo
Presto!

See You Soon! In Italy

Pension Glück im Winkel, Hietzigstrasse 4, O-8051 Dresden. Tel: 3 73 39. Single Room: 16DM, Double Room: 42–50DM. Single room without washing facilities, WC and bath on each floor; 1 double occupancy room with bathroom and balcony; breakfast not available. The pension is located 200 metres from the Parkhotel.

Pension Preusche, Wilhelm-Müller-Strasse 19, O-8029 Dresden. Tel: 4 32 81 15. Double Room: 24–30DM. WC, shower, radio, TV and breakfast included.

Pension Jarosch, Wilhelm-Müller-Strasse3, O-8029 Dresden. Tel: 4 32 67 90. Single Room: 30DM, Double Room: 40DM. Additional beds available, radio, TV, some rooms with bathroom facilities, breakfast available upon request.

Pension Deckwer, Rädestrasse 26, O-8038 Dresden. Tel: 4 32 71 92. Per bed: 25DM. TV, radio, rooms have washing facilities, WC and shower on each floor, breakfast included.

Pension Eichlepp, Dr Rudolf-Friedrichs-Strasse 15, O-8122 Radebeul. Single Room: 35DM, Double: 50DM. TV, radio, refrigerator, rooms have washing facilities, shower and WC located on each floor, common room, breakfast available upon request.

Pension Eggert, Wurgwiltzer Strasse 1b, O-8027 Dresden. Tel: 4 32 52 41. Per bed: 21DM. TV, radio, rooms include washing facilities, WC and shower located on each floor, breakfast available upon request, additional beds available.

For private rooms enquire at:
Dresden-Information, Prager Strasse 10/11, O-8010. Tel: 495 50 25, Telex: 2-61 98, Fax: 495 12 76.

CAMPING

It is illegal to simply camp wherever you happen to find a spot. There are campsites in and around Dresden which are open from 1 May until 30 September. It is also possible to find a suitable campsite for a trailer or caravan. If you're planning to stay longer than 3 days, it's advisable to register in advance. Some campgrounds offer cottages for rent; the cost is 20DM a day per person. A bed in a camp cabin costs between 3–10DM per person. Campground fees run from between 3–17DM per day.

CAMPSITES (WITH CABINS)

Mockritz, Boderitzer -Strasse 8, O-8020 Dresden. Tel: 47 82 26. 10DM per bed; lavatory facilities located approximately 30 metres away.. 20DM per bed; (2-6 beds), shower and WC in cottage.

Reichenberg, Am Bad Sonnenland, O-8105 Reichenberg. Tel: 7 50 70. 3–10DM per bed. Lavatories.

Wosta, located on the banks of the Elbe and has an outdoor swimming pool. Trieskestrasse 100, O-8046 Dresden. Tel: 2 23 19 03. 4DM per person, 4–6DM per tent. Cottages: from 10DM per bed. Tent and sleeping-bag rentals.

YOUTH HOSTELS

Junior rates range between 4-5DM per night. **Seniors** pay between 11–13DM per night. **Bed linen** can be rented for 6DM and breakfast costs an additional 4DM. Potential guests must not necessarily have an International Youth Hostel Card.

Young Tourist Hotel "Schloss Eckberg" (Eckberg Castle), Bautzner Strasse 134, O-8060 Dresden. Tel: 549 07, Telex: 21 20. Comfortable lodgings for young people where the standard is about the equivalent of a 3-star hotel. The hotel is wonderfully located on a hill overlooking the Elbe.

Rudi Arndt Youth Hostel, Hübler Strasse 11, O-8027 Dresden. Tel: 47 06 67. Junior rates (to 26 years old): 5.50DM; senior rates: 13DM. Bed linen is available for 6DM, breakfast and/or dinner cost 3.60DM each. There are washing facilities in each room, WC and communal washrooms on each floor.

Oberloschwitz Youth Hostel, Sierksstrasse 33, O-8054 Dresden. Tel: 366 72. Junior rate: 4.50DM; senior rate 11.50DM. Breakfast and/or dinner are available for 4DM each; bed linens cost 5.50DM.

Wilhelm Dieckmann Youth Hostel, Weintraubenstrasse 12, O-8122 Radebeul. Tel: 747 86. Junior rate: 5DM; senior rate: 12.50DM. Bed linen/towels are 8.50DM, breakfast and/or dinner cost 4DM each. There is a shower and WC on each floor.

FOOD DIGEST

SAXON SPECIALITIES

Saxon cuisine tends to be quite heavy and is certainly not particularly calorie-conscious! It is reminiscent of Bohemian cuisine, even if the equivalent of the ubiquitous Bohemian dumpling is nowhere to be found. Meat, particularly pork, is consumed in great quantities. Boiled pork knuckle served with sauerkraut is an especially popular dish amongst Dresden natives. A simple, also quite popular meal often consists of a stew made of either mainly potatoes, lentils, noodles or rice. Dresden cake has quite a famous reputation: "Dresdner Eierschecke" dominates the sweet-treat scene throughout the year and "Dresdner Stollen" is the speciality during Advent and Christmas-time. It's traditional to eat pancakes at Shrovetide.

BEVERAGES

The Meissen Wine-Growers Co-operative produces some truly splendid wines, which can be recommended to professed lovers of dry wines. The fruit used by the co-op is cultivated in the northernmost grape-growing areas in Europe, near Radebeul and Meissen, in Dresden itself and Pillnitz. Dresden beer is also highly recommended, especially "Radeberger Pilsner".

RESTAURANTS

At the present time it is all but impossible to definitively recommend any one restaurant as the gastronomic situation in Dresden is currently undergoing radical change. In the wake of the general tendency to privatise, nearly all dining establishments have been taken over by new owners. Many will probably close in the due course of time and as of yet, there aren't any that seem to deserve outstanding praise. The thing to do is to just follow your nose and try your luck!

International, Prager Strasse, O-8010 Dresden. Tel: 49 52 65. Hours: 11am–midnight Monday–Sunday. Polish specialities.

Am Zwinger, Ernst-Thälmann-Strasse 24, O-8010 Dresden. Tel: 495 11 81, Hours: 11am–midnight Monday–Sunday; Saturday until 1am. Terrace café.

Kulturpalast, Altmarkt, O-8010 Dresden . Tel: 486 63 06. Hours: 10am–midnight Monday–Sunday.

Szeged, Ernst-Thälmann-Strasse 4, O-8010 Dresden. Tel: 495 13 71. Hours: 11am–midnight Monday–Sunday. Hungarian Specialities.

Gastmahl des Meeres, Grunaer Strasse 5, O-8010 Dresden. Tel: 485 36 12. Hours: 11am–10pm Monday–Sunday. Seafood Banquet.

Kügelenhaus, Strasse der Befreiung 13, O-8060 Dresden. Tel: 5 27 91. Hours: 11am–midnight Monday–Sunday. Meeting place for intellectuals.

Blockhaus, Neustädter Markt 19, O-8060 Dresden. Tel: 5 36 30 and 5 44 21. Hours: 11am–midnight. Russian cuisine.

Meissner Weinkeller, Strasse der Befreiung 1b, O-8060 Dresden. Tel: 5 58 14 and 5 59 28. Hours: 6pm–midnight Monday–Sunday. Elbe wines.

Opernrestaurant, Theaterplatz 2, O-8010 Dresden. 10am–10pm Monday–Sunday.

Ostrawa, Fetscherstrasse 30, O-8019 Dresden. Tel: 459 31 31. Hours: 10am–11pm Monday–Thursday; 10am–midnight Friday and Saturday. Czechoslovakian specialities.

OUTSIDE THE CITY CENTRE

Luisenhof, Bergbahnstrasse 8, O-8051 Dresden. Tel: 3 68 42. Hours: 11am–11pm Monday–Thursday; 11am–midnight Friday and Saturday. This restaurant is referred to as the "Dresden Balcony" because of its wonderful view of the city. It can be reached via the mountain railway and offers a cultural programme. Tables should be booked in advance.

Maygarten Linie 6, Schaufusstrasse 24, O-8021 Dresden. Tel: 302 68. Hours: 5–11pm Tuesday–Thursday; 11am–11pm Friday and Saturday.

Hubertusgarten, Bautzner Landstrasse 89, O-8051 Dresden. Tel: 3 60 74. Hours: 5pm–midnight Wednesday–Friday; 11am–midnight Saturday; 11am–4pm Sunday. Game specialities.

Café Prag, Altmarkt 16, O-8010 Dresden. Tel: 495 11 35. Hours: 10am–10pm. Cabaret programme and dancing.

Café Haus Altmarkt, Ernst-Thälmann-Strasse 19, O-8101 Dresden. Tel: 495 12 12. Hours: 9am–9pm Monday–Saturday; 1–9pm Sunday. Restaurant serving good plain home-style fare.

Ring Café, Wallstrasse 7, O-8010 Dresden. Tel: 495 60 83. Hours: 9am–11pm, daily.

Mokkastube (Mocca Room), Altmarkt 16/17, O-8010 Dresden. Tel: 495 11 35.

Café Kästner, Alaunstrasse 1, O-8060 Dresden. Tel: 57 04 45. Hours: 11am–10pm Monday–Sunday.

Café Toscana, Schillerplatz 7, O-8053 Dresden. Tel: 3 07 44. Hours: 9am–6pm Monday–Friday; 8am–5pm Saturday. This is a popular, traditional-style café with its own bakery on the premises.

Café im Fernsehturm (TV Tower Café), Oberwachwitzer Weg 37, O-8054 Dresden. Tel: 3 67 59. Hours: 10am–4pm, daily. Café with panoramic view.

Café Hausberg, Hoher Steig 4, O-8054 Dresden. Tel: 392 00. Café with a wonderful panoramic view.

NIGHTLIFE

BARS

Parkhotel, Bautzner Landstrasse 7, O-8051 Dresden Weisser Hirsch. Tel: 3 68 51. Hours: 8pm–2am Wednesday and Thursday; 8pm–3am Friday and Saturday; 10pm–4am Sunday.

Etagenbar im Zwinger, Ernst-Thälmann-Strasse 24, O-8010 Dresden. Tel: 495 12. Hours: 2–9pm Monday–Sunday.

BEER GARDENS

Bühlauer Waldgärten, Nachtflügelweg 25. Tel: 36 45 7. Hours: 2–10pm Monday–Sunday.

Die 100, Alaunstrasse 100, O-8060 Dresden. Daily from 10pm until the small hours of the morning.

Planwirtschaft, Louisenstrasse 20. Hours: 4pm–1am daily.

DANCING

Mazurkabar in the Hotel International, Prager Strasse, O-8010 Dresden. Tel: 495 25 65. Hours: 8pm–3am Monday–Sunday.
Altmarktbar, Ernst-Thälmann-Strasse 19, O-8010 Dresden. Tel: 495 12 12. Hours: 8pm–4am Monday–Sunday.
Lindengarten, Otto-Buchwitz-Strasse 121a, O-8010 Dresden. Tel: 5 59 21. Hours: 8pm–3am Monday and Tuesday.

DISCOS

Many student clubs and youth centres organise disco nights. At Sachs, an ultra-modern disco complete with a laser light show and other assorted high-tech accoutrements costing several million German marks, made its grand debut in 1991.
Sachs, Stephensonstrasse 6, O-8045 Dresden. Tel: 229 25 55

NIGHTCLUBS

Hotel Dresdner Hof, An der Frauenkirche 5, O-8010 Dresden. Tel: 484 17 76. Hours: 8pm–3am Monday–Sunday.
Hotel International, Prager Strasse, O-8010 Dresden. Tel: 455 25 65. Hours: 8pm–3am Monday–Sunday.
Am Zwinger, Ernst-Thälmann-Strasse 24, O-8010 Dresden. Tel: 495 12 81. Hours: 8pm–4am Monday–Sunday.
Jupiterbar in the Hotel Bellevue, Köpckestrasse 15, O-8010 Dresden. Tel: 5 34 25. Hours: 9pm–4am Monday–Sunday.

GAMBLING CASINOS

Hotel Bellevue, Köpckestrasse 15, O-8010 Dresden. Tel: 5 34 25. Hours: 7pm–1am daily.
Pirnaisches Tor, Grunaer Strasse 5, O-8010 Dresden. Tel: 459 36 12. Hours: 10am–2pm Monday–Sunday.
Brauerei Mockritz (Mockritz Brewery), Gostriltzer Strasse 30, O-8020 Dresden. Tel: 47 75 33. Hours: 4pm–midnight Wednesday and Thursday; 5pm–midnight Friday. Restaurant and bar on the premises.

"IN" SPOTS

For those wanting to get to know the alternative, "in" scene in Dresden Neustadt–Bunte Republik Neustadt (BRN) (Multi-coloured Republic), the following pubs can be recommended (keeping in mind that "in" pubs, in Dresden like everywhere else, have a tendency to change names and locations frequently):
Die 100, at the corner of Alannstrasse and Bischofsweg, O-8060 Dresden. Hours: 8pm–4am Monday–Sunday.
Planwirtschaft, Louisenstrasse 15, O-8060 Dresden. Hours: 4pm–2am.

Projekttheater, Louisenstrasse 15, O-8060 Dresden. Hours: 4pm–2am Monday–Sunday.
Raskolnikow, Böhmische Strasse 36, O-8060 Dresden. Hours: from 9pm Wednesday–Sunday.
Stillos, Hechtstrasse 64, O-8060 Dresden. Hours: 7pm–4am Wednesday–Monday.
Tivoli, Louisenstrasse 10, O-8060 Dresden. Hours: from 10pm Monday–Sunday.

FAST FOOD

The following self-service restaurants can be recommended if you're looking for quick, inexpensive bite to eat:
Am Zwinger, (commonly referred to as the "Fresswürfel"), Ernst-Thälmann-Strasse/Postplatz, O-8010 Dresden. Tel: 495 12 81. Hours: 6am–6pm Monday–Friday; 8am–3pm Saturday.
Wallterrassen, Wallstrasse 11, O-8010 Dresden. Tel: 495 24 81. Hours: 7am–6pm Monday–Friday; 8am–1.30pm Saturday.
Picknick, Grunaer Strasse 28, O-8010 Dresden. Tel: 495 22 27. Hours: 7am–7pm Monday–Saturday; 8am–7pm Sunday.
Narrenhäusel, Köpckestrasse/Augustusbrücke, O-8060 Dresden. Tel: 5 55 02. Open around the clock except between 5–6am when it closes for cleaning.
Passant, Prager Strasse, O-8010 Dresden. Tel: 4 85 60. Hours: 9am–7pm Monday–Sunday.
Schlossschänke Pillnitz, August-Böckstiegel-Strasse 10, O-8054 Dresden. Tel: 3 93 40. Hours: 10am–10pm daily.

THINGS TO DO

IMPORTANT BUILDINGS

Zwinger: Undoubtedly the most magnificent and famous construction in Dresden is located between Postplatz and Theaterplatz. The Zwinger was erected between 1710–1732. It was designed by the architect Matthaeus Daniel Pöppelmann as a square where festivals could be celebrated, surrounded on all 4 sides by architectural structures for Augustus the Strong, Elector of Saxony, and King of Poland. The sculptures were created by Balthasar Permoser. Surrounding the square are the Kronentor (Crown Gate) and opulent, Baroque-style pavilions connected to each other by galleries. The fourth, initially incomplete side was later finished between 1847 and 1854 by G. Semper's art gallery. The

Zwinger, destroyed in 1945, was rebuilt by the year 1964. A number of museums affiliated with the National Art Collections are housed here.

Residenzschloss (Schlossplatz): This palace was erected under the auspices of Duke George the Bearded (which is why the original part is referred to as Georgenbau) between 1530–1535 and was subsequently extended and expanded by Augustus II. From 1889 until 1901 it was transformed into a unified Neo-Renaissance-style building by the architects Frölich and Dunger. The palace was almost completely destroyed in 1945 and is currently undergoing extensive reconstruction. The exhibit on display in the palace documents its reconstruction.

Cathedral: This former court cathedral is the largest Catholic church in all of Saxony. The Italian architect Ciaveri was commissioned by Frederick Augustus II to build the cathedral in the Baroque style. Construction took place between 1738 and 1771. The stone figures gracing the balustrades of the nave and aisles are the work of the Italian sculptor Corenzo Mattielli. Inside the church, the painting hung above the high altar by Raphael Mengs, the pulpit created by Balthasar Permoser and the organ built by Gottfried Silbermann are all worthy of note. The Catholic electoral princes and kings of Saxony are buried in the cathedral's crypt and the heart of Augustus the Strong is kept in a small vessel on the premises.

The Semper Opera House (Theaterplatz 2): Following the fire that destroyed the old building by Semper, the new opera house was erected in the style of the High-Renaissance between 1871 to 1878 according to Gottfried Semper's plans by his son Manfred Semper. Dominating features are the principal axis with its monumental loggia and the main façade facing Theaterplatz with its bronze chariot drawn by 4 panthers which were created by Johannes Schilling. The sculptures of Goethe and Schiller were created by Ernst Rietschel. The opera house's interior has a decidedly festive atmosphere due to its wealth of paintings, mouldings, ornate gilting and fabrics. Also seriously damaged in 1945, it has subsequently been restored to its original state and was reopened in 1985 just in time for the 40th anniversary of the destruction of Dresden.

Brühlsche Terrasse: Also known as the "Balcony of Europe", the Brühlsche Terrasse was named after Count Heinrich von Brühl, the chief minister under Augustus the Strong and his son. It was erected upon the remains of the city fortifications dating from the 16th century. The state parliament building, College of Fine Arts and Sekundogenitur Building (wine restaurants) are all located here.

Kreuzkirche (Altmarkt): Dresden's oldest parish and main church (dating back to the 13th century) with its tall tower (94 metres/315 ft) was constructed in its present classical form between 1764–1792. The church sustained a lot of damage in 1945 and 10 years later was again officially reopened. The Kreuzchor is as old as the church itself.

The Frauenkirche ruins (Neumarkt): The 95 metre-high (320 ft) dome of this once world-famous holy edifice (built between 1726 and 1745 by George Bähr) lent its commanding presence to Dresden's wonderful skyline. Today the ruins stand as a memorial to the destruction of the city in February 1945. Plans are already in the making for the church's reconstruction.

Pillnitz Palace and Pleasure Garden: Pillnitz was gradually built over the course of the 18th century and served the princely and royal families as a summer residence. The "Water" and "Mountain" Palaces were constructed in the "Indian Style" by Daniel Pöppelmann; the New Palace (Schuricht, 1818–26) was erected sometime later. The large pleasure garden is divided into separate English, Dutch and Chinese gardens, all enhanced by lovely pavilions.

Grosser Garten (Fucikplatz): The Great Garten is an impressive example of Baroque-style landscaping. Its focal point is the Garden Palace, surrounded by pavilions created in the early-Baroque style by J.G. Starcke. The large palace pond was designed by Karcher. In the garden there are a number of works by various well-known sculptors. Nowadays, the Great Garten is a place of cultural, recreational and educational enjoyment. The garden is popularly referred to as the "green lung" of Dresden.

CITY SIGHTSEEING TOURS

The following city sightseeing tours are organised by the information centres in Dresden all year round:
Via mini-van departing from Dr-Külz-Ring:
Little City Sightseeing Tour (90 minutes): Daily at 10.30am, noon, 1.30pm, 3pm and 4.30pm.
Big City Sightseeing Tour (3 hours): Daily at 10am, including a tour through the Pillnitz Palace Park.
Via double-decker bus departing from Augustusbrücke:
Little City Sightseeing Tour (90 minutes): Daily at 10am, 11.30am, 1pm, 2.30pm and 4pm.
Via tram departing from Postplatz: Daily except Monday at 9am, 11am and 1pm.
Dresden-Information offers excursions which must be booked at least 6 days in advance at:
Dresden Information, Bereich Stadtrundfahrten (City Sightseeing Tours). Tel: 495 50 25 ext. 10.

Musical tradition in Dresden: This journey takes you to Grupa for a visit to the Richard Wagner Museum. The return trip leads over Hosterwitz and includes a stop at the Carl-Maria von Weber Memorial before arriving in Dresden for a guided tour through the Semper Opera House. The entire outing lasts 5 hours. The tour is offered daily at 9.30am (according to demand) from March until October. Departure point is Dr-Külz-Ring; cost is 55DM per person plus admission fees.

Meissen Porcelain - from invention to manufacture: This tour begins with a stroll over the Brühlsche Terrasse and Böttgerstele, followed by a trip to Meissen for a visit to the porcelain factory (display workshop and hall), and sightseeing at the castle and cathedral before heading back to Dresden. The tour is offered daily at 9am (according to demand) from the end of May until October. Departure point is the Augustusbrücke; cost is 55DM per person plus admission fees. The morning excursion lasts 5 hours.

Moritzburg Baroque Palace: Journey to Moritzburg. Sightseeing tour of the Baroque Palace and the palace grounds. The afternoon excursion lasts 3 hours. This tour is offered daily at 2pm (according to demand) from the end of March (Easter) until October. Point of departure is Augustusbrücke; cost is 34DM per person plus admission fees.

To Saxon Switzerland: This excursion takes you via Pillnitz and Lohmen to Rathen for a sightseeing tour of the Bastei. The journey continues over Hohenstein, the Polenztal Valley and Bad Schandau to Königstein for a visit to the Königsstein fortress before heading back to Dresden. The tour is offered daily at 9am (according to demand) from the end of March (Easter) until October. Departure point is Dr-Külz-Ring; cost per person is 55DM, plus entrance fees.

Life in Antonstadt: A walk through the outer Neustadt suitable for everyone. Tour lasts about 2 hours and is organised by:

Die IG Äussere Neustadt, Louisenstrasse 67, O-8060 Dresden. Tel: 57 08 58.

By lift up the Elbe sandstone mountains: The recently resurrected elevator in Saxon Bad Schandau is a tourist attraction dating from the period of rapid industrial expansion in Germany (beginning in 1871). It is located in the part of the town called Ostrau. Passengers enjoy a panoramic view of the deeply carved out river valley in the Elbe Sandstone Mountains (Elbsandstein Mountains) during the ride up from the Elbuferstrasse to the exclusive residential suburb situated on the mountain top. The actual structure consists of an elevator tower contained in a bridge 50 metres high (165 ft) leading up to the top of the mountain. It was built by Rudolf Sendig in 1904. The iron construction is decorated with Art Nouveau-style ornaments. On the upper, mountainside end of the bridge elevator passengers are confronted with an animal cage in which bears once lived and which now houses two lynxes.

Nostalgic Sightseeing Tour: Dresden Transport Services organise a special kind of city sightseeing tour which departs from the Mickten Tram Station and offers participants the opportunity of getting to know a number of city suburbs. Passengers take a "309" tram car dating from the year 1902 into the historical core of the city for a 30-minute stop and visit the Transport Museum in the Johanneum. The tour continues via Dresden "Büssing" – an old-time bus manufactured in 1938 to the ferry mooring. Here passengers transfer onto the *Johanna* where those in need of a little sustenance can get a bite to eat (food costs are not included in the tour package).

In Dresden-Loschwitz passengers climb aboard the reconstructed suspension railway. The *Grosse Hechtwagen* waits in Bühlau to transport tour participants the final part of the journey back into the city centre. In 1932 the Hechtwagen was the fastest tramcar at 84 km/h (53 mph) in all of Germany.

Tickets can be purchased at any information centre office or directly at the tour departure point. In addition to these excursions, special outings including a tour of the Zwinger and visits to the galleries in the Albertinum, as well as the Grünes Gewölbe (Green Vault) are also available. Qualified guides with a command of one or more foreign languages are available to accompany you individually on city sightseeing rounds. The Information Centre and various travel agencies also offer both single and several-day excursions into the countryside surrounding Dresden. Popular destinations include Pillnitz, the Grosssedlitz Baroque Garden, Stolpen Castle, Königstein, Saxon Switzerland, Radebeul, Meissen and Moritzburg.

Dresden-Information Travel Services, Prager Strasse 12. Tel: 495 11 75. Hours: 9am–6pm Monday–Friday.

Reisewelt Dresden (Travelworld Dresden), Neustädter Markt 5, O-8060 Dresden. Tel: 5 28 01.

Alternative City Sightseeing Tours with programme arrangement, group organisation and guides are offered by: **Igel-Tour**, c/o Johannstädter Kulturtreff, Dürerstrasse 79, O-8019 Dresden. Tel: 495 40 96 and 486 72 81. Office Hours: 8am–noon Monday.

CULTURE PLUS

Dresden has the reputation of being a cultural metropolis and as such hosts quite a diverse assortment of cultural activities and events. Enquire at your hotel reception or in the Information Centre as to what is currently being offered in the city. A calendar of events is published monthly and is available at any newspaper kiosk, in many bookshops and in the Information Centre itself.

MUSEUMS

The city is home to 29 museums. The "Staatlichen Kunstsammlungen" (National Art Collections) are well-known far beyond the country's borders. Museum tours can be arranged either directly through the information office located in the Zwinger or by calling 484 01 01 between 8am and noon. You'll also find leaflets there containing information about special events. As a rule museums are open from 9am–5pm; take note of the different days on which they are closed.

Alte Meister (Old Masters') Gallery: In the Zwinger (Semper Building), Julian-Grumman-Allee. Tel: 495 23 81. Hours: 9am–5 pm; Wednesday until 6pm; closed Monday. An important collection containing works dating from the early Renaissance to the late Baroque period. In addition to German, French and Spanish, Dutch and Italian painters are also particularly well-represented. One of the most famous paintings in the collection is Raphael's *Sistine Madonna*. Note: At the time of writing the gallery is closed; the most important paintings are currently on view in the Albertinum.

Neue Meister (New Masters') Gallery: In the Albertinum (Brühlsche Terrasse), O-8010 Dresden, Tel: 495 30 56. Hours: 9am–5pm; Wednesday until 6pm; closed Monday. The collection includes paintings from the Classical to the present. The Dresden Romantic painters (including Caspar David Friedrich and Ludwig Richter) are especially well-represented.

Grünes Gewölbe (Green Vault): Presently in the Albertinum; entrance on Georg-Treu-Platz, O-8010 Dresden. Tel: 495 30 56. Hours: 9am–5pm Friday–Monday and Wednesday; 9am–6pm Tuesday; closed Thursday. German and Italian treasures of priceless artistic and material value dating from the Middle Ages up until the Baroque Period. The highlight of the collection is the work of J.M. Dinglinger. When reconstruction work on the Royal Palace is completed, the treasures will be returned to their original home.

Sculpture Collection: In the Albertinum, O-8010 Dresden. Tel: 495 30 56. Hours: 9am–5pm Friday–Monday and Wednesday; 9am–6pm Tuesday; closed Thursday. Due to a lack of space, only a small portion of the entire ancient art collection is on exhibit in the vaulted cellar of the Albertinum. A number of sculptures dating from the 19th and 20th centuries are housed in the Neue Meister Gallery.

Porcelain Collection: In the Zwinger, O-8010 Dresden. Tel: 484 01 27. Hours: 9am–5pm Saturday–Thursday; closed Friday. In addition to exquisite samples of Chinese and Japanese porcelain from the 17th and 18th centuries, the Böttger Collection – examples of fine china manufactured in the Meissen workshops – is also quite outstanding.

Kraszewski Museum: Nordstrasse 28, O-8060 Dresden. Tel: 5 44 50. Hours: 1–5pm Wednesday–Friday; 11am–5pm Saturday and Sunday.

Museum für Kunsthandwerk (Museum of Arts and Crafts): In Pillnitz Palace, O-8054 Dresden. Tel: 3 93 25. Hours: closed Monday and from November–April. Arts and crafts masterpieces dating from the 14th–20th centuries.

Münzmuseum: In the Albertinum (entrance on Georg-Treu-Platz), O-8010 Dresden. Tel: 495 30 56. Hours: 9am–5pm Friday–Monday and Wednesday; 9am–6pm Tuesday; closed Thursday. A variety of coins, medallions, banknotes and stamps are on display here. Exhibits document the development of ancient and German monetary systems, as well as the development of German medallions in both the Renaissance and Baroque Periods.

Kupferstichkabinett (Engravings Cabinet): Situated in Günzstrasse 34. Tel: 59 38 13. Hours: 9am–4.30pm Monday, Wednesday and Friday; 9am–6pm Tuesday and Thursday; closed Saturday and Sunday. One of the most extensive graphic collections in the world. Regularly changing exhibits.

Museum für Volkskunst (Folk Art Museum): In Köpckestrasse 1, O-8060 Dresden. Tel: 57 08 17. Hours: 10am–5pm Tuesday–Sunday; closed Monday. Displays of German, predominantly Saxon, folk art from both past and present.

OTHER MUSEUMS

Barockmuseum Schloss Moritzburg (Moritzburg Palace Baroque Museum), O-8105 Moritzburg. Tel: 439. Hours: 9am–11.45am, 1–4.45pm Wednesday–Sunday.

Fasanenschlösschen Moritzburg, O-8105 Moritzburg. Tel: (0297) 207. Hours: 9am–4pm daily from 15 April, weather conditions permitting.

Königsstein Fortress, O-8305 Königsstein. Tel: 374/375. Hours: 9am–5pm daily.

Staatliche Mathematisch-Physicalischer Salon (National Exhibit of Mathematics and Physics), in the Zwinger (entrance on Postplatz). Tel: 495 13 64. Hours: 9am–4pm daily; closed Thursday. Free admission on the last Sunday of every month.

Deutsches Hygiene Museum Dresden (German Museum of Hygiene in Dresden), Lingnerplatz 1, O-8010 Dresden. Tel: 4 84 60. Hours: 9am–6pm Saturday–Thursday; closed Friday.

Carl-Maria von Weber Memorial, Dresdner Strasse 44, O-8054 Dresden. Tel: 3 92 34. Hours: 1–6pm Tuesday, Wednesday, Friday and Saturday; 1–4pm Sunday.

Museum Haus Hoflössnitz, Knohllweg 37, O-8122 Radebeul. Tel: 7 56 16. Hours: 2– 5pm Tuesday–Friday; 10am–5pm Saturday; 2–5pm Sunday.

Landesmuseum für Vorgeschichte (Regional Museum of Prehistory), Karl-Marx-Platz, O-8060 Dresden. Tel: 5 25 91. Hours: 9am–5pm Monday–Thursday; 10am–4pm Sunday.

Militärhistorisches Museum (Museum of Military History), Dr-Kurt-Fischer-Platz 3, O-8060 Dresden. Tel: 59 20. Hours: 9am–5pm Tuesday–Sunday.

Staatliche Porzellanmanufaktur (National Porcelain Factory), Leninstrasse 9, O-8250 Meissen. Tel: 053-541. Hours: Demonstration workshop: 8.30am–noon, 1–4.30pm Tuesday–Sunday.

Albrechtsburg Meissen, Domplatz 1, O-8250 Meissen. Tel: 053-29 20. Hours: 9am–4pm Tuesday–Sunday.

Puppet Theatre Collection, Barkengasse 6, O-8122 Radebeul. Tel: 7 43 73. Hours: 9am–4pm Tuesday–Friday. The last Sunday of every month is "Family Sunday" with a puppet performance; 10am–4pm.

Richard Wagner Museum in Graupa, O-8304 Graupa, Tel: 04-48 229. Admission every hour on the hour. Hours: 10am–4pm Saturday–Thursday.

Staatliches Museum für Völkerkunde (National Museum of Ethnology), Karl-Marx-Platz 11, O-8060 Dresden. Tel: 5 25 91. Hours: 10am–5pm Monday, Tuesday, Thursday, Saturday and Sunday.

Stadtgeschichtliches Museum (Museum of City History), In the Landhaus, Ernst-Thälmann-Strasse 2, O-8010 Dresden. Tel: 495 23 02. Hours: 10am–6pm Monday–Thursday and Saturday; 10am–4pm Sunday; closed Friday.

Technisches Museum (Technical Museum), Reinhold-Becker-Strasse 5, O-8053 Dresden. Tel: 3 54 85. Hours: 9am–6pm Monday–Friday; 11am–4pm Saturday. Groups by prearranged appointment only.

Verkehrsmuseum (Transport Museum), Johanneum am Neumarkt, Augustusstrasse 1. Tel: 495 30 02. Hours: 1 April–30 September 9am–5pm; 1 October–31 March 10am–5pm. Closed Monday.

Museum zur Dresdner Frühromantik (Museum of Dresden Early-Romanticism), Strasse der Befreiung 13, O-8060 Dresden. Tel: 5 47 60. Hours: 10am–5pm Wednesday–Saturday; 10am–4pm Sunday.

Buchmuseum der sächsischen Landesbibliothek (Saxon Regional Library Book Museum), Marienallee 12, O-8060 Dresden. Tel: 5 26 77. Hours: 9am–4pm Tuesday–Friday; tours offered at 2pm on Saturdays.

Karl May Museum, Karl-May-Strasse 15, O-8122 Radebeul. Tel: 76 27 23. Hours: 9am–5pm daily.

Museum für Mineralogie und Geologie (Museum of Mineralogy and Geology), Augustusstrasse 2, O-8010 Dresden. Tel: 495 25 03. Hours: 10am–1pm, 2–4pm Wednesday–Sunday.

Museum für Tierkunde (Museum of Zoology), Augustusstrasse 2, O-8010 Dresden. Tel: 495 25 03.

ARCHIVES

Staatsarchiv Dresden (Dresden National Archives), Archivstrasse 14, O-8060 Dresden. Tel: 57 06 80 and 5 47 22. Hours: 8am–4pm Monday–Friday.

Stadtarchiv (City Archives), Marienallee 3, O-8060 Dresden, Tel: 5 47 50, Hours: 9am–4pm Tuesday–Friday.

EXHIBITIONS

Exhibition Centre at Fucikplatz, Stübelallee 2a, O-8019 Dresden. Tel: 459 81 14. Changing art, flower, animal, industrial etc. exhibits.

Galerie der Verbände bildender Künstler (The Association of Fine Artists Gallery), Rähmitzgasse 8, O-8060 Dresden. Tel: 5 14 56 or 5 15 82. Hours: 10am–4pm Tuesday–Sunday; 10am–6pm Wednesday.

Albertinum, Art Gallery, Neue Meister (New Masters)/Alte Meister (Old Masters), entrance on Brühlsche Strasse, O-8010 Dresden. Tel: 493 30 56. Hours: 9am–5pm Wednesday–Sunday.

Galerie "Kunst der Zeit" (Contemporary Art Gallery), Ernst-Thälmann-Strasse 7, O-8010 Dres-den, Tel: 495 24 67. Hours: 9am–6pm Monday and Tuesday; 9.30am–6pm Wednesday; 9am–6.30pm Thursday; 9am–7pm Friday; 9am–1pm Saturday. Co-operative of Dresden Fine Artists.

Dresdens Neue Galerie (Dresden's New Gallery), Ernst-Thälmann-Strasse 16, O-8010 Dresden. Tel: 495 51 98. Hours: 10am–6pm Monday–Friday; 10am–1pm Saturday.

Leonhardi Museum/Galerie Ost, Grundstrasse 26, O-8054 Dresden. Tel: 3 65 13. Hours: 2–6pm Wednesday–Friday; 10am–6pm Saturday and Sunday.

Galerie Mitte, Fetscherplatz 7, O-8019 Dresden. Tel: 459 00 52. Hours: 2–6pm Wednesday, Thursday and Friday; 10am–6pm Saturday and Sunday.

Galerie Comenius, Bautzner Strasse 30, O-8060 Dresden. Tel: 5 58 02. Hours: 2–6pm Tuesday–Friday; 10am–1pm Saturday. "Dresdner Sezession 90", an organisation of female painters.

Kunstausstellung Kühl (Kühl Art Exhibition), Zittauer Strasse 12, O-8060 Dresden. Tel: 5 55 88. Hours: 10am–1pm, 2–6pm Tuesday–Friday; 10am–3pm Saturday; 11pm–1pm Sunday. Most of the art works on display in the gallery are offered for sale.

In addition to these galleries, a number of "Graphic Designer Markets" take place scattered around the city. Look for announcements in newspapers or posted around the city.

CONCERTS

Renowned names like the "Staatskapelle Dresden" (Dresden National Orchestra), the "Dresdner Philharmonie", and the "Dresdner Kreuzchor" all attest to the high standard of the Dresden music world. Symphony concerts are held in the Festival Hall of the Kulturpalast while smaller concerts take place in the Semper Opera House, in the Blockhaus and in a variety of other cultural facilities. Of all the open-air concerts performed at various spots during the warmer seasons of the year, those held in the Pillnitz Palace Park are the most popular. A variety of organ concerts are conducted in many of the city's churches and the Kreuzchor sings regularly on Sunday evenings at 6pm in the Kreuzkirche. The "Zentrum für zeitgenössische Musik" (Centre for Contemporary Music) features modern music performances.

For concert information and advance ticket sales:

Konzert- und Gastspielagentur GmbH, Schillerstrasse 4, O-8054 Dresden. Tel: 3 43 26

Veranstaltungsbetrieb, Tiergartenstrasse 36, O-8020 Dresden. Tel: 47 50 97

Staatskapelle Dresden, in the Semper Opera House. Tel: 4 84 20

Dresdner Philharmonie, Kulturpalast Festsaal. Tel: 4 86 62 86

Zentrum für zeitgenössische Musik, Schevenstrasse 17, O-8054 Dresden. Tel: 37 82 81

Kulturpalast, Ernst-Thälmann-Strasse (due to be renamed), O-8010 Dresden. Visitors' Service, tel: 486 63 30 / 486 63 33. Hours: 10am–noon, 1–6pm Monday–Friday.

Gedenkstätte Carl-Maria von Weber (Carl-Maria von Weber Memorial), Dresdner Strasse 44, O-8054 Dresden. Tel: 3 92 34

Haus der Freundschaft, Blockhaus, Neustädter Markt 19, O-8060 Dresden. Tel: 5 49 85

Kreuzkirche, Am Altmarkt.

Kathedrale, Schlossplatz.

Freilichtbühnen (Open-air stages), Schlosshof Pillnitz. Via Bus 85 all the way to the last station Pillnitz.

Konzertplatz "Weisser Hirsch", via the tram 11 to Plattbreite.

Freilichtbühne "Junge Garde" (Open-air stage), in the Great Garten. Karchealle or Tiergartenstrasse.

OPERA, OPERETTA & BALLET

The Dresden National Opera has a long and illustrious tradition due to the efforts of a number of famous musicians including Carl-Maria von Weber, Richard Wagner and Richard Strauss. It was reopened in 1985 hoping to do justice to this past tradition. The operetta theatre is devoted to the less-serious muse and ballet performances take place both in the Opera House as well as on various other stages.

Zentrale Vorverkaufskasse (Central advance-booking office), Theaterplatz (Schinkelwache), O-8010 Dresden. Tel: 4 84 20. Hours: 4–8pm Monday; 10am–noon, 1–5pm Tuesday; 1–5pm Thursday; 1–3pm Friday; closed Wednesday, Saturday and Sunday.

This visitors' service supplies tickets for the National Opera, the National Operetta, national theatres, the Saxony Regional Theatre and "Young People's Theatre". Up-to-date information regarding performance schedules and ticket prices is available all day, tel: 484 27 31. Tickets may be purchased the night of the performance at some theatre box offices and generally go on sale one hour prior to the show.

Staatsoper, Theaterplatz 2, O-8010 Dresden. Evening box office: Tel: 484 24 91

Staatsoperette, Pirnaer Landstrasse 131, O-8045. Evening box office: Tel: 526 31

Staatskapelle Dresden, Theaterplatz 2, O-8010 Dresden. Tel: 484 23 40

THEATRE

Theatre in Dresden has a good reputation. Especially before the recent momentous political and social changes, theatres frequently put on socially critical, courageous productions which drew massive audiences. Nowadays the number of theatre-goers has somewhat declined with the result that tickets for performances are generally still available at box offices the night of the show.

Staatschauspiel (Grosses Haus) (National Theatre), Ostra Allee (formerly Julian-Grimau-Allee) 1, O-8010 Dresden. Evening box office: Tel: 484 24 29

Staatsschauspiel (Kleines Haus), Glacisstrasse (formerly Togliattistrasse) 28, O-8060 Dresden. Evening box office: Tel: 526 31

Landesbühnen Sachsen (Saxony Regional Theatre), Wilhelm-Pieck-Strasse 152, O-8122 Radebeul. Tel: 70 40

Staatliches Puppentheater (National Puppet Theatre), Leipziger Strasse 220, O-8030 Dresden. Tel: 57 09 80/5 11 24

Theater der Jungen Generation (Young People's Theatre), Meissner Landstrasse 4, O-8938 Dresden. Tel: 43 72 67

Landesbühnen Sachsen (Saxony Regional Theatre), W.-Pieck-Strasse 152, O-8122 Radebeul. Tel: 70 40

Theater im Hof, Ostra Allee 27, O-8010 Dresden.

During the summer months the Saxon Regional Theatre Ensemble performs at the Felsenbühne Rathen (the Rathen amphitheatre) in Saxon Switzerland. Theatre tickets may be purchased at the advance ticket booking office in Schinkelwache.

SMALL THEATRES

Theater 50, Pantomime theatre, Clara-Zetkin-Strasse 21, O-8028 Dresden. Tel: 4 32 76 42

Projekttheatre, Luisenstrasse 47, O-8060 Dresden.

Kleine Szene, Bautzner Strasse 107, O-8060 Dresden. Tel: 48 42 Ex. 595

Freilichtbühne "Junge Garde", open-air stage in the Great Garden, O-8020 Dresden. Tel: 2 39 10 12

Schichttheater, Kleines Theater Reick, Reicker Strasse 89, O-8036 Dresden. Tel: 4 86 62/47 20 79

Kabarett "Die Herkuleskeule", Sternplatz, O-8010 Dresden, Tel: 4 95 14 46

Dresdner Brettl, Maternistrasse 17, O-8010 Dresden. Tel: 4 95 41 23. Cabaret, music and literature performances.

Podium, Strasse der Befreiung 11, O-8060 Dresden. Tel: 5 32 66

Parktheater am Palaisteich, in the Great Garden, Fucikplatz, O-8010 Dresden.

Kabarett-Theatre, Die "Heruleskeule", Sternplatz (formerly Hans-Beimler-Platz), O-8010 Dresden. Tel: 495 51 91. Advance ticket booking at the theatre. Hours: 3–6pm Tuesday; 10am–2pm Wednesday; 3–5pm Thursday.

"die Bühne", the Dresden University little theatre, Teplizer Strasse 28, O-8020 Dresden. Tel: 463 63 51

CINEMAS

The relatively few cinemas (11) in Dresden are having difficulties surviving in the free-market economy. Cinemas that have been accustomed to showing predominantly artistic films must now offer more commercially-oriented films in order to attract enough viewers. There is a group initiative concerned with presenting non-commercial films, which can be reached by calling 57 05 37. Nearly all movies are dubbed and you'll find cinema programmes posted around the city.

UFA-Palast, Prager Strasse, O-8010 Dresden. Tel: 495 20 25

Rundkino, Prager Strasse, O-8010 Dresden. Tel: 495 20 25. The largest cinema in Dresden with two theatres and exhibits.

Filmtheater am Hauptbahnhof (cinema at the main railway station), Leninplatz, O-8010 Dresden. Tel: 47 05 32

Programmkino Ost, Schandauer Strasse 72, O-8021 Dresden. Tel: 33 37 82

Faunpalast, Leipzigerstr 76, O-8023 Dresden. Tel: 5 45 50

Schauburg, Otto-Buchwitz-Strasse 55, O-8051 Dresden. Tel: 3 65 85

Olympia Lichtspiele, Dohnaer Strasse 55 , O-8020 Dresden. Tel: 47 97 17

Kleines Theater Reick, Reicker Strasse 93, O-8020 Dresden. Tel: 47 20 79

Fimtheater Glückauf am Gittersee, Karlsruher Strasse 136, O-8040 Dresden. Tel: 47 83 47

Kino vor Ort, in the Casemates under the Brühlsche Terrasse.

Klubkino Turmhaus Cotta, Grillparzerstrasse 31, O-8029 Dresden. Tel: 43 43 04

Nickelodeon, Marschnerstrasse/Dürerstrasse, University auditorium , O-8019 Dresden. Tel: 47 20 79

Casablanca, Friedenstrasse 23, O-8060 Dresden.

YOUNG PEOPLE'S CLUBS

There are quite a number of young peoples' clubs in Dresden where young folks come together for a night of disco music and dancing. Events and programmes at each are remarkably diverse.

Jazzclub Tonne, Tzschirnerplatz 3, O-8010 Dresden. Tel: 495 13 54. Predominantly featuring jazz concerts; snack-bar on the premises.

Club Für Dich, Martin-Luther-Platz 21, O-8060 Dresden. Tel: 519 84. Featuring literary evenings and other events; café on the premises.

Clubhaus Am Wasaplatz, Wasaplatz 1, O-8020 Dresden. Tel: 47 85 09. Featuring public, "try-out" stages, literary and musical performances, dancing.

Jugendclub Scheune, Alaunstrasse 36, O-8060 Dresden. Tel: 5 16 71 and 555 32. Featuring a variety of events, including dancing.

Schülerfreizeitzentrum Louise, Louisenstrasse 41, O-8060 Dresden. Tel: 51 39 41

Jugendclub Kunst und Literatur, Strasse der Befreiung 5b, O-8060 Dresden. Tel: 5 39 58

Club Bärenzwinger, Brühlscher Garten (Linie 3, 5, 7, 8). Disco, films.

SHOPPING

Since the union of East and West currency, business has been booming. These days you can buy just about anything your heart desires in Dresden! The formerly typical queues in front of shops have disappeared and new department and discount stores have sprung up everywhere. Private vendors also sell their various and abundant wares along city streets and on the squares. Those interested in unusual clothing will do well to wander through the many boutiques, prepared of course, to dig a little deeper into their pockets to pay the price of individuality. The folk art produced in the Erzgebirge mountains is abundant and popular among tourists. Visitors hoping to find great bargains in second-hand bookshops and antique stores will be disappointed. In the past few years the once plentiful supply of antique items has been drastically reduced. The few articles that are still available are sold at considerably inflated prices. Dresden's once prodigious collection of cultural treasures has, unfortunately, made its way out of the country (both by legal and illegal means).

DEPARTMENT STORES

Karstadt Warenhaus, Prager Strasse 17, O-8010 Dresden. Tel: 4 84 70

Kinderkaufhaus, Webergasse, O-8010 Dresden. Tel: 4 95 24 02

Jugendmoden, Dr Rudolf-Rüdrich-Strasse 12, O-8010 Dresden. Tel: 4 95 31 37

A few private stores have also managed to survive the recent changes:

Claus Dieter Löwe, Kesseldorfer Strasse 40, O-8028 Dresden. Tel: 43 63 00

Firma Rausch, Otto-Buchwitz-Strasse 91, O-8060 Dresden. Tel: 57 49 86

Firma Dienemann, Antiquariat und Sortiment, Antonstrasse 35, O-8060 Dresden. Tel: 5 37 47

ANTIQUES

Dresdner An- und Verkauf (Dresden Buy and Sell), Bautzner Strasse 23 (1st floor), O-8060 Dresden. Tel: 5 39 36

Staatlicher Kunsthandel (National Art Dealers), Strasse der Befreiung 17, O-8060 Dresden. Tel: 57 07 40

Antiquitätengalerie, Dresdner Strasse 55, O-8210.

SOUVENIRS

You can purchase an inexpensive memento of your stay in Dresden at the stands and kiosks located throughout the city. For those not averse to paying a bit more, wood-carvings from the Erzgebirge such as pyramids and Räuchermännchen (little incense-burning figures), or world-famous Meissen porcelain are popular souvenirs.

MARKETS

At the present time the big market hall located on the Strasse der Befreiung is undergoing renovation. Following the closing of the open-air market on Postplatz, market vendors are scattered throughout the outer city districts. The legally-sanctioned open-air markets now take place at Schillingplatz (Löbtan) and along Holbeinstrasse (Johannstadt). There is not yet a permanent place for a main flea market in Dresden. However, smaller flea markets are held at different places. Currently, they're most frequently found at Fucikplatz.

The famous Dresdner Striezelmarkt (Dresden Pastry Market) goes back a long way. Every year this market, held at Christmas-time, attracts throngs of visitors to nibble and buy. At the festively decorated stalls you can buy the well-known *Dresdner Christstollen*, *Pflaumentoffel* (plum-dumplings), *Pulsnitzer Lebkuchen* (gingerbread), toys made in the Erzgebirge and Christmas trees already hung with decorations.

Sports

Athletics were very much promoted in what used to be East Germany. However, this support only applied to competitive sports; there was relatively little done in support of popular sports. Opportunities for athletic activities for holiday-makers in Dresden are therefore fairly limited, a situation that will most certainly change within the next few yearsFor instance there's already talk about creating a new golf course. Opportunities to play tennis, go horseback riding or bowling are also few and far between. The fitness centres located in the two luxury-class hotels Bellevue and Dresdner Hof are both equipped with swimming pools, saunas, solariums and bowling alleys as well as with other athletic facilities.

ATHLETIC OPPORTUNITIES

Sportstätten (Athletic Facilities), Freizeitzentrum im Sachsenbad (Leisure Centre), Wurzener Strasse 18, O-8023 Dresden. Tel: 5 28 36. Hours: 10am–10pm Monday–Saturday; 10am–6pm Sunday. Table tennis, billiards, a bowling alley, solarium and indoor swimming pool.

Freizeitzentrum, in the Great Garden (Bahnhof Zoo), Fucikplatz. Mini-golf, table tennis and sporting equipment rentals. Hours: 10am–2pm daily; 2–6pm Saturday and Sunday.

Dynamo Stadium, Dr-Richard-Sorge-Strasse, O-8010 Dresden. Tel: 4 95 60 46

Heinz Steyer Stadium, Pieschener Allee 1, O-8010 Dresden. Tel: 43 72 77

Horse Race Track, Oskar-Röder-Strasse 1, O-8036 Dresden. Tel: 2 37 11 03/2 37 11 25

SWIMMING

INDOOR SWIMMING POOLS

Volksschwimmhalle, Steinstrasse 4, O-8010 Dresden. Tel: 4 59 30 48

Freiberger Strasse, O-8010 Dresden. Tel: 4 95 11 80

Dohnaer Strasse 135, O-8036 Dresden. Tel: 274 31 61. Hours: 6.45am–9pm Monday–Friday; 8am–5pm Saturday and Sunday; FKK (nude swimming) 8–9pm Wednesday.

Sachsenbad, Wurzner Strasse 18, O-8023 Dresden. Tel: 5 28 36. Hours: 6am–10pm Monday–Friday; FKK (nude swimming) 8–10pm Tuesday.

OUTDOOR SWIMMING POOLS

Summer hours: 10am–8pm Monday–Friday; 8am–8pm Saturday and Sunday.

Georg-Arnhold-Bad, Dr-Richard-Sorge-Strasse 10, Fucikplatz, O-8010 Dresden. Tel: 495 20 97. Hours: 5.30am–8pm Monday–Friday, 8am–6pm Saturday and Sunday until 15 September.

Freibad Bühlau, Bachmannstrasse 6, O-8051 Dresden. Tel: 3 69 55. Via Line 11 to the Bühlau Tram Station.

Freibad Dölzschen, Luftbadstrasse, O-8028 Dresden. Via tram 12 to the stop Fritz-Schulze-Strasse. Open from 15 May until 15 September.

Freibad Mockritz, Munztrichweg, O-8020 Dresden. Tel: 47 82 01. Via bus 76, 81 until Mockritz, the last stop. Open from 15 May until 15 September.

There are areas for sunbathing, playing and engaging in athletic activities at all of the outdoor swimming pools. A variety of sports and play equipment can be rented and food is also available on the premises.

SAUNAS

Sachsenbad, Wurzener Strasse 18, O-8023 Dresden. Tel: 5 28 36. Irish-Roman steam bath.

TENNIS COURTS

Tennisplätze Weisser Hirsch, Kurparkstrasse, O-8081 Dresden. Tel: 3 71 91

Tennisplätze Wiener Strasse 46, O-8020 Dresden. Tel: 47 74 91

Tennisplätze Rudolf-Renner-Platz 9a, O-8028 Dresden. Tel: 43 62 61. During the winter these facilities are used for ice-skating.

WINTER SPORTS

Ostragehege Ice Sport Arena and Speed-Skating Rink, Pieschener Allee 1, O-8010 Dresden. Tel: 43 72 11. Hours: 7–9pm Monday, Tuesday and Thursday; 2–4pm Saturday and Sunday.

From September until March some tennis courts are transformed into ice-skating rinks; it's also possible to ice-skate on the frozen Zwinger Pond and on Lake Carola in the Great Garden.

RIDING

Race Track, Oskar-Röder-Strasse 1. Tel: 237 11 03 or 237 11 25. Horse races are held here every Saturday at 2pm.

SPECIAL INFORMATION

Dresden-Information, Prager Strasse 10, O-8010 Dresden. Tel: 495 50 25, Telex: 2-6198. Hours: April until September from 9am–8pm Monday–Saturday; 9am–2pm Sunday. 9am–6pm Monday–Wednesday; 9am–6.30pm Thursday; 9am–7pm Friday; 9am–2pm Sunday.

Dresden-Information Branch Office, Neustädter Markt (in the underpass). Tel: 5 35 39. The staff here will be able to answer any questions you might have, in a number of different languages.

TRAVEL AGENCIES

Elbe-tourist, the district office in charge of all travel agencies, will help you to plan activities in Dresden as well as in the surrounding countryside, will provide you with information in all travel matters and can accept bookings.

Servicebüro in Dresden-Information, Prager Strasse 11, O-8010 Dresden. Tel: 495 11 75. Hours: 9am–6pm Monday–Friday; 9am–noon Saturday and Sunday.

Reisebüro, Ernst-Thälmann-Strasse 22, O-8010 Dresden. Tel: 4 86 50, Telex: 23 40

Reisebüro, Neustädter Markt 5, O-8060 Dresden. Tel: 5 28 01

GAY CONTACTS

Arbeitskreis Homosexualität (Homosexual Study-Group), Hüblerstrasse 3, O-8091 Dresden.

Gerede-Homosexuelle Initiative Dresden e.V. (Dresden Homosexuals in Conversation Initiative), Wiener Strasse 41, O-8020 Dresden. Tel: 464 02 20. Hours: 6–9pm Tuesday.

WOMEN

"Sowieso" Frauenberatungs- und Kommunikationszentrum Dresden ("Sowieso" Dresden Womens' Counselling and Communications Centre), Angelikastrasse 1, O-8060 Dresden. Tel: 5 14 70

Frauenbildungszentrum Hilfe zur Selbsthilfe e.V. (Womens' Educational Centre "Helping You to Help Yourself"), Naumannstrasse 8, O-8053 Dresden. Tel: 3 52 75

Frauenreferat Stadt Dresden (The City of Dresden Women's Issues Office), Dr-Külz-Ring 19, O-8010 Dresden. Tel: 488 22 67

CHILDREN

In Dresden there are all kinds of things for children to do and see. Opportunities range from athletics and playing to theatre performances and more, providing parents with some temporary relief.

Theater der Jungen Generation, Meissner Landstrasse 4, O-8029 Dresden. Tel: 43 72 57. Theatre programme suitable for children six years of age or older.

Staatliches Puppentheater (National Puppet Theatre), Leipziger Strasse 220, O-8030 Dresden. Tel: 57 69 80 or 5 11 24. For children and families.

Puppentheater "Sonnenhäusel" (Sonnenhäusel Puppet Theatre), in the Great Garden. Theatre programme suitable for children four years of age or older.

Freizeitpalast, Schloss Albrechtsberg, Bautzner Strasse 130, O-8060 Dresden. Tel: 5 56 65. In this wonderful, classical palace children of all ages can participate in sports or in a variety of arts and crafts activities. There are athletic and play areas, a swimming pool and nursery located in the palace grounds.

Freizeitzentrum im Grossen Garten (Great Garden), Bahnhof Zoo. During the summer months children's festivals, discos and other events are held here. Numerous events expressly for children are organised in many residential areas and young peoples' clubs as well. For more information, consult the calendar of events put out by Dresden-Information.

Zoologic Garden, southwest of the Great Garden, Tiergartenstrasse 1, O-8019 Dresden. Tel: 47 54 45. Hours: 8am–6pm daily. One of the oldest zoos in Germany. Only a very few animals survived the zoo's destruction in 1945. Since then, the animal population has risen to 2,000. Located on the zoo premises you'll find restaurants, cafés and a concert pavilion. During the summer concerts and other events take place here.

Botanical Garden, northwest of the Great Garden, Stübelallee 2, O-8019 Dresden. Tel: 495 31 85. Hours: during the summer months from 8am–6pm daily. In the winter tours are available by prearranged appointment only.

Parkeisenbahn (Park Railroad), the train departs from Fucikplatz for a tour through the Great Garden. Hours: 1–5pm Monday–Friday; 10am–5pm Saturday and Sunday.

Barockgarten Grosssedlitz (Grosssedlitz Baroque Garden), O-8312 Heidenau. Tel: 25 92 (if you're calling from Dresden the dialling code is 0292).

Schlosspark Pillnitz, O-8054 Dresden. Hours: 5am–8pm daily.

TU Dresden Forts Botanical Garden, O-8223 Tharandt. Tel: 62 31. Hours: 8am–5pm Monday, Wednesday, Thursday, Saturday and Sunday.

Moritzburg Game Preserve. Tel: 488 (the dialling code from Dresden is 0297). Hours: 9am–4pm daily; tours at 2.30pm.

It's easiest to meet students at either the young peoples' clubs or in the clubs which cater especially to students. Here you'll also find the most inexpensive drinks and meals around.

Studentenclub Bärenzwinger, Brühlscher Garten, O-8010 Dresden. Tel: 595 14 09 (club), 463 46 99 (office).

Studentenclub Pauker, Wigardstrasse 17, O-8060 Dresden. Tel: 5 99 04 04

Studentenclub Spirale, Nöthnitzer Strasse 46, O-8027 Dresden. Tel: 4 63 60 38

Studenten-Club der Hochschule für bildende Künste (The College of Fine Arts Students' Club), Terrassenufer, O-8010 Dresden. Tel: 495 24 57. Open to everyone. Hours: 8pm–1am Thursday.

Studentenclub der Hochschule für Musik (The College of Music Students' Club), Fritz-Heckert-Platz 13, O-8010 Dresden.

Club Neue Mensas, Bergstrasse 47, O-8077 Dresden. Tel: 4 63 64 95

Studentenclub CD, Marschnerstrasse, O-8019 Dresden

FURTHER READING

Bailey, George. *Germans*. (1972)

Bradley, John. *The Illustrated History of the Third Reich*. (1978)

Calleo, David. *The German Problem Reconsidered: 1860-1978*. (1980)

Craig, Gordon. *The Germans*. (1982)

Dawson, William H. *German Life in Town and Country*. (1977)

Holborn, Hajo. *A History of Modern Germany: 1840-1945*. (1969)

Jones, Brangwyn G. *Germany: An Introduction to the German Nation*. (1970)

Kirsch, Henry. *German Democratic Republic: A Profile*. (1985)

Lowie, Robert H. *Toward Understanding Germany*. (1979)

MacDonald, Ian. *Get to Know Germany*. (1975)

Marsh, David. *New Germany at the Crossroads*. (1990)

To get to know and understand the German mentality, read any of the classical works by Goethe and Schiller, Heinrich Heine and Friedrich Hölderlin, to name a few. Below is a selection of German and English/American authors:

Grass, Günter. *Headbirths*; *The Germans Are Dying Out*; and *The Flounder*.

Mann, Thomas. *Buddenbrooks*.

Mansfield, Catherine. *In A German Pension*.

Stael, Madame de. *Germany*.

Twain, Mark. *A Tramp Abroad*.

ART/PHOTO CREDITS

263

INDEX

INSIGHT *pocket* GUIDES

EXISTING & FORTHCOMING TITLES:

Aegean Islands 57
Algarve 57
Alsace 57
Athens 57
Bali 58
Bali Bird Walks 58
Bangkok 58
Barcelona 58
Bavaria 59
Berlin 59
Bhutan 59
Boston 59
Brittany 60
Brussels 60
Budapest &
Surroundings 60
Canton 60
Chiang Mai 61
Costa Blanca 61
Costa Brava 61
Cote d'Azur 61
Crete 62
Denmark 62
Florence 62
Florida 62
Gran Canaria 63
Hawaii 63
Hong Kong 63
Ibiza 63

Ireland 64
Istanbul 64
Jakarta 64
Kathmandu
Bikes & Hikes 64
Kenya 65
Kuala Lumpur 65
Lisbon 65
Loire Valley 65
London 66
Macau 66
Madrid 66
Malacca 66
Mallorca 67
Malta 67
Marbella/
Costa del Sol 67
Miami 67
Milan 68
Morocco 68
Moscow 68
Munich 68
Nepal 69
New Delhi 69
New York City 69
North California 69
Oslo/Bergen 70
Paris 70
Penang 70

Phuket 70
Prague 71
Provence 71
Rhodes 71
Rome 71
Sabah 72
San Francisco 72
Sardinia 72
Scotland 72
Seville/Grenada 73
Seychelles 73
Sikkim 73
Singapore 73
South California 74
Southeast England 74
Sri Lanka 74
St Petersburg 74
Sydney 75
Tenerife 75
Thailand 75
Tibet 75
Turkish Coast 76
Tuscany 76
Venice 76
Vienna 76
Yogyakarta 77
Yugoslavia's
Adriatic Coast 77

● ●

United States: **Houghton Mifflin Company, Boston MA 02108**
Tel: (800) 2253362 Fax: (800) 4589501

Canada: **Thomas Allen & Son, 390 Steelcase Road East**
Markham, Ontario L3R 1G2
Tel: (416) 4759126 Fax: (416) 4756747

Great Britain: **GeoCenter UK, Hampshire RG22 4BJ**
Tel: (256) 817987 Fax: (256) 817988

Worldwide: **Höfer Communications Singapore 2262**
Tel: (65) 8612755 Fax: (65) 8616438

" I was first drawn to the Insight Guides by the excellent "Nepal" volume. I can think of no book which so effectively captures the essence of a country. Out of these pages leaped the Nepal I know – the captivating charm of a people and their culture. I've since discovered and enjoyed the entire Insight Guide Series. Each volume deals with a country or city in the same sensitive depth, which is nowhere more evident than in the superb photography. **"**

Sir Edmund Hillary